"This is a fantastic resource. Bill and Eric have really done their homework and provided an insightful and easy-to-use reference with answers to the most common questions Mormons ask. We highly recommend it."

JOSH MCDOWELL & SEAN MCDOWELL
Coauthors of *More Than a Carpenter*

"*Answering Mormons' Questions* is a very useful handbook that should be kept close at hand by anyone engaged in faith conversations with Latter-day Saints. It gives up-to-date answers on a wide range of topics that actually come up in discussion. Answers are brief but not shallow. The issues are treated in a thoughtful and civil manner. With practical tips and thought-provoking questions, this tool shows us how to have more dialogue with our Mormon friends and neighbors."

ROSS ANDERSON
Author of *Understanding Your Mormon Neighbor*

"Mormonism is on the rise. This powerful book will equip you—and your church—to present the truths of the Bible and the love of the true Savior to friends and family members ensnared in Mormon teachings."

MARK MITTELBERG
coauthor of *Becoming a Contagious Christian*, and author of
The Questions Christians Hope No One Will Ask (with answers)

"*Answering Mormons' Questions* is an informative study that specifically addresses the unique challenges of twenty-first-century Mormonism. Under the guise of "Christianity," the modern day LDS Church is seeking to launch a most sinister deception on an unsuspecting world. This book offers simple yet profound answers that will equip the Christian community to meet the LDS challenge head-on."

CHIP THOMPSON
Director, Tri-Grace Ministries

"Bill McKeever and Eric Johnson draw from their extensive experience and expertise in one-on-one witnessing to Mormons, along with their fair, balanced research into the teachings of the LDS Church, to give Christians who desire to reach Mormons the tools they need to do so in a loving fashion that honors God's truth. *Answering Mormons' Questions* is a great addition to any believer's library, as well as an excellent introduction to the work of evangelizing a religious group that sorely needs to hear about the one true God and the gospel of grace."

DR. JAMES WHITE
Alpha and Omega Ministries

"McKeever and Johnson are right up there at the top of my list for producing some of the most credible resources for helping Christians reach their Mormon friends and loved ones for Christ. Truth is, they know their Mormon doctrine better than many Mormons do. This new edition is long overdue and very much needed."

Dr. Ronald Huggins
Associate Professor of New Testament
Midwestern Baptist Theological Seminary

"Answering Mormons' Questions is a book that every Mormon should read. It is well-written and well-documented, responding to those questions and challenges Mormons have raised through the years. A must-read also for Christians desiring to share the true gospel with Mormons."

Dr. James Bjornstad
Professor of Philosophy
Cedarville University

"As a pastor of a local church in Utah, the first resource I recommend inquirers to explore in order to know more about Mormon beliefs is the ministry of Mormonism Research Ministry. In *Answering Mormons' Questions*, Bill and Eric have provided yet another excellent, well-researched, and factual resource that I can heartily recommend to others."

Cory Anderson
Senior Pastor, Shadow Mountain Church
West Jordan, Utah

"What a great guide to help live out Peter's injunction to 'give an answer to everyone'! Bill and Eric know Mormonism and love Mormons. They are the ablest equippers the church today has in responding to the issues that separate Mormonism and Christianity. Right now, more than ever, we need to be ready to answer Mormons' questions, and this book will help you do just that. I hope everyone in my church reads it."

Dr. Bryan Hurlbutt
Lead Pastor, Lifeline Community
West Jordan, Utah

"I have been a missionary in Utah for more than fifty years and I have read and reviewed many books on Mormonism. *Answering Mormons' Questions* is one of the most practical books for helping readers respond to LDS claims with solid, thoughtful answers and still show Christian love in doing so. It will be a great help to anyone who witnesses to Mormons."

Marvin Cowan
Serving with Missions Door in Utah

ANSWERING MORMONS' QUESTIONS

Updated and Expanded Edition

ANSWERING MORMONS' QUESTIONS

Ready Responses for Inquiring Latter-day Saints

BILL MCKEEVER *and*
ERIC JOHNSON

Kregel
Publications

Library of Congress Cataloging-in-Publication Data
McKeever, Bill.
Answering Mormons' questions : ready responses for inquiring
Latter-day Saints / Bill McKeever and Eric Johnson.—Updated
and expanded ed.
    p. cm.
    Includes bibliographical references (p. 323) and index.
1. Church of Jesus Christ of Latter-Day Saints—Controversial
literature.   2. Mormon Church—Controversial literature.
I. Johnson, Eric, 1962– II. Title.
BX8645.M395   2012   289.3—dc23   2012026074

ISBN 978-0-8254-4268-1

To our wives,
Tammy McKeever and Terri Johnson

A wife of noble character who can find? She is worth far more than rubies. . . .
Many women do noble things, but you surpass them all.
—PROVERBS 31:10, 29 (NIV)

And to our parents,
Barbara Lanphere and James and Betty Johnson

Parents are the pride of their children.
—PROVERBS 17:6B (NIV)

But in your hearts set apart Christ as Lord. Always be prepared to give an answer to everyone who asks you to give the reason for the hope that you have. But do this with gentleness and respect, keeping a clear conscience, so that those who speak maliciously against your good behavior in Christ may be ashamed of their slander.

—1 PETER 3:15–16 (NIV)

Do your best to present yourself to God as one approved, a worker who has no need to be ashamed, rightly handling the word of truth.

—2 TIMOTHY 2:15 (ESV)

. . . speaking the truth in love . . .

—EPHESIANS 4:15

Contents

Section 3: God

Section 4: Salvation

Section 5: The Bible

Section 6: Joseph Smith and the Book of Mormon

Foreword

With tens of thousands of Mormon missionaries carrying their message around the world, many Christians find themselves challenged to answer questions about their own faith and trying to understand how Christianity differs from Mormonism. When I left the Church of Jesus Christ of Latter-day Saints many years ago and started to visit other churches, I soon found that there were far greater differences between Christianity and Mormonism than I had originally thought. *Answering Mormons' Questions* addresses many of the same questions I had and prepares Christians to more clearly share the gospel as presented in the Bible.

Bill McKeever and Eric Johnson have been involved in outreach to the LDS people for many years and have authored several books on the subject, including *Mormonism 101*. Through Mormonism Research Ministry, they have taught seminars to equip Christians to be more effective in sharing their faith and to better understand the uniqueness of Mormon doctrine. They are regularly involved in evangelism at various venues such as Mormon temple openings and the Mormon Miracle Pageant in Manti, Utah. They also meet with Latter-day Saint people one-on-one.

I have long valued my friendship with these men and have a great respect for their abiding faith in Christ. Their book represents years of research and countless hours spent in dialogue with Mormons. Theirs is a knowledge born of experience and shared in love.

Sandra Tanner
Cofounder, Utah Lighthouse Ministry
Coauthor, *Mormonism: Shadow or Reality*

Acknowledgments

WE WANT TO THANK Sharon Lindbloom, our associate at Mormonism Research Ministry, who spent many hours looking over the chapters and providing valuable insights. Sharon, we greatly appreciate your valuable help! In addition, we want to acknowledge a number of our friends in ministry for their feedback on certain issues. If we e-mailed you and you responded, know that your response made this book even stronger.

Introduction

THE CHURCH OF JESUS CHRIST of Latter-day Saints (we will also refer to it as the *LDS* or *Mormon Church*, to the religion as *Mormonism*, and to church members as *Latter-day Saints* or *Mormons*[1]) officially began on April 6, 1830, having six initial members. According to the LDS Church's history, Joseph Smith (1805–1844) claimed to have been visited by both God the Father and Jesus Christ, who told him all the churches were "wrong" and that "all their creeds were an abomination in his sight." In addition, they said that the Christian "professors were all corrupt" and that "they draw near to me with their lips, but their hearts are far from me."[2]

Three years later, an angel named Moroni is said to have directed Smith to ancient gold plates (written in "Reformed Egyptian") that were buried near the Smith home in Palmyra, New York. He eventually translated these plates and published the Book of Mormon in 1830. This was the beginning of a church that today numbers in the millions, with more than half its members living outside the United States. It boasts of congregations on every continent and in the vast majority of the world's countries, with its missionary force numbering in the tens of thousands.

Perhaps you are a Christian believer who wants to share your faith with Mormon friends, family, coworkers, or neighbors. Maybe someone you know has recently converted to Mormonism. Or possibly two nicely dressed missionaries recently visited your home and you want to better understand this religion from a Christian point of view. Regardless, we're glad you have a desire to learn more, and we hope this book will facilitate respectful conversations with Latter-day Saints. At the beginning of each chapter, there are possible questions you can ask the Latter-day Saint when that particular topic is introduced. Then, at the end of each chapter, we include a witnessing tip paragraph as well as several study questions; those who are interested in using this book in a study session may want to look at www.mrm.org/amqstudy for possible strategies in using these questions to stimulate dialogue within the group.

Since we are often told to "ask a Mormon" in order to properly learn about Mormonism, we will regularly cite the official LDS standard works—the Bible (unless otherwise noted, we'll quote the official version of the church, the King James Version), the Book of Mormon, the Doctrine and Covenants, and the Pearl of Great Price. In order to understand the historical and current views of Mormon doctrine, we utilize numerous quotations from the LDS Church's General Authorities, who are called prophets, apostles, and seventies. In order to assist the reader with a timeline, we will include the birth/death date of a deceased General Authority the first time he is mentioned in a particular chapter.

As a quick background, here are some facts about the Mormon Church.

Official name of the church: The Church of Jesus Christ of Latter-day Saints
Unofficial names used throughout this book: Mormon or LDS
Founded: April 6, 1830
Founder: Joseph Smith
Headquarters: Salt Lake City, Utah
Leadership: Top leaders are males called General Authorities or the Brethren. They are:
- Prophet or President: The top leader of the church
- First Presidency: The top three members of the leadership, including the prophet
- Apostle: A member of the Quorum of the Twelve Apostles
- Seventy: A member of one of the Quorums of the Seventy

Since we emphasize the teachings of the prophets/presidents, here is the list of these men (and the years they served as the top leader), in chronological order.

1. Joseph Smith (1830–1844)
2. Brigham Young (1847–1877)
3. John Taylor (1880–1887)
4. Wilford Woodruff (1887–1898)
5. Lorenzo Snow (1898–1901)
6. Joseph F. Smith (1901–1918)
7. Heber J. Grant (1918–1945)
8. George Albert Smith (1945–1951)

9. David O. McKay (1951–1970)
10. Joseph Fielding Smith (1970–1972)
11. Harold B. Lee (1972–1973)
12. Spencer W. Kimball (1973–1985)
13. Ezra Taft Benson (1985–1994)
14. Howard W. Hunter (1994–1995)
15. Gordon B. Hinckley (1995–2008)
16. Thomas S. Monson (2008–)

Also utilized throughout are quotations from official LDS Church manuals and magazines. And although their views are not considered authoritative or officially binding, we will also cite Mormon apologists as well as professors from LDS institutions, including Brigham Young University in Provo, Utah. Our goal is to provide pertinent statements showing the membership's prevailing view on particular topics. We have done our best to include as much of the context as possible in order to make the quotes understandable since we realize that not every reader will have access to these sources.

We fully understand that not everyone reading this book will have much exposure to the basic teachings of Mormonism.[3] Therefore, we have included several tools in the back of the book. Appendix 1 has ten potential questions that can help guide a conversation to important topics. Appendix 2 provides a quick reference to Bible verses to use in witnessing situations. There is also a glossary of Mormon terms and their unique definitions; feel free to utilize the glossary any time you might be unaware of the definition of a particular word. While at points some chapters may seem to get very deep and complicated, we encourage you to do your best to stay with it. We purposely didn't call this book *Simple Answers to Mormons' Questions* because, quite frankly, such a title would be terribly misleading. Mormons generally are not going to seriously consider uninformed, thoughtless answers to their honest questions. However, if you work hard and use this book's tools, we believe you can respond with reasonable answers.

Because we emphasize logical arguments, some might mistakenly accuse us of claiming that salvation can come through rational reasoning. Let us say clearly that this is not our view. Of course, truth conforms to logic, meaning that using good thinking skills rather than emotions is crucial. But it is impossible to bring anyone to submission to the gospel through argumentation alone, no matter how reasonable the presentation may be. Faith, not knowledge, allows a person to have a personal relationship with God. And, most important, people are brought to God only through the power of the Holy Spirit.

Still, we are responsible to present the gospel message to open and willing minds in a clear, logical manner that honors the text of Scripture. As the apostle Paul explains, "How beautiful are the feet of them that preach the gospel of peace, and bring glad tidings of good things! . . . So then faith cometh by hearing, and hearing by the word of God" (Rom. 10:15, 17). Let it be known that prayer is the vital ingredient in successful evangelism efforts. Without this as the backbone to evangelism, fruit will never be produced.

Galatians 4:16 asks, "Am I therefore become your enemy, because I tell you the truth?" Knowing that it is common within our culture to equate disagreement with hatred or bigotry, we wish to make known up front that our work is born out of a genuine love and sincere compassion for the Latter-day Saints, many of whom we personally know. We want only the best for them. Our goal is to provide them the truth through God's Word, which Jesus said would set a person free (John 8:32; 17:17). Therefore, this book is not to be used as a bludgeon but rather as an aid to assist you in sharing God's truth. Christian, are you ready to engage in healthy dialogue?

Soli Deo gloria.

Abbreviations

Latter-day Saint Abbreviations

D&C   Doctrine and Covenants
LDS   The Church of Jesus Christ of Latter-day Saints (the LDS Church)
PoGP   Pearl of Great Price

Bible Version Abbreviations

ESV   The English Standard Version
JST   The Joseph Smith Translation, also known as the Inspired Version
KJV   King James Version of the Bible
NIV   New International Version

— Section 1 —

The LDS Church

Why won't you accept Mormons as Christians? Do you think we're a cult?

Response Questions

- Would you please define the meaning of "Christian"?
- Why does it bother you that I, as a Christian, won't accept Mormonism as a part of Christianity?
- If you think Mormonism's beliefs are "Christian," then would you consider my beliefs "Mormon"?
- Why do you think people assume that your religion is a cult?

• • • • • • • • • • • • • • • • •

"I contend that the Latter-day Saints are the only good and true Christians, that I know anything about in the world. There are a good many people who profess to be Christians, but they are not founded on the foundation that Jesus Christ himself has laid."[1]
—President Joseph F. Smith (1838–1918)

————————————————— Summary —————————————

LDS Church leaders not only proclaim that theirs is a Christian organization, but they also insist that theirs is the only church with which God is pleased. Since even before the church was founded in 1830, incredible claims have been made that fall outside the parameters of biblical truth. Their views of the Godhead, salvation, and Scripture, along with many other doctrines, separate Mormons from the rest of the professing Christian world. And while Christians need to be respectful when discussing these topics, differences on central issues cannot be ignored. After all, truth matters.

WHEN DIALOGUING WITH MORMONS, it is not uncommon to hear them say, "We're Christians too." Such an attitude was readily apparent in a 2007 general conference talk given by Seventy Gary J. Coleman. He told the story of fourteen-year-old Cortnee, the daughter of an LDS mission president, who was confused when her high school classmates questioned her Christianity. She went home and asked her mother, "Mom, are we Christians?" Coleman answered,

> As a member of The Church of Jesus Christ of Latter-day Saints, you are a Christian, and I am too. I am a devout Christian who is exceedingly fortunate to have greater knowledge of the true "doctrine of Christ" since my conversion to the restored Church. These truths define this Church as having the fullness of the gospel of Jesus Christ, I now understand the true nature of the Godhead, I have access to additional scripture and revelation, and I can partake of the blessings of priesthood authority. Yes, Cortnee, we are Christians.[2]

Many Latter-day Saints today are easily offended when their claim to Christianity is challenged. Perhaps they think their character or conduct is being judged. While there are many noble, moral Latter-day Saints who are striving to live exemplary lives, more than just minor disagreements exist between Mormonism and Christianity. The very idea that LDS Church founder Joseph Smith (1805–1844) claimed he was told by God the Father and Jesus in the First Vision account that all the churches were "wrong" should show those outside the LDS Church that Mormonism does not view itself as just another Christian denomination.[3] This vision, President David O. McKay (1873–1970) wrote, showed "that no creed in Christendom had the true plan of salvation."[4]

According to Mormon teaching, the period of the "great apostasy" that took place after the death of the apostles "lasted well over a millennium. During this period, man-made creeds and practices were substituted for the plan of salvation that Jesus had taught."[5] In an October 2010 general conference talk, Apostle Neil Andersen said,

> Some ask, "Aren't there many of other faiths who love Christ?" Of course there are! However, as members of The Church of Jesus Christ of Latter-day Saints, having a witness of His reality not only

from the Bible but also from the Book of Mormon; knowing His priesthood has been restored to the earth; having made sacred covenants to follow Him and received the gift of the Holy Ghost; having been endowed with power in His holy temple; and being part of preparing for His glorious return to the earth, we cannot compare what we are to be with those who have not yet received these truths.[6]

A church manual written specifically to instruct Mormon missionaries defines the differences between Mormonism and Christianity in a section describing the gift of the Holy Ghost: "The priesthood authority needed to perform this ordinance, which was lost centuries ago through apostasy, was restored through the Prophet Joseph Smith. Only through membership in the Church can one receive the gift of the Holy Ghost. This authority makes the Church different from any other religion in the world. By the Lord's own declaration, it is 'the only true and living church upon the face of the whole earth' (D&C 1:30)."[7] Saying that his church "accepts many of the same biblical doctrines as other Christian churches," apologist Gilbert Scharffs explained in a book used by Mormon missionaries that "the LDS Church also believes in numerous biblical concepts changed or forgotten by many Christian denominations, which could arguably make the LDS Church more Christian than other Christians."[8]

Within Christian thought, there is room for differences of opinions on peripheral issues. However, when it comes to the fundamentals of the Christian faith, there is no room for compromise. Words have meaning, and thus the word *Christian* is an important title held near and dear by many followers of the biblical Jesus. Princeton theologian B. B. Warfield (1851–1921) declared, "People who set upon calling unchristian things Christian are simply washing all meaning out of the name. If everything that is called Christianity in these days is Christianity, then there is no such thing as Christianity. A name applied indiscriminately to everything, designates nothing."[9] Brigham Young University professor Daniel Peterson said it well when he wrote, "Cherry-picking similarities while failing to mention major differences is a powerful way to misrepresent and mislead."[10] With that in mind, let's consider the following quotes from LDS leaders.

Regarding God . . .

President Brigham Young (1801–1877): "The doctrine that God was once a man and has progressed to become a God is unique to this Church."[11]

Charles W. Penrose (1832–1925), a member of the First Presidency: "The God whom the 'Christians' worship is a being of their own creation—if, indeed, there can be such a being as they describe him to be; they have formed certain notions concerning deity, and then they have formulated those notions into articles of faith or religion."[12]

Seventy B. H. Roberts (1857–1933): "We offend again in our doctrine that men are of the same race with the divine personages we call Gods. Great stress is laid upon the idea that we believe that 'as man is, God once was, and as God now is, man may become.' The world usually shouts 'blasphemy' and 'sacrilege' at one when he talks of such a possibility."[13]

Apostle Jeffrey R. Holland: "So any criticism that The Church of Jesus Christ of Latter-day Saints does not hold the contemporary Christian view of God, Jesus, and the Holy Ghost is *not* a comment about our commitment to Christ but rather a recognition (accurate, I might add) that our view of the Godhead breaks with post-New Testament Christian history and returns to the doctrine taught by Jesus Himself."[14]

Regarding Jesus . . .

Apostle Orson Hyde (1805–1878): "I discover that some of the Eastern papers represent me as a great blasphemer, because I said, in my lecture on Marriage, at our last Conference, that Jesus Christ was married at Cana of Galilee, that Mary, Martha, and others were his wives, and that he begat children."[15]

Seventy Bernard P. Brockbank (1909–2000): "It is true that many of the Christian churches worship a different Jesus Christ than is worshipped by the Mormons or The Church of Jesus Christ of Latter-day Saints."[16]

President Gordon B. Hinckley (1910–2008): "As a church we have critics, many of them. They say we do not believe in the traditional Christ of Christianity. There is some substance to what they say."[17]

Regarding salvation . . .

Apostle James Talmage (1862–1933): "Yet in spite of the plain word of God, dogmas of men have been promulgated to the effect that by faith alone may salvation be attained, and that a wordy profession of belief shall open the doors of heaven to the sinner."[18]

Seventy LeGrand Richards (1886–1983): "One erroneous teaching of many Christian churches is: By *faith alone we are saved*. This false doctrine would relieve man from the responsibility of his acts other than to confess a belief in God, and would teach man that no matter how great the sin, a confession would bring him complete forgiveness and salvation."[19]

Apostle Bruce R. McConkie (1915–1985): "Certain saved-by-grace-alone fanatics flatter their followers into believing they can be saved through no act other than confessing Christ with their lips."[20]

President Spencer W. Kimball (1895–1985): "One of the most fallacious doctrines originated by Satan and propounded by man is that man is saved alone by the grace of God; that belief in Jesus Christ alone is all that is needed for salvation."[21]

Regarding the Bible . . .

Joseph Smith: "There are many things in the Bible which do not, as they now stand, accord with the revelations of the Holy Ghost to me."[22]

The First Presidency: "The Bible, as it has been transmitted over the centuries, has suffered the loss of many plain and precious parts."[23]

Apostle Jeffrey R. Holland: "Some Christians, in large measure because of their genuine love for the Bible, have declared that there can be no more authorized scripture beyond the Bible. In thus pronouncing the canon of revelation closed, our friends in some other faiths shut the door on divine expression that we in The Church of Jesus Christ of Latter-day Saints hold dear: the Book of Mormon, the Doctrine and Covenants, the Pearl of Great Price, and the ongoing guidance received by God's anointed prophets and apostles. Imputing no ill will to those who take such a position, nevertheless we respectfully but resolutely reject such an unscriptural characterization of true Christianity."[24]

Regarding Christianity . . .

Apostle Bruce R. McConkie: "Modern Christians, as part of their various creeds and doctrines, have inherited many myths, legends, and traditions from their ancestors—all of which views they falsely assume are part of true religion. . . . Indeed, it would be difficult to assemble a greater number of myths into one philosophical system than are now found in the philosophies of modern Christendom."[25]

The LDS Newsroom: "The primary purpose of temple work is to 'seal' or unite families together, with the expectation that those relationships continue beyond death. The same temple rites can be performed for those who have died. There is no counterpart to temple practices in other Christian churches."[26]

Apostle Dallin H. Oaks: "The Church of Jesus Christ of Latter-day Saints has many beliefs in common with other Christian churches. But we have differences, and those differences explain why we send missionaries to other Christians."[27]

Is Mormonism a Cult?

The definition of "cult" varies depending on the source. It comes from the Latin word *cultus,* which was originally a general word meaning worship of a god. In the twentieth century, it came to refer to a religious group— often considering itself Christian—that varied from biblical Christianity in a variety of ways. Alan W. Gomes, professor of historical theology at Biola University in California, defines the word this way: "A cult of Christianity is a group of people, which claiming to be Christian, embraces a particular doctrinal system taught by an individual leader, group of leaders, or organization, which (system) denies (either explicitly or implicitly) one or more of the central doctrines of the Christian faith as taught in the sixty-six books of the Bible."[28] Among these central doctrines are "the Trinity, the deity of Christ, the bodily resurrection, the atoning work of Christ on the cross, and salvation by grace through faith. These doctrines so comprise the essence of the Christian faith that to remove any of them is to make the belief system non-Christian."[29]

Although some think the word *cult* should be discarded altogether, Gomes believes it should be retained for several reasons. He argues that it has an "established history of usage, long before the secular media or social sciences got hold of it," and it is "well suited to describe theological heterodoxy, which is determined by an absolute, objective, and unchanging standard."[30] While the word has become a pejorative term in recent years, perhaps being improperly used to poke fun or to be mean-spirited, Gomes adds that a label, when applied objectively, can be "exceedingly helpful" because, for one, "the purpose here is objective classification. Of course, some or even many cults may have unsavory aspects about them, but that must be determined on a case-by-case basis."[31]

While Mormonism certainly denies important doctrines of the Christian faith, we don't encourage using *cult* as a label in a typical dialogue, since it could unnecessarily offend the hearer and possibly hinder what otherwise may be a very positive conversation. At the same time, this hasn't stopped past General Authorities from using this term to describe others outside of the LDS faith. Referring to the role of the LDS leadership, Apostle Mark E. Petersen (1900–1984) told a general conference crowd, "They will protect you from the false teachings of cultists and splinter groups and from the misleading philosophies of men."[32] McConkie wrote, "Only when the Church is fed the bread of life are its members kept in paths of righteousness. It is the spiritually illiterate who become cultists and who forsake the faith."[33] He even likened those who hold to the Trinity and the Athanasian Creed as belonging to such a group:

> A false Christ is not a person. It is a false system of worship, a false church, a false cult that says: "Lo, here is salvation; here is the doctrine of Christ. Come and believe thus and so, and ye shall be saved." It is any concept or philosophy that says that redemption, salvation, sanctification, justification, and all of the promised rewards can be gained in any way except that set forth by the apostles and prophets. We hear the voice of false Christs when we hear the Athanasian Creed proclaim that "whosoever will be saved" must believe that the Father, Son, and Holy Ghost are incomprehensible and uncreated, that they form a Trinity of equals, who are not three Gods but one God, and not one God but three Gods, and that unless we so believe we "cannot be saved," and "shall perish everlastingly."[34]

In fact, in a complaint about polygamous groups who call themselves "Mormon," Apostle M. Russell Ballard told a fall 2011 general conference audience, "Others may try to use the word *Mormon* more broadly to include and refer to those who have left the Church and formed various splinter groups. Such use only leads to confusion."[35] How is Ballard's effort to protect the word *Mormon* any different from professing Christians who want to protect the word *Christian* from those who are doctrinally outside the traditional definition? We recommend using the word *cult* cautiously, as it should be used in a descriptive, not an accusatory, manner.

Questions for Discussion

- In your estimation, what is the greatest danger in allowing Mormonism to be called a "Christian" religion?

- What advantages might Mormon missionaries have if they were able to convince Christians at their doorsteps that there are more similarities than differences between the two faiths?

- How could you respond to your Mormon friend who is genuinely hurt by those who say Mormons are not true Christians?

Evangelism Tip

When your Latter-day Saint friend claims to be a Christian, ask, "If we are both called Christians, are you suggesting our faiths are alike? Would you then feel comfortable if I called myself a Mormon or a Latter-day Saint?" Explain how you reject basic Mormon teachings such as Joseph Smith as a true prophet, the Book of Mormon as a historical work, and the LDS Church as a restored church from ancient times. You will probably be met with incredulity. If so, this shows that serious differences involving vital issues really *do* divide Mormons and Christians. Words have meaning and thus do matter.

Why won't you let us define our own doctrine rather than telling us what we believe?

Response Questions

- In what way do you feel that I have erroneously defined your doctrine?
- Without becoming a Latter-day Saint, what would be a good way for someone to better understand just what it is that Mormonism teaches?
- While you certainly might disagree with your leaders, shouldn't the authoritative words of these men reflect the actual doctrines of your church?

• • • • • • • • • • • • • • • •

"How grateful we are that the heavens are indeed open, that the gospel of Jesus Christ has been restored, and that the Church is founded on the rock of revelation. We are a blessed people, with apostles and prophets upon the earth today."[1]

—President Thomas S. Monson

Summary

When Christians attempt to define important doctrines as taught in Mormonism, a dispute potentially can arise over whether or not a particular teaching is truly LDS doctrine. Some Mormons even back away from more controversial teachings of their church leaders, especially when those particular leaders are deceased. However, if there is any authority in the Mormon Church, surely it must lie in the pronouncements provided by the leaders, along with official curriculum produced by the church.

WHEN A CHRISTIAN PRESENTS information as taught by Mormon leaders, it is not uncommon to hear the words, "That's not Mormon doctrine!" At this point, many Christians retreat, thinking, "Well, they're the Mormons, so they ought to know what is or is not their doctrine." The Mormon is then able to switch topics and leave the issue at hand. In fact, when asking Latter-day Saints what Mormonism teaches, the answers can differ from one member to the next.

Yet it was Joseph Smith (1805–1844) who criticized the Christian churches of his day, saying *they* were the ones who were confused. According to his official First Vision account, when he claimed he saw God the Father and Jesus Christ in 1820, "the teachers of religion of the different sects understood the same passages of scripture so differently as to destroy all confidence in settling the question by an appeal to the Bible." Smith claimed the heavenly beings insisted he must "join none of them" and "that all their creeds were an abomination in his sight."[2]

If every Mormon is allowed to personally decide the veracity of a particular doctrine—even if that person's conclusion disagrees with the LDS leadership—then progress in a conversation will be hindered. According to the law of noncontradiction, something cannot be A and non-A at the same time. Mormonism is either true or it is false. Only when the objective teachings of the Mormon religion are understood can it be determined whether or not Mormonism is true.

Defining Truth in Mormonism

According to one LDS Church manual, "The Church of Jesus Christ of Latter-day Saints accepts four books as scripture: the Bible, the Book of Mormon, the Doctrine and Covenants, and the Pearl of Great Price. These books are called the standard works of the Church. The inspired words of our living prophets are also accepted as scripture."[3]

Since Mormonism began in 1830, church leaders have rejected the idea of a closed canon, claiming that inspired teachings from God can be given to their living prophet. "Since Latter-day Saints believe in the genuine gift of prophecy, it follows that the revelations received by modern prophets should be esteemed as highly as those received by ancient ones. Hence, the LDS canon of scripture can never be closed."[4]

The job of clarifying the position of the church has been entrusted to the Mormon prophet, as well as to his two counselors. These three men make up the First Presidency. A church manual for Mormon missionaries explains the role of the Mormon "prophet, seer, and revelator": "A living prophet directs the Church today. This prophet, the President of The Church of Jesus Christ of Latter-day Saints, is the authorized successor to Joseph Smith. He and the present Apostles trace their authority to Jesus Christ in an unbroken chain of ordinations through Joseph Smith."[5] One place to hear the words of the leaders are at the semiannual general conference. As Dieter F. Uchtdorf of the First Presidency explained, "Listen to general conference with an ear willing to hear the voice of God through his latter-day prophets."[6]

Giving a general conference message in April 2012, Apostle D. Todd Christofferson explained, "In 1954, President J. Reuben Clark Jr., then a counselor in the First Presidency, explained how doctrine is promulgated in the Church. Speaking of members of the First Presidency and Quorum of the Twelve Apostles, he stated: '[We] should [bear] in mind that some of the General Authorities have had assigned to them a special calling; they possess a special gift; they are sustained as prophets, seers, and revelators, which gives them a special spiritual endowment in connection with their teaching of the people. They have the right, the power, and authority to declare the mind and will of God to his people, subject to the over-all power and authority of the President of the Church. . . . the President of the Church has a further and special spiritual endowment in this respect, for he is the Prophet, Seer, and Revelator of the whole Church."[7]

Several biblical passages typically are used as support for this unique position. One is Amos 3:7, which reads, "Surely the Lord God will do nothing, but he revealeth his secret unto his servants the prophets." Prior to this claim, God asked if it is possible for two to walk together unless they are in agreement (v. 3). He then gave several rhetorical questions that can be answered only in the negative (vv. 4–6). Mormons usually insist that verse 7 is a general rule, implying that the New Testament church will be led by a living, mortal prophet who will reveal the Lord's "secrets" to the church. However, the context of this passage is speaking of impending danger and judgment upon the nation of Israel for the people's iniquities (see v. 2). In other words, God used mortal men to warn theocratic Israel on His behalf. To disobey a prophet in the Old Testament often resulted in judgment and punishment. Their words were considered final, authoritative, and, ultimately, binding.

Nothing is implied in the Amos passage that this refers to the governmental role of a prophet living in post-Old Testament times. In fact, Christian theologian Wayne Grudem notes, "There is no convincing evidence that New Testament prophets in their role as prophets ever governed

early churches through 'charismatic leadership' by means of prophetic dec-
larations about the direction of the church. This theory is based on some
people's ideas of how the church 'must have' or 'could have' developed, but it
is not supported by the facts of the New Testament itself."[8] Grudem points
out that the role of a New Testament prophet is quite different from that
of the Old Testament prophet. He writes, "It is not surprising, then, that
when we read the New Testament we find several times when the *apostles* are
connected with the Old Testament prophets, but New Testament *prophets*,
by contrast, are never connected with Old Testament prophets in the same
way."[9]

Though the LDS Church claims to be a restoration of how things were
done in ancient times, it breaks with Scripture by insisting there can be only
one "living prophet" whose authority is above all others. This pattern is not
found in the New Testament. For instance, Paul wrote in 1 Corinthians
14:29 that when two or three prophets spoke, those who heard them were
allowed to weigh, or judge, what was said. How were they to be judged?
Grudem explains, "As a prophet was speaking, each member of the congregation would listen carefully, evaluating the prophecy in the light of the
Scripture and the authoritative teaching that he or she already knew to be
true."[10] In 1 Thessalonians 6:21, Paul told the Thessalonian believers that
they should not despise prophecies but were to prove, or test, "all things; hold
fast that which is good." Obviously this would include prophetic utterances.

Another passage often cited by Mormons is Ephesians 2:20. The apostles
and prophets mentioned here form the foundation of the church insofar as
they fit with Jesus Christ the chief cornerstone. Hebrews 1:1–2 states how
God spoke previously through the prophets but has "in these last days spoken unto us by his Son." First Corinthians 3:11 explains, "For other foundation can no man lay than that is laid, which is Jesus Christ." A foundation
must align with the cornerstone that sets its trajectories and measurements.
In the same way, the proclamations given by the apostles and prophets
always were to be measured by how they matched with Jesus' message and
life. As prophesied in the Old Testament and declared as the fulfillment in
the New Testament, Jesus Christ—who is clearly presented as God manifest
in the flesh—*is* the living prophet for the Christian. And while Mormonism
teaches that men are necessary to guide the church with authority, the
Bible says the task of guidance is given to the Holy Spirit. John 16:13 says,
"Howbeit when he, the Spirit of truth, is come, he will guide you into all
truth."

Is the Mormon Prophet a Trustworthy Source?

While Mormons may give lip service to the idea that their church alone has access to modern-day revelation from God, many have brushed aside the claims of leaders with whom they disagree, especially after those particular leaders have died. This position sends a clear message that they consider the "revelation" of these leaders nothing more than the personal opinion of the speaker and not something to be taken seriously. One proponent of this thinking is LDS apologist Michael R. Ash, who states that "the official position of Mormonism is that of a *fallible* prophet, yet few Mormons really seem to believe it. . . . we can know if leaders speak the will of God when we, ourselves, are 'moved by the Holy Ghost' (D&C 68:3–4). The onus is upon us to determine when they speak for the Lord. If we rely solely on the revelations of the prophets, without seeking our own personal confirming revelations, we tend to tacitly accept their revelations as infallible."[11] He also warns, "We need to be aware that sometimes we are too quick to uncritically accept the things we hear or read—even from sources such as Church leaders or in Church magazines."[12]

Ash's claim that church leaders and official church publications can be products of the day and culture means that some false ideas from Salt Lake City possibly could be disseminated.[13] This salad-bar philosophy of picking and choosing among the leadership's teachings is not easily supported by official church manuals and general conference addresses through the years. For example, President Wilford Woodruff (1807–1898) explained the importance of the living prophet: "The Lord will never permit me or any other man who stands as President of this Church to lead you astray. It is not in the programme. It is not in the mind of God. If I were to attempt that, the Lord would remove me out of my place."[14] President George Albert Smith (1870–1951) said, "I may have my own ideas and opinions, I may set up my own judgment with reference to things, but I know that when my judgment conflicts with the teachings of those that the Lord has given to us to point the way, I should change my course. If I desire salvation I will follow the leaders that our Heavenly Father has given to us, as long as he sustains them."[15]

President Harold B. Lee (1899–1973) gave an address to a general conference audience that has been quoted in a number of church manuals. He said, "Now the only safety we have as members of this church is to do exactly what the Lord said to the Church in that day when the Church was organized. We must learn to give heed to the word and commandments that the Lord shall give through his prophet. . . . There will be some things that take patience and faith. You may not like what comes from the authority of the Church. It may contradict your political views. It may contradict your social views. It may interfere with some of your social life. But if you listen to these things, as if from the mouth of the Lord himself, with patience and faith, the promise is that 'the gates of hell shall not prevail against you.'"[16] President Spencer W. Kimball (1895–1985) agreed, saying, "Let us hearken to those we sustain as prophets and seers, as well as the other brethren, as if our eternal life depended upon it, because it does!"[17] Kimball even declared in a church manual that Mormon magazines ought to be studied when he said, "I hope you will get your copy of the [Ensign or Liahona] and underline the pertinent thoughts and keep it with you for continual reference. No text or volume outside the standard works of the Church should have such a prominent place on your personal library shelves—not for their rhetorical excellence or eloquence of delivery, but for the concepts which point the way to eternal life."[18]

Clarifying official church doctrine is not the job of Mormon lay members or employees at church-owned schools. President Ezra Taft Benson (1899–1994) stated, "Doctrinal interpretation is the province of the First Presidency. The Lord has given that stewardship to them by revelation. No teacher has the right to interpret doctrine for the members of the Church."[19] A 2010 LDS teacher's manual reports, "The President of the Church was foreordained in the premortal life and is called in mortality after long, faithful service in the Quorum of the Twelve Apostles. He is set apart to exercise the keys of the kingdom of heaven on earth and formally sustained by the membership of the Church."[20] Apostle M. Russell Ballard declared to a general conference audience, "When we hear the counsel of the Lord expressed through the words of the President of the Church, our response should be positive and prompt. History shows that there is safety, peace, prosperity, and happiness in responding to prophet counsel."[21]

When asked by television interviewer Larry King to describe his role as the leader of a major religion, President Gordon B. Hinckley (1910–2008) replied, "My role is to declare doctrine."[22] This thinking can be traced to Doctrine and Covenants 21:4–5. Speaking specifically of Mormonism's founder Joseph Smith, the commandment supposedly given by God states that members are to "give heed unto all his words and commandments which he shall give unto you as he receiveth them, walking in all holiness before me; for his word ye shall receive, as if from mine own mouth, in all patience and faith." Harold B. Lee taught that this passage applied to LDS prophets in general and should not be limited to just the founder of Mormonism.[23]

While he was serving as a church apostle, Ezra Taft Benson gave a discourse in 1980 called "Fourteen Fundamentals in Following the Prophet." The talk was dusted off and quoted twice at the October 2010 general conference. Seventy Claudio R. M. Costa[24] and Seventy Kevin R. Duncan[25] both listed the main points of this speech given three decades earlier.[26] Consider several of the points.

- First: The prophet is the only man who speaks for the Lord in everything.
- Second: The living prophet is more vital to us than the standard works.
- Third: The living prophet is more important to us than a dead prophet.[27]
- Fourth: The prophet will never lead the Church astray.
- Fifth: The prophet is not required to have any particular earthly training or credentials to speak on any subject or act on any matter at any time.
- Eleventh: The two groups who have the greatest difficulty in following the prophet are the proud who are learned and the proud who are rich.
- Fourteenth: The prophet and the presidency—the living prophet and the first presidency—follow them and be blessed; reject them and suffer.

Costa concluded his sermon, saying, "We are privileged to have the words of our living prophets, seers, and revelators during this wonderful general conference. They will speak the will of the Lord for us, His people. They will transmit the word of God and His counsel to us. Pay attention and follow their instruction and suggestions, and I testify to you that your life will be completely blessed."[28]

Christians who ask Mormons to explain controversial or embarrassing teachings by past leaders often are rebuffed with a comment made by Joseph Smith in 1843. Speaking to two members in a private conversation, he remarked, "A prophet was a prophet only when he was acting as such."[29] Using this quote, Apostle Christofferson explained at the April 2012 general conference, "At the same time it should be remembered that not every statement made by a Church leader, past or present, necessarily constitutes doctrine. It is commonly understood in the Church that a statement made by one leader on a single occasion often represents a personal, though well-considered, opinion, not meant to be official or binding for the whole church."[30] Quoting Apostle J. Reuben Clark, Christofferson then explained that "the Church will know by the testimony of the Holy Ghost in the body of the members, whether the brethren in voicing their views are 'moved upon the Holy Ghost'; and in due time that knowledge will be made manifest."[31]

Clearly this is a case of plausible deniability. Consider the possibility of a member who says he personally prayed about the teaching of the leadership—say, Christofferson's teaching at this official general conference—and did not receive the testimony that what was said is true. Would the lack of a testimony from a member or even a group of members really mean that Christofferson was merely giving a "personal, though well-considered, opinion"? It is doublespeak to say that prophets and other leaders are able to provide "latter-day" revelation but then only can be believed if "the body of the members" received personal revelation that what was taught is actually true. If this is the way to receive revelation from God, then why are the LDS leaders even needed in the first place?

Mormons have even been warned to refrain from any criticism of the prophet and other General Authorities. For example, President George Albert Smith (1870–1951) said in a general conference message, "I stand here to plead with you, my brethren and sisters, not to permit words of criticism or of unkindness to pass your lips about those whom the Lord has called to lead us. . . . If you do, I can say to you that you will find yourselves in the power of the adversary."[32] President Joseph Fielding Smith (1876–1972) wrote, "JUDGMENT AWAITS CHURCH MEMBERS WHO CRITICIZE BRETHREN. But it is not of this class particularly that I desire to refer, but to those members of the Church who have entered into the waters of baptism and have made covenants before the Lord that they will observe his laws and respect his priesthood, who have been persuaded, or who are in danger of being persuaded, by such characters."[33]

Hinckley told a group of students, "'You have been taught to think critically, to explore, to consider various sides of every question. This is all good,' he said. 'But you can do so without looking for flaws in the church or in its leaders.' Hinckley said that church critics 'are wearing out their lives trying to find fault with this church. They mine history. They examine the words of general authorities.' Though they may be 'enjoying their day in the sun, their sun will set and they will not be remembered for good,' he said."[34]

Mormon leaders have admonished teachers who use unofficial sources when preparing their church lessons. Instead, "correlated" material that has been prepared by an "inspired Church-writing committee" and "has been approved by the Quorum of the Twelve and the First Presidency" is stressed.[35]

The Correlation Department of the LDS Church is responsible for protecting the "purity of doctrine" taught in church manuals and making it clear that Mormons are to take such teachings seriously. In practice, leaders have not hidden the fact that correlated material has the church's stamp of approval. One church manual states,

> Explain that Church publications, such as lesson manuals and Church magazines, are produced to help members learn and live the gospel of Jesus Christ. The correlation process helps ensure that these materials are scripture-based, doctrinally accurate, and appropriate for the intended audience. All Church publications are planned, prepared, reviewed, and implemented under the direction of the First Presidency and Quorum of the Twelve.[36]

Instructions for teaching Melchizedek Priesthood and Relief Society lessons can be found in a 2008 article of the general conference edition of the *Ensign* magazine. Listed at the end of this article are pointers on how to lead the lessons. The first two points read, "You may at times be tempted to set aside the conference talks and prepare the lesson using other materials. But the conference talks are the approved curriculum. Your assignment is to help others learn and live the gospel as taught in the most recent general conference of the Church. Review the talk(s), looking for principles and doctrines that meet the needs of class members. Also look for stories, scripture references, and statements from the talk(s) that will help you teach the principles and doctrines."[37] The third point uses the words *principles* and *doctrines* no fewer than five times each.

In the age of the Internet, the Mormon Church's Web site is also considered an authoritative place to procure information that is both official and reliable. The LDS Newsroom site states, "In addition, information on official Church Web sites is reliable and consistent with the doctrines and policies of the Church. All materials on Newsroom and other Church Web sites are carefully reviewed and approved before they are posted . . . In a complementary way, Newsroom, LDS.org and other Church Web sites provide an official voice from the Church."[38]

With all of this said, ultimately the Mormon people are left to depend on living, mortal men for guidance, even when their teachings may deviate from the Bible. Christians, on the other hand, can rest assured that their living Prophet (Jesus) will never lead them astray. Reading the Bible and understanding His special revelation thus becomes the goal of every faithful Christian believer.

Questions for Discussion

- Why do you think some Mormons may sometimes shy away from past teachings of LDS leaders?

- Suppose a Mormon says, "You can't understand Mormon doctrine because you're not a Mormon." What examples might you give to show that this is faulty reasoning?

- Some Mormons might say that the General Authorities, including the prophets, could be wrong at times and should be accepted only based on a Mormon's personal revelation. Do you think most Mormons believe this? Does this test work for or against the LDS leadership? Why do you think so?

————————————— Evangelism Tip —————————————

Mormonism is not an esoteric religion based merely on one's personal opinion. When a Latter-day Saint insists upon a doctrinal position that contradicts LDS scriptures or leadership (past or present), ask, "What position do *you* hold in the church?" The view given by church leaders and correlated church curriculum takes precedence over any member's personal perspective. One shouldn't have to be a Mormon in order to understand the basic teachings of the Latter-day Saint religion, just as one doesn't have to be a Christian to comprehend the fundamental truths of Christianity.

Chapter 3

Doesn't the fact that Jesus Christ is in our church's name prove we are Christian?

Response Questions

- Would it matter if you knew that your church did not always have Jesus' name in it?
- Do you accept non-Mormon churches that also have the name of Jesus in their title as being true?

● ● ● ● ● ● ● ● ● ● ● ● ● ● ● ● ●

"We are decidedly a Christian church. Ours is the only Church that bears the name of the Savior. It is called The Church of Jesus Christ of Latter-day Saints, and that alone, if we are sincere in our belief, and we are, is sufficient proof that we are Christians."[1]
—Apostle Rudger Clawson (1857–1943)

—————————— Summary ——————————

The name of God's church is very important to many Mormons since their leadership makes the claim that theirs is the only true church. LDS mission-aries often point to the name "Jesus Christ" on their black badges attached to their shirts or dresses as certification that they are Christians. But just having the name of Jesus in a church's name does not necessarily make it Christian. A true Christian church must teach true Christian doctrine as set forth in the Bible.

GENERALLY, MORMONS BELIEVE their church should be considered Christian. After all, they like to point out how the name of Jesus is in their church's name. In 1991, Brigham Young University professor Stephen E. Robinson summed up this idea when he asserted, "Is not the name of our church The Church of *Jesus Christ* of Latter-day Saints? Do we not worship Christ? . . . The Utah Saints shook their heads and wondered how it was possible that anyone could seriously doubt that the Latter-day Saints were Christians."[2]

Third Nephi 27:8 from the Book of Mormon reads, "And how be it my church save it be called in my name? For if a church be called in Moses' name then it be Moses' church; or if it be called in the name of a man then it be the church of a man; but if it be called in my name then it is my church, if it so be that they are built upon my gospel." Apostle Bruce R. McConkie (1915–1985) referenced this verse when he wrote, "The resurrected Christ gave to the Nephites this test whereby they might distinguish the true church from any other: 1. It would be called in his name, for 'how be it my church save it be called in my name?'"[3] It seems odd that such a point even needs to be made. While this certainly could be a concern among some living in Joseph Smith's time, it is highly doubtful this would have been an issue with people who lived in A.D. 34 or 35, when 3 Nephi 27 was allegedly written.

If having the name of Jesus was a requirement to be a "true church," why didn't the apostle Paul follow this pattern when he addressed various New Testament churches? For example, he referred to the Thessalonians in both of his letters as "the church of the Thessalonians." In Galatians 1:2 he wrote to the "churches of Galatia," and in 1 Corinthians 1:2 he called the body of believers in Corinth "the church of God which is at Corinth." These were New Testament churches, but should we assume these congregations were not part of Christ's true church because Jesus' name was absent?

Many unfamiliar with LDS history may be unaware that since its founding on April 6, 1830 the church's official title has not always included Christ's name. Doctrine and Covenants 20:1 reports that the original name of the church was the "Church of Christ." In 1834, the name was changed to "The Church of the Latter-day Saints."[4] This took place at a priesthood conference at which Joseph Smith was present. The vote was unanimous. Note that any reference to Christ was completely omitted. This remained the church's official title until April 26, 1838, when Smith claimed that he had a revelation and was told to change it to the name the church bears today. This meant the

A replica of The Christus statue sculpted by Albert Bertel Thorvaldson in the Temple Square North Visitor's Center in Salt Lake City, Utah.

church did not have the name "Jesus" or "Christ" in it from 1834 to 1838. Does this mean the LDS Church was not Christ's church during that four-year span?

Richard Lloyd Anderson, emeritus professor of church history and doctrine at Brigham Young University, attempted to explain the 1834 change. "This alteration was not seen as a deemphasis of Christ," he wrote. "On the contrary, it was done in hopes that the name of the Church would more clearly reflect the fact that Christ was at its head."[5] Anderson believes that even though the official title of the church omitted the name of Christ, it was still known in the minds of many as the Church of Christ, and so he argues that the church's name really never changed. The name "Church of Latter-day Saints," Anderson adds, is "descriptive of divine restoration," indicating "Jesus is at its head."[6]

Book of Mormon witness David Whitmer (1805–1888) did not agree with the 1834 name change. He wrote, "In June, 1829, the Lord gave us the name by which we must call the church, being the same as He gave the Nephites. We obeyed His commandment, and called it the Church of Christ until 1834, when, through the influence of Sidney Rigdon, the name of the church was changed to 'The Church of the Latter Day Saints,' dropping out the name of Christ entirely, that name which we were strictly commanded to call the church by, and which Christ by His own lips makes so plain."[7] Whitmer certainly saw an inconsistency between what the Book of Mormon commanded and how church leaders voted. In addition to the church's name, Latter-day Saints also point to their church's doctrinal and structural unity as proof of its authenticity. However, much of this unity can be attributed to the fact that the LDS Church tends to discipline those who express public opposition to what comes forth from Salt Lake City. Those who openly disagree with church doctrine and policy can be threatened with being disfellowshipped or even excommunicated. Consider also the many "restoration churches" teaching that Joseph Smith was a true prophet of God and the Book of Mormon is ancient scripture. The LDS leadership rejects their claims of authenticity.[8]

Technically, God's church is not an organization or a building. Rather, the body of Christ is composed of redeemed humans whose sins have been forgiven.[9] In the New Testament (KJV), the word *church* appears 115 times. In the great majority of these passages, it refers to a local congregation of believers, but it can also speak of believers everywhere. Jesus used the illustration of a shepherd (Himself) over a flock (believers), and many other images are used in the New Testament to describe the church, including the bride of Christ, the salt of the earth, and branches of the vine.

Neither the title of a church nor a label a person may be given defines true Christianity. Rather, as John 1:12 says, "But as many as received him, to them gave he power to become the sons of God, even to them that believe on his name." Christians are saved individuals who by faith in the work of Jesus Christ on the cross at Calvary have been forgiven their sins. God recognizes His people by their trust in Him, not by a name imprinted on a badge or on a sign posted at the entrance of a building where people meet on Sunday mornings.

Questions for Discussion

- Suppose a Mormon tells you that your church must not be Christian because it does not have the name of Jesus in it. How would you counter this argument?

- Some might insist that Christians' disagreement on such issues as the mode of baptism, the way to administer the Lord's Supper, or even which Bible version is best proves they are all apostate. Why are these issues not of paramount importance in defining a Christian? List several issues about which all Christians should be in agreement.

Evangelism Tip

Given the fact that an organization is free to call itself by any title it wishes, it is not a strong argument to assert that a church is Christian because it believes in Jesus or uses His name in its title. If so, then the Islamic "Mosque of Jesus Christ" in Madaba, Jordan, is also Christian! The better test is whether or not a church's teachings accurately reflect the message God wants to communicate to His creation. If it can be demonstrated that Mormon positions are not biblically supported, then it is inappropriate to assume it is God's church.

Aren't evangelism efforts aimed at Mormons just another act of persecution?

Response Questions

- Why should disagreement with another person's faith position be considered persecution?
- Suppose it is true that members of the LDS Church have been/are being persecuted. How would this make their church true?
- Christians have been persecuted throughout the world. Does this make their faith true?

• • • • • • • • • • • • • • • •

"Since the spring of 1820, Lucifer has led a relentless attack against the Latter-day Saints and their leaders. A parade of anti-Christs, anti-Mormons, and apostate groups have appeared on the scene. Many are still among us and have released new floods of lies and false accusations. These faith-killers and testimony-thieves use personal contacts, the printed word, electronic media, and other means of communication to sow doubts and to disturb the peace of true believers."[1]

—Seventy Carlos E. Asay

—————————————— Summary ——————————————

There have been cases through the years when Mormons have been unduly persecuted. However, the complete history of these events is usually not taken into consideration. Sometimes arrogant attitudes on the part of Mormons themselves, as well as issues not even based in religion, initiated the conflicts. Today, opposition to the LDS faith is often equated to hatred and bigotry. Mere disagreement with a religion and its beliefs should not be considered an act of persecution.

BEFORE CONSIDERING THIS question posed by the Latter-day Saint, we must define the word *persecution*. Webster's dictionary says that to persecute is "to afflict or harass constantly so as to injure or distress; oppress cruelly."[2] Some Mormons have used Matthew 5:11 as a picture of the persecution they have received over the years for their beliefs. There, Jesus said, "Blessed are ye, when men shall revile you, and persecute you, and shall say all manner of evil against you falsely, for my sake."

When the issue arises, many Mormons, especially those who trace their roots back to the nineteenth century, describe the persecution of their forefathers. Mormons were driven from Missouri and Illinois before finally arriving in what is known today as the state of Utah. Such violence against the Mormons can never be condoned. Yet with all the talk of the abuses faced by early Mormons, there is rarely any discussion of the role played by the Mormons themselves in those early conflicts. To be sure, the average Mormon has no idea that both sides had their share of human rights abuses. They simply think of their forebears as innocent victims.

It would be wrong to say the Mormons were treated badly simply because they had theological disagreements with their new neighbors. Historian D. Michael Quinn, a former Mormon, wrote, "Fear of being overwhelmed politically, socially, culturally, economically by Mormon immigration was what fueled anti-Mormonism wherever the Latter-day Saints settled during Joseph Smith's lifetime. Religious belief, as non-Mormons understood it, had little to do with anti-Mormonism. On the other hand, by the mid-1830s Mormons embraced a religion that shaped their politics, economics and society. Conflict was inevitable."[3]

This idea is supported by LDS scholars, including historians James B. Allen and Glen M. Leonard, who wrote, "Impressed by Mormon group solidarity, some old settlers expressed fears that the Mormons were determined to take over all their lands and businesses."[4] Stephen C. LeSueur, another historian, notes, "Non-Mormon land speculators could not hope to compete with the Mormons, who were purchasing large tracts of land with Church funds," and the huge immigration of Mormons to the area also "threatened to displace older towns as the political and commercial centers for their counties."[5]

Arrogance on the part of some Mormon settlers certainly did not help the situation. As Allen and Leonard explain,

> The Saints themselves may not have been totally without blame in the matter. The feelings of the Missourians, even though misplaced,

were undoubtedly intensified by the rhetoric of the gathering itself. They were quick to listen to the boasting of a few overly zealous Saints who too-loudly declared a divine right to the land. As enthusiastic millennialists, they also proclaimed that the time of the gentiles was short, and they were perhaps too quick to quote the revelation that said that "the Lord willeth that the disciples and the children of men should open their hearts, even to purchase this whole region of country, as soon as time will permit" (D&C 58:52). Though the Saints were specifically and repeatedly commanded to be peaceful and to never shed blood, some seemed unwisely to threaten warfare if they could not fulfill the commandment peacefully.[6]

The leadership of Joseph Smith (1805–1844) didn't help to ease the tension. When First Counselor Sidney Rigdon (1793–1876) gave a fiery 1838 speech that threatened the state of Missouri with what he called a "war of extermination," Smith turned it into a pamphlet. Adding to the Missourians' distress were the rumors of Mormon "Danites," a secret band of Mormon hit men known to intimidate non-Mormon "Gentiles" and LDS dissenters. Acts of violence against the Mormon settlers and the Mormons' belief that they would not receive proper redress compelled them to retaliate. LeSueur lays blame at the feet of Joseph Smith for the "plundering and burning committed by Mormon soldiers in Daviess County." He wrote, "Although Mormon military action was generally initiated in response to reports of violence, the Mormons tended to overreact and in some instances retaliated against innocent citizens. Their perception of themselves as the chosen people, their absolute confidence in their leaders, and their determination not to be driven out led Mormon soldiers to commit numerous crimes. The Mormons had many friends among the Missourians, but their military operations undercut their support in the non-Mormon community."[7]

Attempts to get along in Missouri proved fruitless. Each side blamed the other, with each claiming to be the defender rather than the aggressor. The violence came to a head in late 1838 when a group of Missouri militia, led by Captain Samuel Bogart (1797–1861), moved through Ray County, disarming Mormon settlers and ordering them to leave. Reports circulated among the Mormons that Bogart's men had burned and plundered several Mormon homes in their two-day march, despite the lack of evidence to support this claim.[8] The massacre at Haun's Mill, in which the Missouri militia attacked a Mormon settlement and killed seventeen men and boys, is an oft-cited example of persecution. Speaking of the persecution faced by Mormons in the past, Apostle Bruce R. McConkie (1915–1985) wrote, "We have staggered under the iron fist of persecution during our whole latter-day history, and we know that hatred and ill will and death will continue to be spewed out upon us until the coming end of the world. We have been driven and scourged and slain; the blood of our prophets stains Illinois; at Haun's Mill the innocent blood of the martyrs for truth cries unto the Lord of Hosts; and on frozen and desolate hills, across half a continent, lie the lonely graves of suffering saints who chose death in preference to the creeds of compulsion of a decadent Christendom."[9]

McConkie's dramatic rhetoric fails to take into account that the Haun's Mill massacre took place just one week after Mormons attacked Missouri state troops. Quinn reported,

> A generally unacknowledged dimension of both the extermination order and the Haun's Mill massacre, however, is that they resulted from Mormon actions in the Battle of Crooked River. Knowingly or not, Mormons had attacked state troops, and this had a cascade effect. . . . Finally, upon receiving news of the injuries and death of state troops at Crooked River, Governor Boggs immediately drafted his extermination order on 27 October 1838 because the Mormons "have made war upon the people of this state." Worse, the killing of one Missourian and mutilation of another while he was defenseless at Crooked River led to the mad-dog revenge by Missourians in the slaughter at Haun's Mill.[10]

Quinn also noted,

> Likewise, at the beginning of the Battle of Crooked River on 25 October 1838, Apostle David W. Patten (a Danite captain with the code-name "Fear Not") told his men: "Go ahead, boys; rake them down." The highest ranking Mormon charged with murder for obeying this order was Apostle Parley P. Pratt who allegedly took the careful aim of a sniper in killing one Missourian and then severely wounding militiaman Samuel Tarwater. This was after Apostle Patten received a fatal stomach wound. In their fury at the sight of their fallen leader, some of the Danites mutilated the unconscious Tarwater "with their swords, striking him lengthwise in the

mouth, cutting off his under teeth, and breaking his lower jaw; cutting off his cheeks . . . and leaving him [for] dead." He survived to press charges against Pratt for attempted murder.[11]

One commenter on Mormonism Research Ministry's blog site insisted, "The historical facts are clear and irrefutable: persecutions against Mormons and the LDS Church during the 19th century were often violent, vicious, and cruel. Many Mormons were murdered and hundreds died fleeing their persecutors during the Missouri War. Even hundreds more Mormons perished from exposure fleeing their persecutors after the martyrdom of Joseph and Hyrum Smith. This is not fiction, this is historical fact!"[12] To the contrary, deaths during the LDS persecution period were not as high as many Mormons imagine. Speaking during the October 1907 general conference, Seventy B. H. Roberts (1857–1933) stated, "First, let me tell you the net results of the persecution of the Latter-day Saints in Missouri, so far as they can be told in a summary: There were killed outright of men, women and children, so far as careful estimates can be made, more than fifty souls. There were as many more wounded and beaten. How many perished by slow death, suffering untold agonies, by reason of exposure and cruelties, no one knows, nor can it be computed."[13] Mormon historians Ronald W. Walker, Richard E. Turley Jr., and Glen M. Leonard conclude that deaths resulting from persecution of Mormons were in the "dozens."[14] While persecution should always be condemned, exaggerating the facts does not help foster honest discussions.

Christian evangelism efforts aimed at Latter-day Saints should not automatically be considered hateful or mean-spirited. Christians with good motives want nothing more than what is desired by Latter-day Saint missionaries who attempt to share their message with others. They simply want to lovingly share their faith. While Mormons may not like a message that contradicts LDS beliefs, they need to understand that the vast majority of Christians are not attempting to "persecute" Latter-day Saints. This is a good reminder to be kind when Mormon missionaries knock on our doors or approach us on the sidewalk. There is no need for us to be rude or disparaging. As 1 Peter 3:15 says, gentleness and respect is to be the rule, not the exception.

Finally, just because a religious people-group has been persecuted does not prove that their ideas and beliefs are true. Otherwise all religious groups who have suffered at some time during their history must be considered true, an idea that would never be accepted by the Latter-day Saint. In fact, the persecution endured by Mormons cannot match what Christians have suffered over the past two millennia and continue to suffer today.[15] Dwelling on the issue of persecution is a red herring and shouldn't be allowed to derail an otherwise productive conversation.

Questions for Discussion

- Why is it important to show gentleness and respect when sharing one's faith with someone of another religion? Provide at least three reasons.

- Some Mormons have taken offense when approached by Christians who want to share their faith, equating such evangelism efforts with persecution. Why is it incorrect to automatically equate disagreement with hatred and bigotry?

- If the unredeemed dead could speak to us, do you think they would have more contempt for the Christian who feared offense and said nothing to them, or the Christian who felt the sense of urgency and unintentionally offended them in the process? Why?

———————————— Evangelism Tip ————————————

When Mormons bring up past persecution against their church, it is often just a means of diverting the conversation. Explain that while Christianity has more of a history with persecution than Mormonism, this fact does not somehow prove its views to be true. Though the Mormon who misuses the word *persecution* should not be allowed to hinder our evangelism efforts, we should be conscious of exercising gentleness and respect when talking to Mormon acquaintances. Generally, people are more apt to listen to an opposing viewpoint if they sense that a challenge to their beliefs is based on genuine concern.

If Mormonism is wrong, then why is it one of the fastest-growing churches? And what about the fruit of Mormonism?

Response Questions

- Are you assuming that a church's size (or growth rate) is the determining factor in whether or not a particular religion is true?
- If another organization or church had more or "better" works, should we consider it to be just as legitimate or truthful?

• • • • • • • • • • • • • • • •

"[LDS Public Relations officials] know why this is the fastest-growing religious element in the United States and in the world, almost."[1]

—President Gordon B. Hinckley (1910–2008)

--------- Summary ---------

It is common for Mormons to point to their church's growth rate in contrast to the stagnation or even loss of church membership in some Protestant denominations. However, the perception that growth and success of a religion equals legitimacy is without foundation. And while the LDS Church is growing, it hardly has the largest numbers or percentage growth in either the United States or the world. Likewise, just because a church displays good works does not necessarily mean that it is Christian. Its teachings need to be biblically based, or the religion ought to be rejected.

Does the accelerated growth of any religion or the good works coming from its adherents somehow validate what it teaches? To many Latter-day Saints, the success of their church is a proof that Mormonism is true. Despite the boasting by many of its members, however, the LDS Church does not encourage this attitude. On its Newsroom Web site is this statement: "The Church of Jesus Christ of Latter-day Saints is the second-fastest growing church in the United States. However, despite its increasing numbers, the Church cautions against overemphasis on growth statistics. The Church makes no statistical comparisons with other churches and makes no claim to be the fastest-growing Christian denomination despite frequent news media comments to that effect."[2]

Still, many LDS members like to point to the growth of the church as somehow validating Mormonism. In light of this, let's first consider the convert growth of the church since 1990. Although it has continually added to its numbers, the LDS Church has not maintained the percentage growth it was enjoying at the end of the twentieth century. Brigham Young University professor Daniel Peterson acknowledged this downturn in recent years, writing, "Today, we have been allotted tools for sharing the gospel of which [Book of Mormon prophet] Alma could never have dreamed. But we may have become complacent. Don't we send out full-time missionaries? Isn't that enough? Aren't we 'the fastest growing religion'? Actually, we're not. Church growth has been falling for many years, and our current rate of missionary success is the lowest it's been for decades. The harvest is great, but the laborers are still too few."[3]

According to a Reuter's article, Church Historian and Recorder Marlin Jansen addressed a religious studies class at Utah State University in the fall of 2011. Answering a student's question about whether LDS leaders knew that members were leaving in droves, he said he was "aware" of the situation. Then he added, "And I'm speaking of the 15 men that are above me in the hierarchy of the church. They really do know and they really care." Jensen said that "not since a famous trouble spot in Mormon history, the 1837 failure of a church bank in Kirtland, Ohio, have so many left the church." The article also reported that "census data from some foreign countries targeted by clean-cut young missionaries show that the retention rate for their converts is as low as 25 percent. In the U.S., only about half of Mormons are active members of the church, said Washington State University emeritus sociologist Armand Mauss, a leading researcher on Mormons. Sociologists estimate there are as few as 5 million active members worldwide."[4]

During the first half of the 1990s, the church consistently grew by more than 3 percent per year. Beginning in 1998, however, the rate of growth never reached 3 percent again, even dipping under 2 percent in three of the six years between 2005 and 2010. One possibility for this decline is the popularity of the Internet, which provides seekers with information that was previously inaccessible to potential converts. In addition, David Stewart, a Mormon who has spent many years studying the church's growth statistics, sees problems in how growth is reported. For example, he discovered that when polled, "less than half of individuals claimed as members by the LDS Church worldwide identify the LDS Church as their faith of preference." Noting that the church loses three-quarters of its converts within a year in some foreign mission fields, he wrote,

> The LDS missionary program has not been as effective in either the United States or in international areas as one would like to believe. . . . Data from Latin America, the Philippines, and other international areas demonstrate that three quarters of converts are entirely lost to the church within a year after baptism. While raw LDS membership numbers may appear impressive on paper, these numbers have only a fractional relationship to the far more modest number of converts who have experienced a genuine, lasting, and life-changing conversion and who experience the blessings of active participation in the work of the Church. The available evidence suggests that the primary responsibility for these fractional retention rates lie with quick-baptize tactics which have traditionally focused more on meeting monthly baptismal goals than on ensuring that converts have been adequately prepared for baptism.[5]

One can only wonder how many baptized members remain on the church rolls, years or even decades after they left the church.[6] But even if the convert numbers are correct, the percentage of growth has gone down in recent years. Compare the LDS Church statistics with another nineteenth-century American religious movement, the Brooklyn, New York–based Watchtower Bible and Tract Society, whose members are known as Jehovah's Witnesses. Unlike Latter-day Saints, the Watchtower Society considers all members to be missionaries who are expected to go door-to-door and evangelize on a regular basis.

In 2010, this organization—which is about half the size of the LDS

George Q. Cannon (center with white beard), a member of the LDS First Presidency, sits among other convicted Mormon polygamists in 1888.

Church—grew by 294,000 converts (as compared to Mormonism's 272,000 converts in the same time frame). This is a 4 percent increase from the previous year's numbers, doubling the total percentage of growth listed by the LDS Church. It is doubtful a Mormon would consider the Watchtower Society true just because its numbers are growing at this rate! As far as total numbers, the LDS Church could never compete with Roman Catholicism, Islam, or Hinduism. In terms of percentage growth, Mormonism is not even the fastest-growing religion in the United States.

Should growth be an indicator of truth? Actually, Jesus Himself said in Matthew 7:13, "Enter ye in at the strait gate: for *wide* is the gate, and *broad* is the way, that leadeth to destruction." As hard as these words are, Jesus said that the majority of people are not on the narrow path but on the broad road to destruction. He also said in Matthew 24:11, "And many false prophets shall rise, and shall deceive many." The apostle Peter confirmed this idea in 2 Peter 2:1–2 when he said that false teachers will cause "many" to follow their "pernicious ways." Even though there is one example of growth statistics in the book of Acts (with the adding of three thousand people as mentioned in Acts 2), there is absolutely no insinuation from this statistic that this was proof of the truthfulness of the message Peter spoke on Pentecost. While Jesus said in Matthew 7:20 that "by their fruits ye shall know them," nowhere does the Bible equate numerical growth with that fruit.

The Financial Fruit of Mormonism

Mormons often point with pride to their church's prosperity, as seen in its many beautiful buildings, including dozens of temples located around the world. Such prosperity, generously used in charitable works, is seen as the "fruit" that attests to the perceived truth of Mormonism. LDS Church public relations news releases often feature the church's donation of food and supplies throughout the United States and the world whenever there is a time of disaster or crisis. However, in the late 1990s, journalists Richard and Joan Ostling wrote,

> In the fourteen years from 1984 to 1997, the church says, it made a total of $30.7 million in cash donations to non-Mormon humanitarian aid (not counting the worth of commodities and goods shipped) in 146 countries, including the United States. . . . In 1997 U.S. congregations of the similarly sized Evangelical Lutheran Church in America raised $11.8 million in cash donations for worldwide hunger. The same year it raised $3.64 million for domestic and international disaster response, for a one-year humanitarian cash total of $15.44 million, more than half the amount the LDS provided over fourteen years. Then there were the Lutherans' many assistance programs apart from simple cash donations. Like the Lutherans, many Protestant and Catholic agencies at home and abroad do extensive—and expensive—medical and educational work. The LDS Church no longer maintains hospitals, and its short-term missionaries concentrate on proselytizing for converts.[7]

According to its own almanac, the LDS Church gave $1.116 billion in humanitarian aid to 167 countries from 1985 through 2009. The totals included more than 12,000 tons of medical supplies, 61,000 tons of food, and 84,000 tons of clothing.[8] Breaking this down over twenty-five years (1985–2009), an average of about $45 million worth of aid per year was given. During those twenty-five years, the church had an average membership of about 9 million members. For each year, this equates to roughly $5 annually for each member of the church.

The church's humanitarian concerns are certainly admirable. However, even if the church decided to increase its giving by, say, ten times, it would still fall far short of the annual giving by three of the biggest Christian humanitarian agencies around the world. In just 2009 alone, Feed the Children distributed $1.2 billion worth of food, supplies, and aid, an annual total that is more than the LDS Church has donated over two and a half decades. In addition, World Vision ($1.1 billion) and Samaritan's Purse ($294 million) took care of the needs of the less fortunate and responded in times of natural disasters. These groups also work to increase agricultural output and improve living conditions.

Numbers from churches are often difficult to decipher. For example, the Catholic Church does not release official numbers, but it finances many hospitals and orphanages around the world, and billions of dollars are certainly spent on these projects. Many Protestant churches are very active in humanitarian works as well, including the Salvation Army, which believes that "God raised up The Salvation Army according to his purposes for his glory and for the proclamation and demonstration of the gospel."[9] Even some atheists, perhaps because they have been asked (usually tongue-in-cheek) for the location of their charitable hospitals, are boldly letting the world know that charity is not reserved only for the religious.[10]

Suppose for a moment, though, that pragmatic results really could determine truth. Who gets to decide who is producing the best fruit? Whatever presuppositions are brought to the decision-making process by the one doing the judging certainly will be the overriding factor in choosing a "winner." Understand that we are not criticizing the LDS Church for giving aid to needy causes or even implying that it should give more. Rather, the point is that good works do not determine the validity of the truth claims of any church or organization. Indeed, Mormons would have to admit that they are not the only ones striving to help others, and there are other groups that very well could be doing it better.

The Social Fruit of Mormonism

Social issues also must be factored into the "fruit" of Mormonism. Consider that a Mormon who decides to leave the church can end up sacrificing family relationships, sometimes even a marriage. Indeed, the reality that they will never be able to leave the religion without giving up relationships most precious to them has caused many Mormons to remain in the church. Responding in a survey that asked, "If you could speak with a top church leader, what would you ask or tell him?" one male said, "Stop hurting marriages by driving a wedge between spouses on this issue. I have gone through hell and back and nearly divorced. We desperately need a General Conference address telling spouses to not divorce an otherwise good spouse over non-belief. I have several friends who have been divorced over primarily this issue, and my own marriage is still on the rocks due to it, even though I am fully active."[11]

While approximately 70 percent of Utah's population are members of the LDS Church, it has a higher depression rate per capita than any other state. According to one health report, one in five Utah women use anti-depressants. One Ogden, Utah, psychiatrist said these numbers "may be

The following information was taken from the May conference editions of the *Ensign* magazine from 1990–2011. Charts courtesy of Mary Ann Rankel.

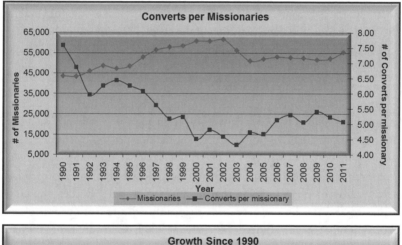

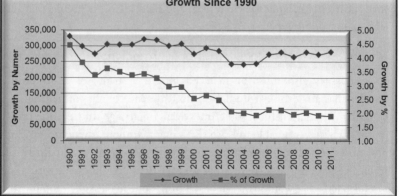

a good thing because it means people are getting help for their depression rather than ignoring the problem."[12] Lifelong Mormon physician Kent Ponder interviewed nearly three hundred LDS women and in a 2003 paper concluded:

> Utah residents currently use more antidepressant drugs, notably Prozac (fluoxetine hydrochloride, introduced in 1987), than the residents of any other US state. This problem is closely and definitely linked to The Church of Jesus Christ of Latter-day Saints. Approximately 70 percent of Utahans are affiliated with the LDS Church. Jim Jorgenson, director of pharmacy services for the University of Utah, confirmed that Utah has the highest percentage of anti-depressant use, hypothesizing that large families, larger in Utah than in other states, produce greater stress. (Large Utah families are primarily Mormon families).[13]

Mormon apologetic groups and researchers from LDS Church–owned Brigham Young University have complained that Ponder's conclusion is faulty. Regardless, there is no doubt that antidepressant drugs are heavily used in the state of Utah. Meanwhile, a study from 2002–2007 conducted by the organization Mental Health of America concluded that "Utah was the most depressed state" in the nation, reporting, "Among adults in Utah, 10.14 percent experienced a depressive episode in the past year and 14.58 percent experienced serious psychological distress. Among adolescents in Utah, 10.14 experienced a major depressive episode in the past year. Individuals in Utah reported having on average 3.27 poor mental health days in the past 30 days."[14]

According to a 2011 study done by the Centers for Disease Control and Prevention, almost one in fifteen people (more than 8 percent of women and more than 5 percent of men) living in Utah contemplated suicide.[15] This statistic, of course, doesn't necessarily indicate that Mormonism is driving people to have suicidal thoughts, as everyone is susceptible to depression. Just as it is erroneous to conclude that positive statistics make a religion true, it is equally erroneous to assume that negative statistics automatically make a religion false. But if a Mormon chooses to look at membership behavior as religious "fruit," then both the positive and negative aspects should be considered. All religious groups have their good and bad examples.

The Fruit of Jesus

How, then, should the truth claims of a church/organization be judged? If indeed the LDS Church espouses doctrine contrary to what is revealed in the Bible, how could this be considered "good"? Jesus said, "By their fruits ye shall know them," but two verses later He predicted that "many" will stand before the Great White Throne on Judgment Day, making a case for themselves and explaining why they deserve salvation. "Lord, Lord," they will say, "have we not prophesied in thy name? and in thy name have cast out devils? and in thy name done many wonderful works?" (Matt. 7:22). Notice Jesus' response: "And then will I profess unto them, I never knew you: depart from me, ye that work iniquity" (v. 23).

Can you imagine the shocked look on the faces of many who are trusting in their own "good" works to qualify them for eternal life? The startling difference between Christianity and Mormonism is made very clear by the Matthew 7 passage so commonly used by Mormons. Instead of pointing to beautiful Mormon temple buildings, the financial prosperity of their organization, their well-oiled missions program, and other factors that, on the surface, look like good works, the Mormon needs to ask this very important question: Is Mormonism true? If it is, then its teachings will align with what God clearly teaches in His Word, the Bible. If not, then this religion—no matter how good it looks on the outside—needs to be avoided at all costs.

Questions for Discussion

- A Mormon has just told you that the fruit of the LDS Church, including its welfare program and beautiful temples located throughout the world, proves that Mormonism really is true. Explain the fallacy of this assertion.

- The LDS Church did not grow as fast in the first decade of the twenty-first century as it did in the last decade of the twentieth century. Perhaps the Internet and the amount of information freely available on Mormonism have played a role in this stunting of growth. Would you agree? What other reasons could have contributed to the church's declining rate of growth?

———————————— Evangelism Tip ————————————

Many Mormons make the mistake of thinking that the perceived success of their church—from nice buildings to successful programs—points to its authenticity. However, the LDS Church is nowhere close to being the largest or fastest-growing religious organization, a fact that should be emphasized to those who point to such "fruit." In addition, most religions have adherents who strive to be good citizens and help their fellow men and women. This, however, does not legitimize the religion's truth claims. If "good" fruit is to be found, it must be hanging on the tree that is leading people to the true God of this universe.

Chapter 6

Why do so many equate our church to splinter groups when we no longer practice polygamy?

Response Questions

- Are you saying polygamy is a completely dead issue in the Mormon Church?
- Doesn't the LDS Church still "seal" living men to more than one woman in LDS temples?
- If polygamy is declared legal, should the church reinstate this practice?

• • • • • • • • • • • • • • • •

"Much of the development of Mormonism can be linked to the introduction, promotion, and eventual abnegation of polygamy. To those who accept Joseph Smith as a prophet of God, plural marriage can be evidence of his divine calling; to those who question or reject his prophetic claims, polygamy is more readily explained as evidence of his downfall."[1]

—Richard Van Wagoner (1946–2010)

Summary

The LDS Church has tried to distance itself from its own past, when marriage to more than one living woman was taught to be essential for eternal exaltation. Leaders also have tried hard to disassociate their religion from splinter groups that practice plural marriage while holding just as strongly to the teachings of Joseph Smith and the Book of Mormon. Mormon leaders adamantly deny that polygamy is a part of current LDS doctrine. However, polygamy is not a completely dead issue, for rather than abandon the idea altogether, the Mormon Church has merely redefined how plural marriage is to be practiced.

IN SECTION 132 OF THE Doctrine and Covenants, Joseph Smith (1805–1844) claimed that God gave him a "new and everlasting covenant." Verses 4 and 6 state unequivocally that "no one can reject this covenant and be permitted to enter my glory . . . he that receiveth a fulness thereof must and shall abide the law, or he shall be damned, saith the Lord God." This covenant refers to polygamy, also known as plural marriage, which for the Mormons meant one man could have more than one wife.[2] Such a radical change in nineteenth-century sexual norms was met with expected resistance. Don Carlos Smith (1816–1841), the brother of Joseph Smith, is reported to have said, "Any man who will teach and practice the doctrine of spiritual wifery will go to hell, I don't care if it is my brother Joseph."[3] Joseph Smith's wife Emma (1804–1879) never liked the doctrine of plural marriage. In Doctrine and Covenants 132:52, she is warned to "receive all those that have been given unto my servant Joseph." Verse 54 states that "if she will not abide this commandment she shall be destroyed, saith the Lord."

It isn't difficult to find examples of polygamy in the Old Testament. Its first mention is found in Genesis 4:19, when Lamech took both Adah and Zillah as his wives. But one thing is certain: while polygamy was tolerated in ancient Israel, it was never commanded or ever meant to be a requirement for true salvation. Genesis 2:24 makes it clear that God's norm for His creation was that a husband would "cleave unto his wife," not wives. Old Testament scholar Paul Copan notes, "If God commended or commanded such a practice, this would be a deviation from the assumed standard of heterosexual monogamy in Genesis 2:24 and elsewhere."[4] Copan also observes, "From Lamech's wives to those of Abraham, Esau, Jacob, David, and Solomon, wherever we see God's ideal of monogamy ignored, we witness strife, competition, and disharmony. The Old Testament presents polygamy as not only undesirable but also a violation of God's standards. Old Testament narratives subtly critique this marital arrangement."[5]

But why would Joseph Smith introduce a practice that is not mentioned even once in the New Testament? While many suggestions have been offered, there seems to be no official answer other than that God commanded it. A group of LDS scholars insists that members "practiced plural marriage because God commanded them to do so. Plural marriage was a religious principle, and this is the only valid explanation as to why the practice was maintained despite decades of opposition and persecution."[6] Some saw plural marriage as a means of providing for widows within the Mormon fold. But couldn't assistance to these women have been given without the men having to marry them? And while some claim the practice was necessary because of an alleged surplus of women in the Mormon community, this assumption is refuted by statistical data. Even Apostle John A. Widtsoe stated, "The United States census records from 1850 to 1940, and all available Church records, uniformly show a preponderance of males in Utah, and in the Church."[7]

Polygamy certainly is not encouraged in the Book of Mormon. Speaking of David and Solomon's "abominable" practice of having many wives and concubines, Jacob 2:26–27 warns, "Wherefore, I the Lord God will not suffer that this people shall do like unto them of old. Wherefore, my brethren, hear me, and hearken to the word of the Lord: For there shall not any man among you have save it be one wife; and concubines he shall have none."

Jacob 2:30 does offer a single exception: "For if I will, saith the Lord of Hosts, raise up seed unto me, I will command my people; otherwise they shall hearken unto these things." In an essay titled "Notes on Mormon Polygamy," writer Stanley Ivans states, "While polygamy increased the number of children of the men, it did not do the same for the women involved. A count revealed that 3,335 wives of polygamists bore 19,806 children, for an average of 5.9 per woman. An equal number of wives of monogamists taken from the same general group bore 26,780 for an average of 8. This suggests the possibility that the overall production of children in Utah may have been less than it would have been without benefit of plurality of wives."[8]

Mormon historian Todd Compton states that Joseph Smith had thirty-three wives,[9] and it is also generally accepted that among those Smith married were women with living husbands. Compton writes that "fully one-third of his plural wives, eleven of them, were married civilly to other men when he married them. If one superimposes a chronological perspective, one sees that of Smith's first twelve wives, nine were polyandrous."[10] Nowhere in Mormon scripture do we find polyandry as an acceptable practice.

If plural marriage were allowed only to increase the population, why is there no evidence of Smith having any children with these women? Some have suggested that Josephine Lyon Fisher, the daughter of Sylvia Sessions, one of Joseph Smith's wives, may have been fathered by Smith. "It is possible that Joseph had children by his plural wives, but by no means certain. The data are surprisingly ephemeral."[11]

The Manifesto

With the passing of the Edmunds-Tucker Act in 1887, the United States government began putting pressure on the LDS Church to abandon what has been called "the principle." At the October 1890 general conference, a statement that has come to be known as the Manifesto was presented, officially ending the LDS practice of plural marriage. The Manifesto was unanimously accepted and appears in Mormon scripture as "Official Declaration—1" at the end of the Doctrine and Covenants. It reads more like a press release than a typical revelation. President George Albert Smith (1870–1951) said, "The practice of plural marriage ceased because the government of the United States forbade it. Our Heavenly Father has always directed that we sustain the constitutional law of the land, and the Supreme Court being the highest authority had declared the law forbidding plural marriage was constitutional."[12]

According to one LDS manual, "Some, however, claimed that President [Wilford] Woodruff gave in to pressure and that the Lord had not really revealed that plural marriage was to cease. The fact that the declaration did not specifically mention revelation as the reason for stopping the practice seemed to fuel the criticism. A year later at a quarterly conference in Brigham City, Utah, President Woodruff made it clear why he made the decision to stop the practice of plural marriage." In that talk, Woodruff (1807–1898) said the Lord showed him "by vision and revelation" exactly what would take place if the church did not stop this practice.[13] This included the confiscation and loss of all the temples, which, of course, would put an end to the ordinances practiced in those temples, as well as the "imprisonment of the First Presidency and Twelve and the heads of families in the Church, and the confiscation of personal property of the people."[14]

Despite the denials and promises contained in the 1890 Manifesto, historical records reveal that plural marriages were still being performed. Kenneth L. Cannon notes, "As early as 1893, however, new plural marriages were performed in Mexico, an idea initially proposed by George Q. Cannon. Woodruff agreed with his first counselor's idea, letting Cannon direct this new polygamy so that he would not participate directly as Church President. Cannon's responsibility included choosing and setting apart certain Church leaders to perform the marriages. In that year at least two couples were married in Mexico, apparently with the approbation of Wilford Woodruff and his two counselors. Throughout the mid-1890s the following scenario was repeated on numerous occasions."[15] According to Cannon, "Among the Quorum of the Twelve and the First Presidency between 1890 and 1898, at least 58 percent of the members took an active part in post-Manifesto polygamy."[16]

Redefining Celestial Marriage

Until the late nineteenth century, celestial marriage was synonymous with plural marriage.[17] Historian Thomas G. Alexander explained, "Generally, the terms 'new and everlasting covenant' of marriage, 'celestial marriage,' and plural marriage were thought to be equivalent."[18] This can easily be demonstrated from the *History of the Church*.

> On the morning of the 12th of July, 1843, Joseph and Hyrum Smith came into the office in the upper story of the brick store, on the bank of the Mississippi river. They were talking on the subject of plural marriage. Hyrum said to Joseph, "If you will write the revelation on celestial marriage, I will take it and read it to Emma, and I believe I can convince her of the truth, and you will hereafter have peace." Joseph smiled and remarked, "You do not know Emma as well as I do." Hyrum repeated his opinion, and further remarked, "The doctrine is so plain, I can convince any reasonable man or woman of its truth, purity and heavenly origin," or words to that effect. Joseph then said, "Well, I will write the revelation and we will see."[19]

In a sermon given on August 31, 1873, Brigham Young (1801–1877) declared, "You will recollect, brethren and sisters, that it was in July, 1843, that he [Joseph Smith] received this revelation concerning celestial marriage. This doctrine was explained and many received it as far as they could understand it. Some apostatized on account of it; but others did not, and received it in their faith."[20] If celestial marriage were always just another term for eternal marriage, why would it cause those who understood it to apostatize? Why would Emma, or any other Mormon man or woman, strongly object to being sealed to their spouse if that was all that was meant by the term *celestial marriage*? The answer is simple. Celestial marriage was originally equated with plural marriage.

Rather than expunge section 132 from the Doctrine and Covenants, the LDS Church leadership chose instead to simply redefine the phrase. Historian B. Carmon Hardy stated, "In early 1908 a committee consisting of Anthon H. Lund, Orson F. Whitney, Brigham H. Roberts, and James E. Talmage, after researching the question, recommended to the First Presidency that 'celestial marriage' not be equated exclusively with 'plural' or 'patriarchal' marriage. The crucial, saving principle, said the report, was simply the eternal nature of the marriage covenant."[21]

In a message from President Heber J. Grant (1856–1945) and his counselors, Anthony W. Ivins (1852–1934) and J. Reuben Clark (1871–1961), the membership was told, "Celestial marriage—that is, marriage for time and eternity—and polygamous or plural marriage are not synonymous terms. Monogamous marriages for time and eternity, solemnized in our temples in accordance with the word of the Lord and the laws of the Church, are Celestial marriages."[22] Seventy B. H. Roberts (1857–1933) noted, "The marriage covenant which unites immortal beings is eternal, hence the eternity of the marriage covenant which Joseph Smith introduced in our dispensation, called the 'New and Everlasting Covenant of Marriage';—sometimes called 'Celestial Marriage'—by which marriages under the law of God, are made in sacred places for time and eternity."[23] Of course, nineteenth-century leaders gave these terms a much broader definition.

A Doctrine That No Power on Earth Can Suppress?

Even though marriage to more than one living woman is not taught today in the LDS Church, early church leaders were adamant that it was to be a permanent practice. For example, First Presidency member George Q. Cannon (1827–1901) stated, "If plural marriage be divine, as the Latter-day Saints say it is, no power on earth can suppress it, unless you crush and destroy the entire people."[24] Ironically, Wilford Woodruff, the same Mormon leader who officially ended the practice, also once stated,

> Were we to compromise this principle by saying, we will renounce it, we would then have to renounce our belief in revelation from God, and our belief in the necessity of Prophets and Apostles, and the principle of the gathering, and then to do away with the idea and practice of building Temples in which to administer ordinances for the exaltation of the living and the redemption of the dead; and at last we would have to renounce our Church organization, and mix up and mingle with the world, and become part of them. Can we afford to do this? I tell you no, we can not; but we can afford to keep the commandments of God.[25]

Woodruff also declared at the 1888 dedication of the Manti temple, "We are not going to stop the practice of plural marriage until the coming of the son of man."[26] While a Mormon might argue that the illegality of plural marriage reflects God's will regarding this subject, pressure from the United

States to eliminate polygamy was looked upon by the church leadership as a direct refusal to recognize God's will.

The Current Status of Polygamy

In reference to the subject of plural marriage, Apostle Bruce R. McConkie (1915–1985) wrote, "Obviously the holy practice will commence again after the Second Coming of the Son of Man and the ushering in of the millennium."[27] In a sense, plural marriage still officially exists today in the LDS Church since Mormon males, under certain circumstances, can be sealed to more than one wife. In a conference message delivered in October 2005, James E. Faust (1920–2007), a member of the First Presidency, declared, "Temple blessings seal husband and wife together, not only for this life but for eternity. Children and posterity can be linked together by this sealing."[28]

According to the 2010 LDS *Church Handbook of Instruction*, "A living woman may be sealed to only one husband." The next paragraph states, "If a husband and wife have been sealed and the wife dies, the man may have another woman sealed to him if she is not already sealed to another man."[29] The manual then states, "A deceased man may have sealed to him all women to whom he was legally married during his life if they are deceased or if they are living and not sealed to another man."[30] Thus, Mormon men who are sealed to more than one wife certainly expect all of their marriages to be binding in the next life.

During a devotional address he gave at Brigham Young University on January 29, 2002, Apostle Dallin H. Oaks spoke about his former wife, June Dixon Oaks, who died of cancer in 1998. Then he said, "Two years later I married Kristen McMain, the eternal companion who now stands at my side."[31] June had been sealed to Dallin H. Oaks in the Salt Lake temple on June 24, 1952. McMain was sealed to Oaks—also for time and eternity in the same temple—on August 25, 2000. When Oaks referred to Kristen McMain as his "eternal companion," he didn't hide the fact that she, like his first wife June, will be his wife for eternity. Apostles L. Tom Perry and Russell M. Nelson also have remarried after their first wives died, and both have been sealed to their new wives for "time and eternity" in temple ceremonies.

Mormon publisher George D. Smith wrote, "Although polygamy has been repeatedly condemned by the contemporary LDS Church, the Nauvoo beginnings of the practice remain in LDS scripture as Section 132 of the Doctrine and Covenants and in the church's temple sealings."[32] Thus, it is misleading for the LDS Church to give the impression that plural marriage plays no role in LDS theology.

Questions for Discussion

- Polygamy was practiced by some of the patriarchs and kings in the Old Testament. List just a couple of them. What were the consequences of their polygamy?

- A Mormon might insist, "Polygamy is a dead issue in the Mormon Church." What would be a good response?

- Since polygamy as a doctrine apparently was banned by the LDS Church due to political pressure in the United States, what do you think the church would do if polygamy were to be legalized in the future? Do you think the church would officially restart the practice? Why or why not?

Evangelism Tip

Though not considered one of the more productive topics of conversation for evangelistic purposes, polygamy continues to spark differences of opinion among practicing LDS members. Some look forward to its future implementation, while others do not. Still, Mormons can be offended when their church is linked to Mormon splinter groups that continue to practice plural marriage in a nineteenth-century manner. Christians who are interested in sharing their faith need to be very sensitive should this topic be introduced. Like using the word *bomb* in an airport, making light of polygamy, even as an innocent joke, generally will be received negatively.

Section 2

Christianity

Chapter 7

If the LDS Church is not true, which church is?

Response Questions

- Do you believe Christian denominations disagree on the major issues such as the Godhead and salvation by grace through faith?
- Do you think all followers of Joseph Smith agree about important issues such as polygamy and church authority?

● ● ● ● ● ● ● ● ● ● ● ● ● ● ● ●

"The Latter-day Saints are the only ones who bear the authority of our Heavenly Father to administer in the ordinances of the Gospel. The world has need of us."[1]

—President George Albert Smith (1870–1951)

Summary

Frustrated when Christians say they do not believe the Church of Jesus Christ of Latter-day Saints is a Christian church, many Mormons like to ask which denomination the Christian believes is true. The assumption is that all denominations contradict each other. However, Christian churches *do* agree on the essential issues crucial to the Christian faith. While there may be disagreement on secondary/peripheral issues, believers from different churches can fellowship together when they understand their commonality in Christ. One's denomination doesn't matter. What is important is the relationship one has with God.

IN A FALL 2011 GENERAL conference address, Tad R. Callister, a member of
the Presidency of the Seventy, said, "Have you ever wondered why there are
so many Christian churches in the world today when they obtain their doctrines from essentially the same Bible? It is because they interpret the Bible
differently. If they interpreted it the same, they would be the same church."[2]
This typical assumption misunderstands the role of Christian denominations. There is no denying that Christianity has had its share of mixed messages and that Christian history is replete with unsavory characters who
have attached to themselves the Christian label. However, to conclude that
the Christian faith is wrong because of the rise of various denominations is
flawed thinking.

When Mormonism began in the 1830s, there was already a serious movement in the United States to steer the Christian church back to its "primitive" roots. Probably the best-known leader of this movement was Thomas
Campbell (1763–1854), an Irish Presbyterian who came to America when
Mormonism's founder Joseph Smith (1805–1844) was barely a toddler. Long
before Smith's First Vision account, Campbell insisted that Christianity had
collected too much traditional baggage over the centuries. He insisted that
the faith needed to be restored to its original purity. Thomas Campbell left
the Presbyterian Church and, together with his son Alexander (1788–1866),
formed a new church that would eventually move to Zanesville, Ohio, in
1814.

New Testament scholar Craig Blomberg lists the unique positions held by
the Campbellites, as they were often called; they include belief in the apostasy
of the early church, the necessity of being baptized for salvation, preaching
against "faith only" salvation, and rejection of a paid clergy.[3] To those familiar with Mormonism, this list will sound very similar to emphases in Joseph
Smith's new movement. If nothing else, this shows that Smith was not original when it came to his views of a needed "restoration." Though some may
argue that Campbell was well intentioned in his desire to unify and "restore"
Christianity, his efforts actually resulted in adding three more denomina-
tional movements: Independent Christian Churches, Disciples of Christ, and
Churches of Christ. Over the years there have been more than two hundred
splinter groups that have claimed to be the true followers of Joseph Smith.[4]
Aside from the LDS Church, the largest of these groups is the Community
of Christ, based in Independence, Missouri, and formerly known as the
Reorganized Church of Jesus Christ of Latter-day Saints. In addition, there
are dozens of churches following Smith and practicing polygamy.

One Church Under Smith?

A month prior to his death, Smith proclaimed, "I have more to boast of than ever any man had. I am the only man that has ever been able to keep a whole church together since the days of Adam. A large majority of the whole have stood by me. Neither Paul, John, Peter, nor Jesus ever did it. I boast that no man ever did such a work as I. The followers of Jesus ran away from Him; but the Latter-day Saints never ran away from me yet."[5]

Smith's bravado becomes especially suspect when it is understood that there were plenty of dissenters at this time. If Mormons wish to point to division within Christianity as proof of apostasy, then consistency would demand an acknowledgment that apostasy has also tainted Smith's newer movement. While honest enough to admit that other groups exist, the LDS Church is quick to brush aside competing claims of authenticity, readily dismissing other restoration churches that claim to more closely represent the church that Smith had in mind. If contradictory teaching and bad behavior among adherents negate the entire faith, then doesn't Mormonism's claim to truth also become spurious? What makes the Utah LDS Church's claim to be the one true church any more believable than the same claim made by dozens of other groups still active today who claim Smith as *their* leader and insist that the Utah-based church is apostate?

Mormon history is full of division, cover-ups, contradictory doctrines, and abhorrent behavior among prominent members. Standing alone, does this mean Mormonism is false? Christianity also has had its share of controversy, and at times it is difficult to wade through some of the confusing things done in the name of "Christ." Yet when there are a billion people in the world claiming to be Christian, it should come as no surprise that questionable behavior and teachings will arise. And, without doubt, one of the biggest problems with Christianity is that fallen members, as well as outright imposters, have infiltrated the ranks.

Throughout history, Christians have struggled to properly understand what God is instructing them in the Bible. Because Christians are not omniscient, they must acknowledge that at times they can miss what God intends for them to believe and do. As a result, Christians will always have their disagreements over the peripheral issues of faith—such things as the mode of baptism or details of the end times. Generally, they are willing to agree to disagree on such issues.[6] Still, there are core beliefs Christians have long shared that cannot be compromised. It is in these core beliefs—for example, that the Bible is the supreme rule of faith, that there is one true God, and that salvation comes by grace through faith and not by works—where Mormonism goes astray. In true Christianity, there is great unity in diversity; the gospel message remains the same, even though there are other differences among the various denominations and churches.

Questions for Discussion

- Choose a Christian denomination other than your own, and explain how its views and your own (along with those of the church you attend) are similar. How are they different? Are these differences so big that you couldn't have fellowship with someone who belongs to the other church? Why or why not?

- Mormons differ among themselves on various beliefs. For example, some Mormons avoid all caffeinated sodas, while others drink them because they are not specifically prohibited by the Word of Wisdom. Some Mormons even disagree on whether life begins at conception. How could these examples help the Christian explain the differences between denominations?

─────────────── Evangelism Tip ───────────────

Good churches may differ on such issues as church government (congregational, episcopal, presbyterian), the songs they sing (hymns versus choruses, with or without instruments), the approach to worship (liturgical versus nonliturgical), the view of the end times (premillennial, postmillennial, amillennial, preterist), and even ways of celebrating Communion (once a month or once a week, individual cups or communal cup). Explain that while they may have differences, Christians from different denominations can agree on the essential doctrines of the faith. Maintaining unity in the midst of such diversity, while praising the God of the universe, can actually be a very positive aspect of Christian denominationalism.

Chapter 8

Didn't the Bible predict the apostasy of the Christian faith?

Response Questions

- Was Jesus not telling the truth when He said He would be with us always?
- Does this apostasy mean that everyone who is not LDS does not have authority from God?

• • • • • • • • • • • • • • • •

"[Referring to the church's official name] *Of Latter-day* explains that it is the same Church as the Church that Jesus Christ established during His mortal ministry but restored in these latter days. We know that there was a falling away, or an apostasy, necessitating the Restoration of His true and complete Church in our time."[1]

—Apostle M. Russell Ballard

—— Summary ——

Mormonism is based upon the idea there was an apostasy of Christianity that took place soon after the death of Jesus' disciples. Founder Joseph Smith believed that he was responsible for returning priesthood authority to the earth. If the Christian church really did need a restoration and God decided to use the LDS Church in this manner, then Mormonism could quite possibly represent true Christianity. However, if God's authority never left the earth, then there is no need for a restoration.

SINCE THE TIME WHEN the Church of Jesus Christ of Latter-day Saints was founded in 1830, LDS leaders have maintained that Christendom very early on fell into irreparable error. According to one church manual, "During the Great Apostasy, people were without divine direction from the living prophets. Many churches were established, but they did not have priesthood power to lead people to the true knowledge of God the Father and Jesus Christ. Parts of the holy scriptures were corrupted or lost, and no one had the authority to confer the gift of the Holy Ghost or perform other priesthood ordinances."[2]

Another manual adds, "Men changed the ordinances and doctrines that He and His Apostles had established. Because of apostasy, there was no direct revelation from God. The true Church was no longer on the earth. Men organized different churches that claimed to be true but taught conflicting doctrines. There was much confusion and contention over religion."[3] President Gordon B. Hinckley (1907–1995) agreed with this assessment, stating in a general conference message, "We acknowledge without hesitation that there are differences between us [other faiths and Mormons]. Were this not so there would have been no need for a restoration of the gospel."[4]

Church founder Joseph Smith (1805–1844) claimed that God told him that "all their [the Christian churches'] creeds were an abomination in his sight; that those professors were all corrupt; that: 'they draw near to me with their lips, but their hearts are far from me, they teach for doctrines the commandments of men, having a form of godliness, but they deny the power thereof.'"[5] Succeeding LDS presidents have clearly reaffirmed the Mormon belief that a universal apostasy tainted the authority of the Christian churches, including the churches found in Eastern Orthodox, Catholic, and Protestant traditions.[6] As Apostle James E. Talmage (1862–1933) wrote, "If the alleged apostasy of the primitive Church was not a reality, The Church of Jesus Christ of Latter-day Saints is not the divine institution its name proclaims."[7] A manual used by Mormon missionaries is very clear regarding the church's stance on the state of Christianity between the death of the apostles and Joseph Smith seventeen hundred years later. It states,

> The priesthood authority given to Christ's Apostles was no longer present on the earth. The apostasy eventually led to the emergence of many churches. . . . Investigators must understand that a universal apostasy occurred following the death of Jesus Christ and His Apostles. If there had been no apostasy, there would have been

no need for a Restoration. As a diamond displayed on black velvet appears more brilliant, so the Restoration stands in striking contrast to the dark background of the Great Apostasy. As guided by the Spirit, teach investigators about the Great Apostasy at a level of detail appropriate to their needs and circumstances. Your purpose is to help them understand the need for the Restoration of the gospel of Jesus Christ.[8]

When Peter declared in Matthew 16:16 that Jesus was "the Christ, the Son of the living God," Jesus responded, "Upon this rock I will build my church; and the gates of hell shall not prevail against it" (v. 18).[9] Despite Jesus' clear indication that nothing would prevail against Christ's church, Apostle Orson Pratt (1811–1881) stated, "Jesus made his appearance on the earth in the meridian of time, and he established his kingdom on the earth. . . . the kingdoms of this world made war against the kingdom of God, established eighteen centuries ago, and they prevailed against it, and the kingdom ceased to exist."[10]

Mormonism teaches that this "rock" upon which the church is built is "revelation," even though the Bible plainly declares the rock is none other than Jesus Christ. Acts 4:11–12 verifies this: "This is the stone which was set at nought of you builders, which is become the head of the corner. Neither is there salvation in any other: for there is none other name under heaven given among men, whereby we must be saved." Mormons often cite 1 Timothy 4:1 to substantiate their claim of a complete apostasy that necessitated the need for a restoration brought forth through Joseph Smith and the LDS Church. However, Paul says that only "*some* shall depart from the faith." While there certainly have been many different apostasies, it is historically inaccurate to say that God's Spirit and power completely left the world, along with His authority.

Ephesians 5:25–32 illustrates Christ's concern for the welfare of His church. When speaking on the subject of husbands and wives, Paul used the comparison of Christ and the church:

Husbands, love your wives, even as Christ also loved the church, and gave himself for it; that he might sanctify and cleanse it with the washing of water by the word, that he might present it to himself a glorious church, not having spot, or wrinkle, or any such thing; but that it should be holy and without blemish. So ought men to love their wives as their own bodies. He that loveth his wife loveth himself. For no man ever yet hated his own flesh; but nourisheth and cherisheth it, even as the Lord the church . . . This is a great mystery: but I speak concerning Christ and the church.

God has always had a people. Even in the Old Testament when it seemed that everyone in Israel had failed God and turned to idol worship, there was always a remnant who refused to serve any other god. The prophet Elijah thought he was the only one who remained faithful to the Lord, but God told him there were still seven thousand men in Israel who had not bowed their knees to Baal (1 Kings 19:18). Jesus loves the church as much as a husband loves his wife. He promised that He would be with His people to the very end (Matt. 28:20), and He always keeps His promises.

Questions for Discussion

- Consider the implications of the "Great Apostasy." What divine authority could anyone outside the LDS Church have if God's authority on earth had been taken away?

- The history of the Christian church is certainly littered with many potholes, but it seems that there have always been people throughout the centuries who desired to seek God and were filled with the Holy Spirit. Some prominent names include Augustine, Tyndale, Wycliffe, and Luther. What other historical examples of people or events can you cite to show that Christ's authority never left the earth?

--------- Evangelism Tip ---------

Although the claim of a universal Christian apostasy is offensive to Christians, Mormons will often introduce the idea. After all, Joseph Smith claimed he was told that all the churches were corrupt and that a restoration was needed. And as one LDS leader stated, there is no need for Mormonism unless the church had lost all authority. Thus, when this issue comes up, explain that you believe Jesus was sinless and could not lie. He expressly stated in Matthew 28:20, "I am with you always, even unto the end of the world."

Chapter 9

Why not just promote what you believe and not judge our faith?

Response Questions

- If judging is always wrong, why are you judging me?
- If you believe that you're correct about Mormonism being the true way to God, then aren't you really saying that I am "wrong"?
- Since truth is singular, shouldn't all truth claims be challenged?

• • • • • • • • • • • • • • • •

"I am willing to exchange all the errors and false notions I have for one truth, and should consider that I had made a good bargain."[1]
—President Wilford Woodruff (1807–1898)

———————————— Summary ————————————

Sadly, in this twenty-first-century culture, many people consider it a gross violation of common decency for someone to say that truth is exclusive and all other views are "wrong." Many Mormons have adopted this same attitude, especially when confronted by Christians who "judge" LDS teachings. Yet the belief that Joseph Smith is a true prophet of God, that the Book of Mormon is historical scripture, and that the LDS Church alone has complete priesthood authority are also exclusive truth claims that presume to judge other views as wrong. People reveal their inconsistency when they insist that "judging is wrong" because such a statement is itself a judgment call. Because truth matters, ideas ought to be considered "fair game" as long as the person holding a different viewpoint is not personally attacked.

Is MAKING A JUDGMENT always wrong? If not, is it wrong to critique what Christians believe to be doctrinal error? A common proof text cited by Mormons who insist that their church is above criticism is Matthew 7:1. This verse—Matthew 7:2 in the Joseph Smith Translation (JST) cited here—reads, "Judge not unrighteously, that ye be not judged; but judge righteous judgment."[2] "Why are you judging me?" is too often asked by those who believe that religious criticism is shameful and unchristian. But is that what this verse teaches?

The context of any passage is the primary factor in determining its meaning. Matthew 7 is part of Jesus' Sermon on the Mount. In verses 1–6 Jesus spoke against hypocrites by using the analogy of the log and the speck. The JST says, "Ye hypocrites, first cast out the beam out of thine own eye; and then shalt thou see clearly to cast out the mote out of thy brother's eye."[3] Jesus' point was that believers must guard their judgmental opinions of others, especially when they themselves are guilty of far greater offenses.

John 7:24 reads, "Judge not according to the appearance, but judge righteous judgment." The religious leaders of Jesus' day stressed the outward appearance, judging on what they could see in regard to cleanliness and the outward observance of the letter of the law. Jesus turned the tables on them constantly, pointing out in Matthew 23:27 that they were like whitewashed tombs, which looked good on the outside but inside were "full of dead men's bones, and of all uncleanness." Indeed, they were the subjects of Jesus' ire throughout the Gospels.[4]

The admonition against hypocrisy is found elsewhere in the Bible. Romans 2:1 says that those who judge unrighteously are without excuse and are self-condemning. The story of the adulterous woman (John 7:53–8:11) shows how Jesus condemned her hypocritical accusers, many of whom may have been guilty of their own sexual sins. Isn't it amazing that they dropped their stones when He invited the one who was without sin among them to begin the woman's punishment?

In dealing with the adulterous woman and her accusers, did Jesus really mean sin and hard-heartedness should never be pointed out? If so, was He being hypocritical when He judged the religious leaders and other sinners? Was Paul guilty when he judged Peter in Galatians 2:11–21 or when he condemned the Judaizers throughout the book of Galatians? In fact, what right did Paul have to make it a habit to preach in places like the Jewish synagogues or on Mars Hill in Athens? The gospel is a truth claim. As Christian apologist Ravi Zacharias has correctly noted, "If truth does not exclude, then no assertion of a truth claim is being made; it's just an opinion that is being stated. Any time you make a truth claim, you mean something contrary to it is false. Truth excludes its opposite."[5]

It is important to understand that Mormon leaders have made some incredible religious truth claims. Should they really be shocked that Christians feel compelled to offer rebuttals to accusations that are purposely meant to undermine beliefs that have long been held by Christians who love and respect the Bible? Joseph Smith (1805–1844) himself said, "One of the grand fundamental principles of 'Mormonism' is to receive truth, let it come from whence it may."[6]

President Brigham Young (1801–1877) boldly proclaimed, "Take up the Bible, compare the religion of the Latter-day Saints with it, and see if it will stand the test."[7] Young also said, "If I should hear a man advocate the erroneous principles he had imbibed through education, and oppose those principles, some might imagine that I was opposed to that man, when, in fact, I am only opposed to every evil and erroneous principle he advances."[8] President Joseph F. Smith (1838–1918) said, "The truth must be at the foundation of religion, or it is in vain and it will fail of its purpose."[9] Apostle Bruce R. McConkie (1915–1985) stated, "If we believe the truth, we can be saved; if we believe a lie, we shall surely be damned."[10]

These are just a few quotes to demonstrate that even the Mormon leadership believes in an open invitation to discern between truth and error. A religion certainly can hold to a belief in God and virtue, have nice programs, be financially prosperous, and grow in numbers, but if it is founded on error rather than truth, it is false—regardless of its perceived success. Truth, such as gravity or the necessity of water to sustain human life, is very narrow. The law of noncontradiction states that either gravity exists or it doesn't exist; there is no middle ground. Humans either need water for survival or they do not; both cannot be true at the same time. In the same way, while there are many religions and philosophies in pluralistic societies, two competing worldviews cannot both be true at the same time. Thus, if atheism is true, then by definition no God exists, negating both Mormonism and Christianity. If Islam is true, then Judaism and Christianity are in error, and so on.

Christians must not share their faith with Mormons in order to show themselves superior in knowledge and rhetoric. Rather, Christians should want to share the truth because they care about those who have not embraced the truth that makes one free. If something is in error, then it must be shown. In the words of Princeton Seminary professor Charles Hodge (1797–1878),

"But truth is at all times sacred, because it is one of the essential attributes of God, so that whatever militates against, or is hostile to truth is in opposition to the very nature of God."[11]

George A. Smith (1817–1875), a member of the First Presidency, ridiculed the notion held by some that personal faith should be excluded from scrutiny. He said in 1871, "If a faith will not bear to be investigated; if its preachers and professors are afraid to have it examined, their foundation must be very weak."[12] Apostle Orson Pratt (1811–1881) challenged his listeners to "convince us of our errors of doctrine, if we have any, by reason, by logical arguments, or by the word of God, and we will be ever grateful for the information, and you will ever have the pleasing reflection that you have been instruments in the hands of God of redeeming your fellow beings from the darkness which you may see enveloping their minds. Come, then, let us reason together, and try to discover the true light upon all subjects."[13] If Latter-day Saints believe theirs is a religion of truth, then we would expect Mormons everywhere to be doing everything in their power to proclaim its message. Indeed, if today's LDS leaders didn't believe that their religion was true—thus negating any opposing philosophy such as atheism, Islam, Christianity, and Buddhism—then why do they devote so much of their church's resources to evangelism and encourage their people to serve missions? Christians should not be defensive or have any ill thoughts when Mormon missionaries knock on their doors. They should take up the challenge invited by Mormon leaders themselves.

For Christians, to not tell others the gospel would be akin to passing by a burning house and not even attempting to let the residents know about the disaster, because some might take the message of a burning house as overly negative. After all, what should be concluded about a doctor who doesn't tell his patient that he or she has cancer because the information is so bleak? Or what would we think of a person who would not tell his friend that she had spinach between her teeth for fear it would ruin her self-esteem?

All these scenarios demand the truth, no matter how difficult it might be to deliver the news. Christians ought to be committed to declaring truth claims when it comes to issues of eternal consequence. This does come with risks, however, for the message could be met with enmity. Yet, as Paul stated in Galatians 4:16, "Am I therefore become your enemy, because I tell you the truth?" While there will be disagreement with a Mormon's doctrine, it is important to convey a spirit of kindness and mutual respect. The hope is that truth will prevail.

Questions for Discussion

- Suppose someone says, "That's your truth, and I have my truth. Nobody has a claim on exclusive truth." What questions can you ask to show that such a viewpoint itself is a claim of exclusive truth, making this a self-defeating argument?

- Sensitive discussion topics, such as differences in religious systems, often end up with the two parties raising the tone (and even harshness) of their voices. Why is it important to stay calm and eliminate the word "you" from evangelism encounters?

- What are some effective ways that have helped you discuss the issue of truth in a kind and gentle manner?

──────────────────── Evangelism Tip ────────────────────

The question raised in this chapter is asked too often in our culture today. Even some Christians have found themselves caught up in this postmodern way of thinking. As Matthew chapter 7 shows, Jesus wasn't condemning "judging" itself, just hypocritical judgment. When someone says you're not supposed to judge, ask, "But didn't you just judge me with that admonishment?" Or you might say, "Correct me if I'm wrong, but are you saying that it is wrong to judge ideas? Isn't that a judgment call itself?" Many people who criticize "judging" often do not see that their effort to censor is born out of making their own judgments.

Chapter 10

Why are your clergy members paid?

Response Questions
- Where does the Bible forbid Christian leaders being paid?
- Doesn't LDS scripture say that the local leaders such as bishops should be paid?
- Do you believe that the Mormon prophet, apostles, and other full-time leaders are "volunteers"?

• • • • • • • • • • • • • • • •

"One of the important and distinguishing features of The Church of Jesus Christ of Latter-day Saints is that its affairs are administered by the lay members of the Church rather than by paid clergy."[1]
—Apostle Franklin D. Richards (1821–1899)

————————————— Summary —————————————

While some Mormons might feel that having a paid clergy is wrong, the Bible points out that receiving financial support as a Christian minister or worker is not only acceptable but an obligation on the part of those who benefit from their service. While it is true that Mormon men who serve terms as bishops do not receive remuneration (even though LDS scripture says such workers should be paid), this is not true of higher level, full-time leaders in the church, including mission presidents all the way up to the General Authorities.

BEFORE LDS CHURCH LEADERS made major changes to the temple ceremony in 1990, Christian pastors were portrayed as being on Satan's payroll. In the endowment ceremony, Lucifer was portrayed as approaching a Christian pastor and saying to him, "If you will preach your orthodox religion to these people and convert them, I will pay you well." This idea that Christian workers have improper motives can be seen in the words of President Brigham Young (1801–1877):

> How much tithing do you pay? The professing Christians, apostates and others have a great deal to say about the Saints paying tithing. Now let us compare notes. The Elders of this Church travel and preach without purse or scrip, and labor at home as Bishops, Presidents, High Counselors, and Ministers, free of charge. Now take the Christians, how many of their Ministers preach without pay? Go to their meetings, in their churches, halls, schoolhouses, or any of their public gatherings, and you have a box, a plate, or a hat put under your face, and it is, "Give me a sixpence, give me a sixpence, give me a sixpence!" Show me the Elder of this Church that does this? [*sic*] We preach the Gospel without purse or scrip and work for our own bread and butter.[2]

According to President Joseph Fielding Smith (1876–1972):

> It can be said also that the officers of the Church of Jesus Christ of Latter-day Saints who labor without salaries coming out of the pockets of the members, are just as spiritually minded, have just as good judgment and wisdom in directing the temporal as well as the spiritual welfare of the people, as are any of the ministers who spend their entire time in what may be called spiritual counsel. For instance, the bishops of our wards and the presidents of our stakes and other officers give their time freely without any monetary compensation paid by members of the Church. It is equally true that the young men and women who are distributed over the face of the earth as missionaries of the Church pay their own way, or their parents do. We do not have a paid ministry, yet these brethren put in as much time in spiritual and Church duties, as do ministers of other denominations who devote their entire time, and in addition, they are under the necessity of earning their own living by their daily

employment in industry. They do this because they have an abiding testimony of the divinity of the work the Church requires of them.[3]

A Paid Ministry According to the Bible

The Bible not only allows for but mandates the compensation of Christian workers. Jesus supported this concept when He stated in Luke 10:7, "The labourer is worthy of his hire." Acts 18:3 says the apostle Paul worked as a tent-maker; however, the apostle himself never said it was wrong for a minister to receive a salary for his labors in the Lord's work. In fact, when the immature Corinthians objected to Paul's receiving financial support, he reminded them, "I robbed other churches, taking wages of them, to do you service" (2 Cor. 11:8).

In 1 Corinthians 9:4–5 Paul declared that Christian ministers must eat, support their families, and pay their bills. He used the example of a soldier who, according to verse 7, never goes to war at his own expense. He further stated that a farmer eats the fruit of what he has planted and a shepherd drinks the milk of his flock. In light of these examples, he asked in verse 11 whether it is wrong for the pastor, who feeds his flock spiritually, to partake of material things; after all, the pastor spends his day serving his people, just as the farmer serves his customers by selling the products of his livelihood. In verse 13, Paul further reminded the Corinthians that the priests in the temple lived by "the things of the temple." The entire job of the priestly tribe of Levi was ministering to the people (Num. 18:1–7). To guarantee priestly service, the tribe of Levi was not granted an inheritance in the Promised Land as the other tribes were. Instead, a tithe (tenth) was gathered from all the children of Israel to sustain the Levites (Num. 18:21).

Paul insisted that the Lord has consecrated those who have devoted their entire lives to ministering to the spiritual needs of their people, meaning they should be supported by that flock. In 1 Corinthians 9:14, he wrote that the Lord ordained that those "which preach the gospel should live of the gospel." Paul dealt with this issue again in 1 Timothy 5:17–18, saying that elders who serve well in the church should have "double honour." This is especially true of those who minister in the "word and doctrine." After this, he immediately cited the words of Jesus, who said, "The labourer is worthy of his reward."

It is true that local LDS leaders such as the bishops are not paid for their service; they must have outside jobs to sustain their households. But many Latter-day Saints seem to believe their higher-level leaders work full-time without being compensated at all. Yet the only logical way this can be accomplished is if each and every General Authority in the LDS Church is financially independent. This, of course, is not the case. According to the *Encyclopedia of Mormonism*, "Because the General Authorities are obliged to leave their regular employment for full-time Church service, they receive a modest living allowance provided from income on Church investments."[4]

Several points must be made. First, their "employment" is full-time, preventing them from working outside the church. There is no problem with this scenario. Yet isn't this the same situation as Christian pastors, missionaries, and other church leaders, who forego full-time employment in order to dedicate themselves full-time to their ministries? Second, what is a "modest living allowance"? Isn't a living allowance just another term for a "wage"? Since the LDS Church does not release itemized financial statements, it is unknown just what "modest" really means in this context. Whether the wage is $10,000 a year or $100,000, does it really matter? The mere fact that a General Authority gets anything at all undermines the original objection posed by the Mormon's question.

Despite the stereotype that many Mormons may have, Christian pastors, missionaries, and other church leaders typically do not receive exorbitant paychecks. It is hardly the norm that pastors command huge incomes. In fact, many serve for little or no compensation at all. One Mormon counterargument is that while Mormon leaders are offered compensation, some choose not to accept this living allowance. That may be commendable, but it does not erase the fact that some do.

A Paid Ministry According to LDS Scripture

It may surprise some Latter-day Saints that their own written scripture supports the idea of a paid ministry. Doctrine and Covenants 42:71–73 states that bishops (as well as elders and high priests who assist these bishops) are to receive "a just remuneration for all their services." Two LDS authors write, "The law of remuneration is that those who administer in spiritual affairs must have their stewardships and labor for their living, 'even as the members.' This is wisdom. For in that position they are absolutely independent and can preach the truth without fear. Those who administer in temporal affairs and give their entire time to public business are to have a just remuneration. If they were to earn a living for themselves they could not give all their time and energy to the community."[5] So why are bishops not paid today? At best, it probably could be argued that the church is no longer subject to this agreement because bishops no longer work "full-time." While Section 42 in the Doctrine and Covenants never explicitly says this is the only qualification for "just remuneration," many hardworking bishops might argue the point that they're not full-time.

Further, Doctrine and Convenants 75:24 specifically names certain men who were called as missionaries and states that "it is the duty of the church to assist in supporting the families of those [missionaries], and also to support the families of those who are called and must needs be sent unto the world to proclaim the gospel unto the world." The *Encyclopedia of Mormonism* concedes, "Missionaries or their families generally cover the major costs of serving a mission. Missionaries called from developing nations may receive needed financial assistance from the general missionary fund of the Church. This assistance covers only basic living costs, as the Church has no paid ministry. No one is paid for missionary service."[6]

Other leaders who receive salaries include mission and temple presidents. Their church is free to pay as little or as much as it wants. But it works both ways. It is a silly notion even to insinuate that Christian laborers are corrupt because they receive financial support for their services when Mormon leaders are supported by their church. Mormons who argue for the superiority of the LDS Church because it has an "unpaid" clergy need to realize how hypocritical, as well as unscriptural, their argument really is.

Questions for Discussion

- Why do you think the Bible allows for Christian workers to receive wages for what they do?

- How would you respond to a Mormon who says that an unpaid clergy brings a higher level of sincerity to their service?

- Does a volunteer clergy really guarantee purer motives? Why or why not?

―――――――――――――――― Evangelism Tip ――――――――――――――――

When Mormons criticize Christian churches because their pastors are paid, they tend to imply that those who volunteer are more admirable than those who receive paychecks. Yet many Mormons are unaware that the Bible encourages Christians to financially provide for those who minister to them. Don't allow a Mormon to discredit Christianity just because pastors and other workers might be compensated. It is important to get off rabbit trails like this and return to issues of more importance.

Chapter 11

Where do you get your authority?

Response Questions
- Where do female members of the LDS Church get their authority?
- Do you know the Bible teaches that true Christian believers—both male and female—hold a priesthood given to them by God and therefore have authority?

• • • • • • • • • • • • • • • •

"Presumptuous and blasphemous are they who purport to baptize, bless, marry, or perform other sacraments in the name of the Lord while in fact lacking his specific authorization."[1]
—President Spencer W. Kimball (1895–1985)

Summary

In Mormonism, having authority to preach the restored gospel on this earth is essential. This authority comes from the priesthood held by Mormon men. Mormonism claims that Christians do not have this authority, meaning that God does not recognize the ordinances performed in Christian churches. Yet the Bible teaches that every Christian believer has been given priesthood authority directly from God. This allows the Christian direct access to God and the right to be called a child of God.

ACCORDING TO MORMONISM, priesthood authority from God left the earth soon after the death of Jesus' apostles. "". . . with the death of the Apostles, priesthood keys and the presiding priesthood authority were taken from the earth. . . . Priesthood keys provided the authority to govern the work of the priesthood. Without apostles, priesthood, and priesthood keys, much of the true knowledge of God was lost and the doctrine of the gospel was distorted. No ordinances required for salvation, such as baptism, could be properly performed."[2]

Joseph Smith (1805–1844) claims to have restored this priesthood authority shortly before he founded his church on April 6, 1830. According to President Joseph Fielding Smith (1876–1972), "'ALL PRIESTHOOD IS MELCHIZEDEK.' How many priesthoods are there? The answer is there is *one priesthood*, but the Lord divided it into *two divisions* known as the *Melchizedek* and the *Aaronic Priesthood*."[3] Joseph Smith and his friend Oliver Cowdery (1806–1850) claimed to have been baptized on May 15, 1829, in the Susquehanna River by a resurrected John the Baptist, who bestowed the lesser "Aaronic Priesthood" on them. On a later date that wasn't recorded, the two were purportedly visited by the biblical apostles Peter, James, and John and given the greater "Melchizedek Priesthood."[4]

Today Mormons believe that these priesthoods are given to worthy male members of the church and provide them with "priesthood power" to marry, baptize, and even bless with God's approval. The Aaronic priesthood, which is given to Mormon boys at the age of twelve, allows them to administer the sacrament. The Melchizedek priesthood is given to males eighteen years or older. It bestows on them the office of "elder" and, among other things, allows them to confer the gift of the Holy Ghost and to provide blessings by the laying on of hands.

Speaking at a general conference, Apostle Russell M. Nelson said, "Every elder in the Church holds the same priesthood as the President of the Church."[5] These priesthoods are necessary to qualify for the highest level of heaven, called the celestial kingdom. According to President Spencer W. Kimball (1895–1985), "No man will ever reach godhood who does not hold the priesthood. You have to be a member of the higher priesthood—an elder, seventy, or high priest—and today is the day to get it and magnify it."[6] Apostle Boyd K. Packer taught an October 1981 general conference audience, "The *power* you receive will depend on what you do with the sacred, unseen gift. Your authority comes through your ordination; your power comes through obedience and worthiness. . . . Power in the priesthood comes from doing

Apostles Peter, James, and John confer the Melchizedek priesthood upon Joseph Smith and Oliver Cowdery. The date of this event is unknown.

your duty in ordinary things: attending meetings, accepting assignments, reading the scriptures, keeping the Word of Wisdom."[7]

Latter-day Saint leaders have said that the priesthood provides their people authority from God, differentiating Mormons from Christians. President George Albert Smith (1870–1951) wrote, "The churches of the world are trying, in their way, to bring peace into the hearts of men. They are possessed of many virtues and many truths, and accomplish much good, but they are not divinely authorized. Neither have their priests been divinely commissioned."[8] According to Apostle Bruce R. McConkie (1915–1985), "As far as all religious organizations now existing are concerned, the presence or the absence of this [Melchizedek] priesthood establishes the divinity or falsity of a professing church."[9] And Apostle Packer explained, "We do not hear of the priesthood keys being exercised in other Christian churches. It seems odd that we are described by some as being non-Christian when we are the only ones who have the authority and the organization that He established."[10]

Priesthood authority does not extend to females; left to herself, a Mormon female has no authority of her own. Charles Penrose (1832–1925), who was a member of the First Presidency, made this interesting observation:

When a woman is sealed to a man holding the Priesthood, she becomes one with him. Sometimes the man is the one and sometimes he is not, but she receives blessings in association with him. The glory and power and dominion that he will exercise when he has the fulness of the Priesthood and becomes a "king and a priest unto God," she will share with him. Sisters have said to me sometimes, "But, I hold the Priesthood with my husband." "Well," I asked, "what office do you hold in the Priesthood?" Then they could not say much more. The sisters are not ordained to any office in the Priesthood and there is authority in the Church which they cannot exercise; it does not belong to them; they cannot do that properly any more than they can change themselves into a man. Now, sisters, do not take the idea that I wish to convey that you have no blessings or authority or power belonging to the Priesthood. When you are sealed to a man of God who holds it and who, by overcoming, inherits the fulness of the glory of God, you will share that with him if you are fit for it, and I guess you will be.[11]

According to Penrose, a husband who holds the priesthood has the power to raise his wife on the resurrection day.

In the divine economy, as in nature, the man "is the head of the woman," and it is written that "he is the savior of the body." But "the man is not without the woman" any more than the woman is without the man, in the Lord. Adam was first formed, then Eve. In the resurrection they stand side by side and hold dominion together. Every man who overcomes all things and is thereby entitled to inherit all things, receives power to bring up his wife to join him in the possession and enjoyment thereof.[12]

This sounds very similar to what Apostle Erastus Snow said in 1857:

Do you uphold your husband before God as our lord? "What!—my husband to be my lord?" I ask, Can you get into the celestial kingdom without him? Have any of you been there? You will remember that you never got into the celestial kingdom without the aid of your husband. If you did, it was because your husband was away, and some one had to act proxy for him. No woman will get into the celestial kingdom, except her husband receives her, if she is worthy to have a husband; and if not, somebody will receive her as a servant.[13]

Priesthood in the Bible

The spiritual significance of the Aaronic, or Levitical, priesthood ended with the death of Christ. The term *priest* refers to a person who stands up for another person/people, acting as a mediator in his cause. The Old Testament priest stood in the gap for the people and offered animal sacrifices to atone for their sins. Mormon males, who claim to hold the Aaronic priesthood, do not offer animal sacrifices; thus, their office is not a restoration of the original, as church leaders would like the public to believe. Furthermore, Doctrine and Covenants 107:16 specifically states, "No man has a legal right to this office, to hold the keys of this priesthood, except he be a literal descendant of Aaron." This warning sounds similar to that found in Numbers 3:10, which states, "And thou shalt appoint Aaron and his sons, and they shall wait on their priest's office: and the stranger that cometh nigh shall be put to death." However, it is not a modern LDS requirement for a Mormon priesthood holder to trace his family roots back to Aaron, the brother of Moses. Because the LDS Church stresses genealogical research in order to vicariously baptize for the dead, it would seem their leaders should know better than to claim such a priesthood for themselves.

The biblical Melchizedek (Gen. 14:18–20), who was the king of Salem as well as a priest of God, is a mysterious figure in Scripture. He blessed Abram, and Abram tithed to him. Nobody beside Melchizedek held the positions of both priest and king until Jesus came. Hebrews 7:21 declares that Jesus is "a priest for ever after the order of Melchizedec."[14] Verse 24 adds that Jesus has "an unchangeable priesthood." Hebrews 7:2–3 describes this order: "First being by interpretation King of righteousness, and after that also King of Salem, which is, King of peace; without father, without mother, without descent, having neither beginning of days, nor end of life; but made like unto the Son of God; abideth a priest continually."

Christ met these qualifications. He is both Righteousness and Peace (cf. Eph. 2:14; 1 John 3:7). As the Word who became flesh (John 1:14), He continues His advocacy as the Christians' priest. In fact, the Bible says that Christians are free to directly approach the throne of God and pray according to His name. As 1 Timothy 2:5 puts it, "There is one God, and one mediator between God and men, the man Christ Jesus."

The Christian's Priesthood

The New Testament does not support the idea that the Aaronic or Melichizedek priesthoods are necessary for humans; instead, Christians have authority as "children of God" through their belief. Contrasting Christians with the rest of the "world" (who "knew him [God] not"), 1 John 3:1 says, "See what kind of love the Father has given to us, that we should be called children of God; and so we are" (ESV).[15] Paul distinguished between "children of the flesh" and "children of God" in Romans 9:8. Galatians 3:26 says it is "by faith in Christ Jesus" that believers become children of God, while John 1:12 says that "as many as received him, to them gave he power to become the sons of God, even to them that believe on his name."[16]

A royal priesthood is provided to all Christian believers. First Peter 2:9–10 states that Christians "are a chosen generation, a royal priesthood, an holy nation, a peculiar people . . . [who] now have obtained mercy." Even though Christians are priests in this spiritual manner, they are called to offer *themselves* as "living sacrifice[s]" to God (Rom. 12:1). As holders of this priesthood, believers are commanded to stand and intercede for people, not to offer blood sacrifices for the cleansing of their sins but to pray that they might turn to the one who cleanses from sin, namely, Christ Jesus.

While Mormonism offers the priesthood only to males, the New Testament makes no such distinction when it comes to those whom God has called to Himself. This authority is available to all believers, regardless of gender. Paul wrote in Galatians 3:28, "There is neither Jew nor Greek, there is neither bond nor free, there is neither male nor female: for ye are all one in Christ Jesus." It is this priesthood, held by all Christians, that provides authority to pray directly to the God of this universe, to boldly proclaim the gospel truth wherever they go, and to know that when they die they will enjoy eternal life with God. There is no greater authority than this.

Questions for Discussion

- What are the differences between the priesthood of Mormonism and that which Peter calls the "the royal priesthood"?

- A Mormon might say that he has priesthood authority that the Christian does not have. What scriptural evidence could you point out to help this person understand that the Christian believer does indeed have authority from God?

- Mormon women essentially need a male's authority to be eligible to enter into the celestial kingdom. Why should a Christian find this troubling?

—————————————— Evangelism Tip ——————————————

Quite often, the issue of authority comes up in a conversation with Mormons. Christians not only have a High Priest who is King (see Heb. 7) and the "mediator between God and men" (1 Tim. 2:5), but they also have been endowed with a holy and royal priesthood (1 Peter 2:5). Regardless of their skin color, financial status, or gender, believers have the opportunity to personally know God and are encouraged to draw near to the throne of grace with confidence (Heb. 4:16). Because Jesus is the believers' mediator, there is no need for any other.

Chapter 12

Why won't you let your daughter date a Mormon?

Response Questions
- Would you allow someone from another religion to date your daughter?
- If the relationship led to marriage, would the Mormon consider leaving his faith for hers?
- What do you say about the Bible's admonition to not be unequally yoked?

• • • • • • • • • • • • • • • •

"Consider this fact: Your marriage is a laboratory for godhood."[1]
—LDS Church manual *Achieving a Celestial Marriage*

————————————— Summary —————————————

While Mormon leaders still warn their people not to marry non-Mormons, there doesn't seem to be the admonition there once was to refrain from dating outside the LDS faith. More and more, it seems many Christian young people get into romantic relationships with Mormons. When this happens, there will be certain pressure to join the LDS Church, especially if the relationship heads toward marriage. Christians must avoid this type of relationship with a Mormon or anyone else who holds views that are contrary to the teachings of the Bible.

In Mormonism, it is possible (though not encouraged) for members to get married for "time" only, which is a marriage solemnized somewhere other than one of the Mormon temples. However, to be married for "time and eternity"—a union that will last beyond death—a man and a woman must get temple recommends and have their relationship "sealed" in a Mormon temple ceremony. Over and over again, LDS leaders have stressed marriage in a temple as an essential practice.[2] With this as a background, let's consider the wisdom of a Christian getting romantically involved with a Mormon or, for that matter, anyone who doesn't hold to a biblical faith.

Dating Outside the Faith

In earlier days, Mormon leaders discouraged church members from dating nonmembers. For example, Apostle Mark E. Petersen (1900–1984) wrote a fictional book that portrayed a conversation between a young Mormon girl and her mother about a non-Mormon boy she was casually dating. Responding to the daughter's question, "Are other people's ideas of God so different?" the mother answered,

> Yes, very different. You do not know much about other peoples' religions because you have never attended any other church. But there are some so-called Christian churches which do not believe in God as a person at all. They think he is an essence, like an invisible cloud with no shape or substance, and that he is everywhere at once, yet in no place in particular. . . . Many teach that God has neither body, parts, nor passions, which of course is the same as saying that he is not a person at all, but just some indefinable influence and yet so small it can dwell in your heart. Can you see that you and Bob probably don't even worship the same God?[3]

Like Petersen, President Spencer W. Kimball (1895–1985) admonished LDS Church members not to date nonmembers. He wrote, "Clearly, right marriage begins with right dating. . . . Do not take the chance of dating nonmembers, or members who are untrained and faithless. A girl may say, 'Oh, I do not intend to marry this person. It is just a "fun" date.' But one cannot afford to take a chance on falling in love with someone who may never accept the gospel."[4] Kimball instructed LDS youth not to date until they were at least sixteen years old, "and even then there should be much judgment used in selections and in the seriousness."[5]

While this age rule appears to be followed by many Mormon youth throughout the United States, the idea of dating only those in the church seems to have been relaxed. Rather, it seems that high moral behavior has become the main consideration. In an article titled "Dating FAQs" published in a Mormon youth magazine, the question was asked, "Should I date someone who is not LDS?" The answer? "Possibly, but don't date anyone (LDS or not) who, because of low standards, will drag you down."[6]

This apparent open door to dating those outside the church is echoed on the official LDS Church Web site, which says Latter-day Saints should date only "those who have high standards, who respect your standards, and in whose company you can maintain the standards of the gospel of Jesus Christ."[7] Speaking to youth, President Thomas S. Monson stated, "Begin to prepare for a temple marriage as well as for a mission. Proper dating is a part of that preparation. . . . Because dating is a preparation for marriage, 'date only those who have high standards.'"[8]

Many local LDS congregations host weekend dances and other social events to which their young people are encouraged to invite nonmember friends. Nonmembers often end up becoming attracted to the wholesome Latter-day Saints. Over the years we have counseled a number of young people who have become involved in relationships with Mormons of the opposite sex. Typically, these Christians are encouraged to participate in the missionary lessons and join the LDS Church if they hope to take their relationships to the next level. In other words, they are pressured to convert to Mormonism. The Christians usually recognize the falsehoods of Mormonism, but they desperately want to continue their relationships and don't know how to do so unless they become Mormons.

Christian researcher Sandra Tanner of Utah Lighthouse Ministry believes the problem is especially prevalent with those attending college. "I often get calls from Christian parents who are deeply concerned about their son or daughter because they have started to date a Mormon at college and have gotten involved in the LDS college social group," she said. "Often the person has joined the LDS Church without even telling the parents, informing them on their next school break. By that time, the person is often in a serious relationship that will lead to a temple wedding, which the [non-LDS] parents will not be allowed to witness."[9] In our experience, far too many Christians reject their faith in order to pursue romantic relationships with Mormons.

"Mixed faith" marriages are a recipe for disaster, both for the couple and their children. In 2 Corinthians 6:14, Paul wrote, "Be ye not unequally yoked together with unbelievers: for what fellowship hath righteousness with unrighteousness? and what communion hath light with darkness?" While Paul was not specifically talking about dating and marriage in this passage, he could have easily been referencing the lack of wisdom in such situations, especially since he had addressed the problems of mixed marriages earlier in 1 Corinthians 7:12–15. One problem that often arises is a religious stalemate in the marriage. When children come along, the couple has to determine a strategy for church attendance. Often this results in a compromise with the children dividing their attendance between two different churches that profess major doctrinal differences. For children, this can be especially confusing.

If dating is considered a possible precursor to marriage, then it makes sense to set the standards high at these beginning levels. Of course, it's not a given that a dating couple will eventually marry. However, is it more likely that a person will marry someone he or she has never dated? The answer is obvious, as dating is certainly the first step in a possible long-term relationship. The dynamics of a dating relationship between a boy and a girl creates a very dangerous situation for a believer if he or she has chosen to date someone of another faith. A relationship with another human should never mean more than a relationship with God.

In addition, "missionary dating" is neither biblical nor ethical and should not be practiced by faithful Christians. While the Bible does say that believers should be "wise as serpents, and harmless as doves" (Matt. 10:16), using romantic attachment in an attempt to change the faith of those they're dating is certainly a wrong application of this passage. The end does not justify the means. Christians who emotionally manipulate Mormons for the purpose of conversion place their integrity in a precarious situation. Why should the Mormon seriously consider following the Bible when the Christian obviously is not heeding its admonition?

If nothing else, this chapter might be a reminder that Christian parents are biblically mandated to teach their children while they're young and to help them adopt a biblical worldview concerning dating and sex. Instilling Christian values and principles into their lives while helping them develop wisdom is crucial to having them eventually own their own faith rather than merely borrow their parents' faith. To date (and then marry) someone from another faith (or no faith at all) is not God honoring and invites tension in the relationship. God desires marriage to be a union in the same way that Jesus is the groom and the church the bride.

Questions for Discussion

- Suppose someone argues that dating a non-Christian does not necessarily mean the relationship will end in marriage. Provide a response consistent with a biblical worldview.

- If a Mormon and Christian date and it leads to serious discussions about marriage, do you believe it's more likely the Mormon would convert to Christianity or the Christian to Mormonism? Do you know any real-life examples to support your answer?

- Suppose a friend of yours says she is dating a Mormon because she thinks it is possible to convert him to Christianity. Why is this not a good strategy for evangelism?

———————————— Evangelism Tip ————————————

If you have a Christian friend who is involved in a relationship with a Mormon, it's important that you lovingly explain the biblical admonition to be "equally yoked," even in dating. Let your friend know how much you care and, hopefully, biblical wisdom will take precedence over human emotions. Setting high standards, especially early in life, will save much heartache. We have heard, "But I'm witnessing to her." However, Christianity is not an "end-justifies-the-means" philosophy. If our desire is to see our Mormon friends be true to God's Word, we should set the example.

Section 3

God

Chapter 13

Didn't the prophet Jeremiah allude to the premortal existence of humankind?

Response Question

- What do you believe the word "knew" means in Jeremiah 1:5?
- Is it possible that before Jeremiah was born God knew Jeremiah but Jeremiah did not know God?

• • • • • • • • • • • • • • • •

"Although serious Bible scholars acknowledge that a belief in the preexistence of man was a genuine Jewish and early Christian doctrine, only traces of this teaching are found in our modern Bible. It seems probable that because this doctrine was so widely accepted as genuine until the council of Constantinople in A.D. 553, both Old and New Testament writers and early church theologians presupposed its veracity and acceptance by later readers."[1]

—LDS apologist Michael W. Hickenbotham

————————————————— Summary ————————————————

Mormonism teaches that all people once existed in a previous spiritual world before they were born on this earth. While verses are twisted to legitimize this doctrine, the Bible does not support such a view. Neither does the evidence support the idea that the doctrine was once taught but later taken away by early church councils. While there were some early church leaders who did teach that souls may have existed in a previous lifetime, their teachings were dissimilar in nature to the current Mormon doctrine.

To support the LDS doctrine of premortality, also known as preexistence or the first estate, Jeremiah 1:5 is commonly quoted. It says, "Before I formed thee in the belly I knew thee; and before thou camest forth out of the womb I sanctified thee, and I ordained thee a prophet unto the nations." Mormonism teaches that "man was also in the beginning with God,"[2] and thus "the human race lived in a premortal existence with God the Father and His Son, Jesus Christ. . . . But at some distant point in our premortal past, spirit bodies were created for us, and we became, literally, spirit sons and daughters of heavenly parents."[3] A church manual reports, "The first-born spirit son of our Father was Jesus Christ. He was our Elder Brother. He became a member of the Godhead while he was in heaven, before he came to this earth."[4] Another manual states, "Before you were born on earth, you lived in the presence of your Heavenly Father as one of His spirit children. In this premortal existence, you attended a council with Heavenly Father's other spirit children. At that council, Heavenly Father presented His great plan of happiness (see Abraham 3:22–26)."[5]

Church leaders have explained that there was a disagreement in the preexistence over who should be the Savior of the world and how mankind would be saved. Two brothers, Jesus and Lucifer, submitted their plans.

> Jesus was willing to come to the earth, give His life for us, and take upon Himself our sins. He, like our Heavenly Father, wanted us to choose whether we would obey Heavenly Father's commandments. He knew we must be free to choose in order to prove ourselves worthy of exaltation. . . . Satan, who was called Lucifer, also came, saying, "Behold, here am I, send me, I will be thy son, and I will redeem all mankind, that one soul shall not be lost, and surely I will do it; wherefore give me thine honor" (Moses 4:1). Satan wanted to force us all to do his will. Under his plan, we would not be allowed to choose. He would take away the freedom of choice that our Father had given us. Satan wanted to have all the honor for our salvation. Under his proposal, our purpose in coming to earth would have been frustrated.[6]

Satan's plan was rejected and, in response, he

> became angry and rebelled. There was war in heaven. Satan and his followers fought against Jesus Christ and His followers. . . . In this

great rebellion, Satan and all the spirits who followed him were sent away from the presence of God and cast down from heaven. A third part of the hosts of heaven were punished for following Satan (see D&C 29:36). They were denied the right to receive mortal bodies. Because we are here on earth and have mortal bodies, we know that we chose to follow Jesus Christ and our Heavenly Father. Satan and his followers are also on the earth, but as spirits. They have not forgotten who we are, and they are around us daily, tempting us and enticing us to do things that are not pleasing to our Heavenly Father. In our premortal life, we chose to follow Jesus Christ and accept God's plan.[7]

Since humans chose wisely in this premortal state, they had a chance to progress by coming to earth. President George Albert Smith (1870–1951) said good works in the premortal state earned for us "the privilege of coming to this earth. . . . our very existence is a reward for our faithfulness before we came here."[8] President Spencer W. Kimball (1895–1985) wrote,

While we lack recollection of our pre-mortal life, before coming to this earth all of us understood definitely the purpose of our being here. We would be expected to gain knowledge, educate ourselves, train ourselves. We were to control our urges and desires, master and control our passions, and overcome our weaknesses, small and large. We were to eliminate sins of omission and of commission, and to follow the laws and commandments given us by our Father. . . . we said in effect, "Yes, Father, in spite of all those things [sorrows, disappointments, hard work, blood, sweat, and tears] I can see great blessings that could come to me as one of thy sons or daughters; in taking a body I can see that I will eventually become immortal like thee, that I might overcome the effects of sins and be perfected, and so I am anxious to go to the earth at the first opportunity." And so we came.[9]

Brothers and Sisters

Mormon leaders have stated that the "third part of the hosts of heaven" is made up of fellow brothers and sisters of all of humankind. Apostle Joseph F. Merrill (1868–1952) said, "According to our teachings, Satan and an army of supporters were cast down to earth from the premortal spirit world. They are spirit brothers of ours, and are real persons having spirit bodies."[10] Mormon leaders also have insisted that the performance of humans as spirits in their premortality determined their social status here on earth. For instance, President Joseph Fielding Smith (1970–1972) explained, "Is it not a reasonable belief, that the Lord would select the choice spirits to come through the better grades of nations? Moreover, is it not reasonable to believe that less worthy spirits would come through less favored lineage? Does this not account in very large part, for the various grades of color and degrees of intelligence we find in the earth?"[11]

Apostle Mark E. Petersen (1900–1984) stated,

> With all this in mind, can we account in any other way for the birth of some of the children of God in darkest Africa, or in flood-ridden China, or among the starving hordes of India, while some of the rest of us are born here in the United States? We cannot escape the conclusion that because of performance in our pre-existence some of us are born as Chinese, some as Japanese, some as Indians, some as Negroes, some as Americans, some as Latter-day Saints. These are rewards and punishments, fully in harmony with His established policy in dealing with sinners and saints, rewarding all according to their deeds.[12]

In a 2008 devotional, Terry Ball, dean of religious education at Brigham Young University, told the students,

> Have you ever wondered why you were born where and when you were born? Why you were not born 500 years ago in some primitive, aboriginal culture in some isolated corner of the world? Is the timing and placing of your birth capricious? For Latter-day Saints the answer is no. Fundamental to our faith is the understanding that before we came to this earth we lived in a premortal existence with a loving Heavenly Father. We further understand that in that premortal state we had agency. And that we grew and developed as we used that agency.[13]

When it comes to those of African heritage, Mormon leaders were very specific that their preexistent behavior is what prevented them from holding the LDS priesthood. For example, Apostle George F. Richards (1821–1899) said that "the Negro race" was "forbidden the priesthood, and the higher temple blessings, presumably because of their not having been valiant while in the spirit. It does not pay to be anything but valiant."[14] Apostle Melvin J. Ballard (1873–1939) asked, "Why is it in this Church we do not grant the priesthood to the Negroes? It is alleged that the Prophet Joseph said—and I have no reason to dispute it—that it is because of some act committed by them before they came into this life. It is alleged that they were neutral, standing neither for Christ nor the devil. But, I am convinced it is because of some things they did before they came into this life that they have been denied the privilege. The races of today are very largely reaping the consequences of a previous life."[15]

Prior to the thirtieth anniversary of the priesthood revelation that reversed the ban regarding those of African heritage, the *Deseret News* quoted former mission president Sheldon F. Child, a member of the First Quorum of the Seventy:

> Elder Child said he doesn't recall that his missionaries encountered "any problem with someone asking" about why the priesthood ban existed or the folklore that was used to explain why it endured for almost 150 years within the church. "When you think about it, that's just what it is—folklore. It's never really been official doctrine. I know that there have been some misconceptions and some statements made by people in the past, but as Elder (Bruce R.) McConkie said, we've received new and additional light and knowledge through revelation, and even the folklore is obsolete now because of the fact that we have the revelation." . . . "We have to keep in mind that it's folklore and not doctrine," Elder Child said. "It's never been recorded as such. Many opinions, personal opinions, were spoken. I'm just so grateful for this revelation," he said, adding he can recall exactly where he was and what he was doing when he heard the news 30 years ago.[16]

Church spokesman Mark Tuttle explained, "This folklore is not part of and never was taught as doctrine by the church."[17] In response to comments by a BYU professor confirming the aforementioned statements made by LDS General Authorities, the Mormon Church released a statement on its official Web site in 2012 insisting that any explanations for the priesthood ban prior to 1978 were "speculation and opinion, not doctrine. The Church is not bound by speculation or opinions given with limited understanding. We condemn racism, including any and all past racism by individuals both insides and outside the Church."[18]

However, a statement from the First Presidency in 1951 seems to refute such notions rather than confirm them:

> The attitude of the Church with reference to Negroes remains as it has always stood. It is not a matter of the declaration of a policy but of direct commandment from the Lord, on which is founded the doctrine of the Church from the days of its organization, to the effect that Negroes may become members of the Church but that they are not entitled to the Priesthood at the present time. The prophets of the Lord have made several statements as to the operation of the principle. President Brigham Young said: "Why are so many of the inhabitants of the earth cursed with a skin of blackness? It comes in consequence of their fathers' [sic] rejecting the power of the Holy Priesthood, and the law of God. They will go down to death. And when all the rest of the children have received their blessings in the Holy Priesthood, then that curse will be removed from the seed of Cain, and they will then come up and possess the Priesthood, and receive all the blessings we are entitled to."[19]

Notice in this statement that all those who were cursed would not receive the blessing of the priesthood until *after* death. Young said,

> How long is that race to endure the dreadful curse that is upon them? That curse will remain upon them, and they never can hold the Priesthood or share in it until all the other descendants of Adam have received the promises and enjoyed the blessings of the Priesthood and the keys thereof. Until the last ones of the residue of Adam's children are brought up to that favourable position, the children of Cain cannot receive the first ordinances of the Priesthood. They were the first that were cursed, and they will be the last from whom the curse will be removed. When the residue of the family of Adam come up and receive their blessings, then the curse will be removed from the seed of Cain, and they will receive blessings in like proportion.[20]

If Young is right, the lifting of the ban—which took place by revelation in 1978, as described in Doctrine and Covenants—Declaration 2—was premature since all the other descendants of Adam have yet to receive the blessings of the priesthood. And if the priesthood ban was implemented based on folklore, what does this say about the reliability and discernment of those LDS leaders who perpetuated and enforced such folklore?

The Bible and Christian History

In Jeremiah 1:5, Jeremiah is told by the sovereign God of the universe that He has a plan for the prophet, and that plan was formed before Jeremiah's birth. Does this mean that humans had a relationship with God in premortality? The answer is, quite simply, no. Notice that this verse says God knew Jeremiah before his birth; nowhere does it intimate that Jeremiah knew God. If God is omniscient (all-knowing) and sovereign, we would expect Him to know Jeremiah. The Bible is full of passages stating that God is in sovereign control, and, as such, His plans cannot be thwarted by anyone. In fact, it's clear that God has a plan for everyone.[21] It was God who determined who our parents would be (thus determining where we would be born), the color of our skin, the number of hairs on our head, and even our natural temperament. Nothing about our existence surprised God. He knew us, but nowhere is it inferred that we knew Him before birth.

The *Ensign* magazine cited Hebrews 12:9 to support the doctrine of premortality, saying, "God is our Heavenly Father, a literal spiritual parent."[22] The verse from Hebrews reads, "Furthermore we have had fathers of our flesh which corrected us, and we gave them reverence: shall we not much rather be in subjection unto the Father of spirits, and live?" Mormons tend to read too much into this passage. All who have entered into mortality have spirits, so it would be wrong to assume this refers to some preexistent state. The writer of Hebrews is merely making a connection between the discipline of human fathers and that of our heavenly Father.

Another verse sometimes used by Latter-day Saints is Ecclesiastes 12:7, which says, in part, "the spirit shall return unto God who gave it." This poetic book is describing how the body decomposes to "dust" and the spirit returns to God for judgment; this does not imply a preexistent state. Zechariah 12:1 states that God forms "the spirit of man within him." The assumption is not that man was composed solely of spirit in some premortal state but that man has a physical body in which the spirit dwells.

Many Mormons point to the church fathers for support of this doctrine. While it is true that Origen (185–254) advocated a type of preexistence, historians consider this view to be mere speculation. One church historian wrote, "Origen tried to express the Christian faith in terms of the prevailing Platonic philosophical ideas of his time. Some of his speculations, for example about the pre-existence of souls and universal salvation, were repudiated by the church, and helped bring about his later condemnation."[23]

Another observed, "The problem is that Origen was very much enamored with speculation and it sometimes led to conclusions that seem patently unbiblical. . . . According to Origen, this premortal, spiritual probation explains why humans enter the world in such unequal conditions. It is his own form of what some Eastern religions call 'karma.' Such speculation seemed innocent and even helpful to Origen, but it goes far to explain why some other Christians regarded him as a heretic."[24] Origen even admitted that his ideas were his own and not necessarily canonical.[25] In addition, Origen's teaching is not even close to Mormonism's doctrine of premortality. For example, he did not teach that Jesus was the firstborn offspring of God or that humans are the siblings of Jesus.

The doctrine of premotality is nothing more than mere speculation on behalf of the Mormon leadership. With no evidence from the Bible, this doctrine is soundly rejected by Bible-believing Christians.

Questions for Discussion

- What weaknesses do you see in the Mormon arguments to support their doctrine that all humans once existed in premortality?

- Suppose a Mormon uses Jeremiah 1:5 to support this doctrine. How can you answer the Mormon's argument?

- What are some of the problems with assuming that the doctrine of premortality was once taught in Christianity but later removed?

—————————————— Evangelism Tip ——————————————

Mormons might claim that corrupt people over the centuries ignored or changed the original teachings of Christ's followers, including the doctrine of premortality. This is an argument from silence, where a conclusion is based on assumption rather than hard evidence. Jesus Himself said that He was the only person who had preexisted in the presence of the Father.[26] In addition, if this really was a biblical teaching, then ask the Mormon why the Book of Mormon is silent on this issue.

Chapter 14

If God was once a man, why can't men become gods?

Response Questions
- Does the Bible allow for God's people to worship false gods? If the Mormon God was once as we are now, does this mean he was once a sinner?
- If a person must experience mortality prior to godhood, how did the first God become God?

• • • • • • • • • • • • • • • •

"Similarly, [Mormons] have a view of the nature of God and the eternal progression of His children that is found in no other Christian faith."[1]

—LDS Newsroom

———————————— Summary ————————————

The nature of God in Mormon teaching is central to determining whether or not Mormonism is a Christian religion. Mormonism not only introduces a God who once existed as a human being, but it also states that all humans have the potential to achieve godhood in the future. By redefining the biblical God, Mormon leaders have created a God in man's image. Since fallen man has certain defined attributes, the Mormon concept of God and the possibility of man becoming God are doctrinal issues open to serious criticism.

KNOWING FULL WELL THAT THE Mormon view of deity is troubling to Bible-believing Christians, Apostle James Talmage (1862–1933) wrote, "In spite of the opposition of the sects, in the face of direct charges of blasphemy, the Church proclaims the eternal truth: *As man is, God once was; as God is, man may be.*"[2] It was President Lorenzo Snow (1814–1901) who formulated this couplet to describe God's progression to godhood as well as man's potential to achieve the same state.[3]

The Bodily Nature of the Mormon God

In an 1844 funeral sermon called the "King Follett Discourse," founder Joseph Smith (1805–1844) proclaimed, "God himself was once as we are now, and is an exalted man, and sits enthroned in yonder heavens! . . . I am going to tell you how God came to be God. We have imagined and supposed that God was God from all eternity. I will refute that idea, and take away the veil, so that you may see."[4] In Doctrine and Covenants 130:22, Smith taught that "the Father has a body of flesh and bones as tangible as man's."

President Joseph Fielding Smith (1876–1972) explained, "*Our Father in heaven, according to the Prophet, had a Father*, and since there has been a condition of this kind through all eternity, each Father had a Father, until we come to a stop where we cannot go further, because of our limited capacity to understand."[5] However, no support for this view can be found in either the standard works or official positions of the church. Therefore, it is fair to ask how many attributes of humanity God actually possessed. If mortality is really a probationary period for humans to prove themselves worthy of exaltation, did Elohim as a man pass with flying colors and resist every worldly temptation? Or was he just like all humans who, falling short of his God's standards, died because of sin (Rom. 6:23)? There is no official statement in Mormonism to the contrary, leaving Mormons with no definitive answer.

Some Mormons might argue that if their God was a sinner, he is no longer one. This is irrelevant. All this really proves is that Elohim is a redeemed sinner, no different from redeemed mortals. To speak of God the Father as existing as a mere human prior to becoming God is to reject the transcendent God of the Bible. God is distinct from His creation. As Psalm 90:2 puts it, He is God from everlasting to everlasting. Other LDS standard works agree. For example, Moroni 8:18 in the Book of Mormon states that "God is unchangeable from all eternity to all eternity." Doctrine and Covenants 20:17 says, "By these things we know that there is a God in heaven who is infinite and eternal, from everlasting to everlasting, the same unchangeable

God, the framer of heaven and earth, and all things which are in them." Doctrine and Covenants 76:4 adds, "From eternity to eternity he is the same and his years never fail."

Some Mormons see a connection between Acts 17:28 and the notion that the Mormon God literally fathered all of humankind. The verse reads, "For in him we live, and move, and have our being; as certain also of your own poets have said, For we are also his offspring." Mormons should be cautioned about reading too much into this verse since Paul is merely using a concept familiar to the Athenians. The poem he refers to (*Phaenomena*) is actually paying homage to Zeus and asserts the dependence of all things on him. The portion referenced by Paul reads: "From Zeus let us begin; him do we mortals never leave unnamed; full of Zeus are all the streets and all the market-places of men; full is the sea and the heavens thereof; always we all have need of Zeus. For we are also his offspring; and he in his kindness unto men giveth favourable signs and wakeneth the people to work, reminding them of livelihood."[6] Paul's connection was apparently derived from the Greeks' belief that Zeus was the supreme God and that all mortals are dependent on him. It is unlikely that Paul was speaking literally when he used the word *offspring* because the Greeks did not believe that Zeus fathered all of mankind.

Men Becoming Gods

The notion that God progressed from human to God is a great source of comfort to many Latter-day Saints. It gives them the hope that if they too are faithful, they also can achieve godhood. In his King Follett funeral sermon, Joseph Smith declared, "Here then is eternal life—to know the only wise and true God; and you have got to learn how to be Gods yourselves, and to be kings and priests to God the same as all Gods have done before you."[7] President Brigham Young (1801–1877) delivered a message in the Salt Lake Tabernacle on August 8, 1852, affirming this teaching. He said, "The Lord created you and me for the purpose of becoming Gods like Himself."[8] In Mormonism, eternal life, exaltation, and godhood are interchangeable terms. "Thus those who gain eternal life receive exaltation. . . . They are gods."[9] Dieter F. Uchtdorf, a member of the First Presidency, declared at a general conference, "While against the backdrop of infinite creation, we may appear to be nothing, we have a spark of eternal fire burning within our breast. We have the incomprehensible promise of exaltation—worlds without end—within our grasp. And it is God's great desire to help us reach it."[10]

Mormon leaders have offered many details as to what these "gods" will be doing. Young taught, "All those who are counted worthy to be exalted and to become Gods, even the sons of God, will go forth and have earths and worlds like those who framed this and millions on millions of others."[11] He added that these worthy members will create earths "like unto ours and to people them in the same manner as we have been brought forth by our parents, by our Father and God."[12]

Not only will exalted humans be forming and ruling over worlds, but they will also have the ability to procreate throughout eternity. This doctrine is known as eternal increase. A church manual declares,

> Mortal persons who overcome all things and gain an ultimate exaltation will live eternally in the family unit and have spirit children, thus becoming Eternal Fathers and Eternal Mothers. (D&C 132:19–32.) Indeed, the formal pronouncement of the Church, issued by the First Presidency and the Council of the Twelve, states: "So far as the stages of eternal progression and attainment have been made known through divine revelation, we are to understand that *only resurrected and glorified beings can become parents of spirit offspring.*"[13]

Apostle Orson Pratt (1811–1881) said that "the inhabitants of each world are required to reverence, adore, and worship their own personal father who dwells in the Heaven which they formerly inhabited."[14] Spencer W. Kimball wrote, "Each one of you has it within the realm of his possibility to develop a kingdom over which you will preside as its king and god. You will need to develop yourself and grow in ability and power and worthiness, to govern such a world with all of its people."[15]

A 2004 LDS student manual recounts a story about President Lorenzo Snow (1814–1901), who, while visiting a kindergarten class in Provo, Utah, saw several children making clay "spheres." Snow told the school official accompanying him,

> These children are now at play, making mud worlds, the time will come when some of these boys, through their faithfulness to the gospel, will progress and develop in knowledge, intelligence and power, in future eternities, until they shall be able to go out into space where there is unorganized matter and call together the necessary elements, and through their knowledge of and control over the

laws and powers of nature, to organize matter into worlds on which their posterity may dwell, and over which they shall rule as gods.[16]

Citing Spencer W. Kimball, Apostle L. Tom Perry said,

> Peter and John had little secular learning, being termed ignorant. But they knew the vital things of life, that God lives and that the crucified, resurrected Lord is the Son of God. They knew the path to eternal life. This they learned in a few decades of their mortal life. Their righteous lives opened the door to godhood for them and creation of worlds with eternal increase. For this they would probably need, eventually, a total knowledge of the sciences . . . Secular knowledge, important as it may be, can never save a soul nor open the celestial kingdom nor create a world nor make a man a god.[17]

Despite the above references made by LDS leaders and church manuals pointing to the possibility of Mormons being able to make and rule over their own worlds, the Mormon Church posted a statement on its official Newsroom Web site relegating such comments to nothing more than mere speculation. Answering the question "Do Latter-day Saints believe that they will 'get their own planet'?" the statement answered, "No. This idea is not taught in Latter-day Saint scripture, nor is it a doctrine of the Church. This misunderstanding stems from speculative comments unreflective of scriptural doctrine."[18] The statement appears to use semantics to cover up teachings made by past LDS leaders who speak of Mormons making and ruling worlds and earths.

It is not uncommon for a Latter-day Saint to tone down the impact of this teaching by emphasizing that Mormons can merely become "like God," as if this somehow means there is a distinction between what the LDS God is now and what Latter-day Saints hope to become. Though Mormons assume that exalted humans will always be subordinate to God, to insist that exalted beings will be merely "like God" suggests there will always be, to a certain degree, a substantial difference in quality and attributes between Elohim and his offspring. If this is so, is the Mormon Elohim also dissimilar from the God(s) who preceded him? In other words, if every generation of gods lacks in any degree the power, might, and dominion of the gods who preceded them, then it must be assumed that the God worshipped by present-day Mormons is also lesser in power, might, and dominion than the myriad of gods who were exalted before him. This means that the Mormon God is subordinate as well as inferior to the gods who preceded him.

Can Humans Really Become "Gods"?

Mormon apologists often compare exaltation with the Eastern Orthodox doctrine of deification, or *theosis*, meaning "union with God." While speaking about a desire or perceived ability to seek God's holiness, this idea never attempts to undermine the biblical truth that God is one or to give hope to believers that they can expect to become, in an ontological sense, a god. *Theosis* does not support the notion that Christians will ever achieve the essence or being of God. Still, this has not stopped Mormons from misusing the writings of some early church fathers,[19] as well as Christian philosopher C. S. Lewis (1898–1963), in an attempt to give Smith's teaching a bit of historical authenticity. Orthodox Bishop Kallistos (Timothy) Ware, Bishop of Diokleia, refutes such a comparison:

> It is clear to me that C. S. Lewis understands the doctrine of *theosis* in essentially the same way as the Orthodox Church does; indeed, he probably derived his viewpoint from reading such Greek Fathers as Athanasius. On the other hand, the Mormon view is altogether different from what Lewis and the Orthodox Church believe. Orthodox theology emphasizes that there is a clear distinction—in the current phraseology "an ontological gap"—between God the Creator and the creation which He has made. This "gap" is bridged by divine love, supremely through the Incarnation, but it is not abolished. The distinction between the Uncreated and the created still remains. The Incarnation is a unique event. "Deification," on the Orthodox understanding, is to be interpreted in terms of the distinction between the divine essence and the divine energies. Human beings share by God's mercy in His energies but not in His essence, either in the present age or in the age to come. That is to say, in *theosis* the saints participate in the grace, power, and glory of God, but they never become God by essence.[20]

Though some of the language used when speaking of exaltation and theosis may sound similar, the concepts are not. It is misleading, if not outright deceptive, for Mormons to continue making this comparison.

The Most High God

Israel praised God as the "Most High," recognizing that there is none like Him (cf. Pss. 7:17; 9:2; 83:18). He is God alone. Isaiah 43:10 declares, "I am he: before me there was no God formed, neither shall there be after me." If Mormonism is true, this verse quickly becomes meaningless since countless numbers of gods must have preceded Elohim before he achieved his personal exaltation. Furthermore, Isaiah makes it clear that no gods are forthcoming. The argument that this speaks only to man-made idols must be rejected since every idol was made "after" God.

In Isaiah 44:6, 8 the omniscient God of the Bible says there are no other gods. He also adamantly declares in Isaiah 45:5, "There is no God beside me."[21] From eternity past to eternity future, there will never be a "most high" God other than the one presented in the Bible. Still, the Bible does refer to "gods" throughout its pages. Whether this term refers to heavenly beings or representatives (such as angels) or false gods, it is never implied that these "gods" share equality with God the "Most High."

John 10:34 often is cited to connect sinful man with potential godhood. In this account, Jesus stood at the famous "porch of Solomon" and responded to the blindness of the religious leaders of His day. He rebuked their unbelief by quoting from Psalm 82:6, "I have said, Ye are gods." Does this offer hope of eventual exaltation as understood by Latter-day Saints? The problem with this interpretation is that Jesus did not say, "Ye *can become* gods." Instead, the text reads, "Ye *are* [present tense] gods." Not even Mormons believe that they are gods right now. At best, they are what many LDS leaders have called "gods in embryo."[22]

Apostle James Talmage—a well-respected authority to Latter-day Saints even today—explained that Jesus was referring to divinely appointed human judges in John 10:34: "Divinely Appointed Judges Called 'gods.' In Psalm 82:6, judges invested by divine appointment are called 'gods.' To this the Savior referred in His reply to the Jews in Solomon's Porch. Judges so authorized officiated as the representatives of God and are honored by the exalted title 'gods.'"[23] The LDS First Presidency appointed Talmage to write this book and, when completed, it was reviewed by a committee of the First Presidency and the Quorum of the Twelve Apostles.

Some modern Mormon apologists, however, have rejected Talmage's interpretation in favor of one that allows for the gods of Psalm 82:6 to be understood as a divine council of heavenly beings. In doing so, they reject the guidance of the First Presidency. While some Latter-day Saints give the impression that Talmage's conclusion has little scholarly support, his interpretation agrees with that of many Hebrew and Old Testament scholars.[24] While other views could be entertained, many Bible commentators see this view as perfectly plausible. For example, Old Testament scholar Derek Kidner explains that "gods" could refer to human judges, "principalities and powers," or to the gods of the heathen. Regarding this last possibility, he writes, "It is true that 1 Corinthians 10:20 speaks of pagan worship as the worship of demons, but this is to make the point that idolatry is never neutral but a surrender to Belial and his hosts; it is not an acceptance by Paul of heathen mythologies. Likewise the Old Testament never wavers in its abhorrence of heathen gods. For Yahweh to authenticate their claim with the words, 'I say, "You are gods,"' would be totally out of character."[25]

Whether Mormons agree with their apostle, along with the First Presidency, or reject his interpretation for one that allows for a divine council of heavenly beings makes little difference. Neither position consistently supports the LDS view that men can progress to become gods that are ontologically similar to the most high God of the Bible.

Another verse Mormons often use to support their case is 1 John 3:2: "Beloved, now are we the sons of God, and it doth not yet appear what we shall be: but we know that, when he shall appear, we shall be like him; for we shall see him as he is." To be "like him" is taken by Mormons to mean that humans could possibly end up having all of the attributes of God Himself, including omnipotence, or "all-powerfulness." President Spencer W. Kimball said as much when he wrote, "To this end God created man to live in mortality and endowed him with the potential to perpetuate the race, to subdue the earth, to perfect himself and to become as God, omniscient and omnipotent."[26] However, since only one being could hold "all power," having more than one omnipotent being defies the very meaning of the word.

In his commentary on 1 John, Christian theologian Simon J. Kistemaker writes, "Scripture discloses that at the coming of Christ we will be glorified in body and soul. 'We shall be like him.' The Bible nowhere states that we shall be equal to Christ. Instead it tells us that we shall be conformed to the likeness of the Son of God. We share his immortality. However, Christ has the preeminence, for the Son of God is 'the firstborn among many brothers' (Rom. 8:29)."[27] Mormonism's version of who God once was and what man may become hardly concur with the descriptions found in the Bible. This is no small issue.

Questions for Discussion

- The statement "As man is, God once was. As God is, man may be" is something most Latter-day Saints will readily agree is true teaching. Why is understanding this concept crucial to understanding Mormonism?

- If God has sinned, what difference would this make in how Christians should approach Him?

- Mormon leaders have been very clear about the notion that exalted members would make and rule over their own worlds. Why do you think current LDS leadership is distancing itself from this teaching?

Evangelism Tip

For centuries Christians have professed their belief in a God who is alone God (Isa. 44:8), self-existent (Isa. 43:10; 48:12), immutable (Ps. 102:27; Isa. 46:10; Mal. 3:6), eternal (Pss. 90:2; 93:2), omnipresent (1 Kings 8:27; Prov. 15:3; Isa. 66:1; Jer. 23:23–24), omnipotent (Job 42:2; Ps. 115:3; Matt. 19:26), and forgiving (Ps. 103:12; 1 John 1:9). Ask your Mormon friend, "Why are the attributes of the God of Mormonism so different from the God who is declared in the Bible?" Remind your friend that if a person's view of God is tainted, there can be no true worship of Him.

Chapter 15

How do you justify the doctrine of the Trinity?

Response Questions

- Could you please define what you think Christians mean by the word *Trinity*?
- If something is a mystery, does that mean it cannot be true?

• • • • • • • • • • • • • • • •

"We maintain that the concepts identified by such nonscriptural terms as 'the incomprehensible mystery of God' and 'the mystery of the Holy Trinity' are attributable to the ideas of Greek philosophy. These philosophical concepts transformed Christianity in the first few centuries following the death of the Apostles."[1]

—Apostle Dallin H. Oaks

—————————— Summary ——————————

The Trinity is a central doctrine of Christianity and a lightning rod for critics, including the LDS Church. Apart from this doctrine, it is impossible to harmonize the many verses that speak of the Father, Son, and Holy Spirit being God and still be true to the Bible's claim that there is only one God. Rather than being an unbiblical invention of the later Christian church, the concept of the Trinity is supported by the Bible and remains a doctrine cherished by millions of Christians around the world.

HISTORICALLY, THE LDS CHURCH has rejected the idea of the Trinity. Mormonism's founder, Joseph Smith (1805–1844), taught, "Many men say there is one God; the Father, the Son and the Holy Ghost are only one God! I say that is a strange God anyhow—three in one, and one in three! It is a curious organization . . . All are to be crammed into one God, according to sectarianism. It would make the biggest God in all the world. He would be a wonderfully big God—he would be a giant or a monster."[2]

Apostle John A. Widtsoe (1872–1952) declared, "The Bible, if read fully and intelligently, teaches that the Holy Trinity is composed of individual Gods."[3] During a speech at Brigham Young University in 1984, Apostle Bruce R. McConkie (1915–1985) went so far as to say that the Trinitarian view of God was the first and greatest heresy of Christianity.[4] Apostle Jeffrey R. Holland told a general conference crowd that "a Trinitarian notion [is] never set forth in the scriptures because it is not true. . . . So any criticism that The Church of Jesus Christ of Latter-day Saints does not hold the contemporary Christian view of God, Jesus, and the Holy Ghost is *not* a comment about our commitment to Christ but rather a recognition (accurate, I might add) that our view of the Godhead breaks with post-New Testament Christian history and returns to the doctrine taught by Jesus Himself."[5]

Arguing that the Trinity is a creation of later Christianity, LDS author Scott Marshall asserted that the Council of Nicaea was made up of "a bunch of church leaders and government officials [who] got together and voted on 'who God was,' and it wasn't even a unanimous vote. There were about four different versions of God that were voted on. The version that is used by Catholics and Protestants today only won by about a 40 percent margin. Their view of God, as you may know, is that He is like a formless mass of spirit that fills the whole universe and when He comes to earth, part of it breaks off and forms itself into Jesus."[6]

The Historic Christian Teaching of the Trinity

Contrary to the opinion of some, the Christian creeds were not written to supersede the Bible. According to Christian church historian Philip Schaff, they "never precede faith, but presuppose it."[7] He went on to say, "The Church is, indeed, not founded on symbols, but on Christ; not on any words of man, but on the word of God; yet it is founded on Christ as *confessed* by men, and a creed is man's answer to Christ's question, man's acceptance and interpretation of God's word."[8] As New Testament scholar Mark Strauss says, "We can conclude that the later Christological creeds of the church, in which

Jesus is confessed as God the Son and as the Second Person of the Trinity, need not be viewed as distortions or evolutionary transmutations of a Jewish rabbi into a divine Lord. They can rather be seen as a natural development arising from the church's reflection on and contemplation of the words and deeds of the historical Jesus."[9]

Creeds were written as a means of accurately explaining what the Bible conveys. The Athanasian Creed took up the task of describing the Godhead in a way that complements the Bible's teaching on this subject. For example, the early church could not accept the Father, Son, and Holy Spirit as three separate gods (tritheism) because this violated the many verses that confirm the existence of only one God.[10] In part, the Athanasian Creed says, "We worship one God in Trinity, and the Trinity in Unity: neither confounding the Persons: nor dividing the Substance [Essence]. For there is one Person of the Father: another of the Son: and another of the Holy Ghost. But the Godhead of the Father, of the Son, and of the Holy Ghost, is all one: the Glory equal, the Majesty coeternal. . . . And yet they are not three Gods: but one God." It should be noted that the Christian church has historically remained faithful to monotheism (one God). The struggle was *explaining* this "oneness" within the Godhead without rejecting the individuality of each member. Noting "that in most instances where a religious group denies the Trinity, the reason can be traced back to the founder's unwillingness to admit the simple reality that God is bigger than we can ever imagine." Christian apologist James White gives an even more succinct definition for the Trinity: "Within the one Being that is God, there exists eternally three coequal and coeternal persons, namely, the Father, the Son, and the Holy Spirit."[11] As White correctly notes, the Trinity solves problems rather than creates them. After all, the doctrine helps explain the concept of one God while allowing for the three persons being fully and completely God.

A common objection is that the word *Trinity* is never used in the Bible. Mormons who use this argument are vulnerable to the same criticism since unique LDS words like *premortality*, *Heavenly Mother*, and *temple endowments* are never mentioned in the Bible. There is no evidence that marriages took place in Jerusalem's temple or that Communion was served with water. Yet Latter-day Saints have held these to be true concepts.

To argue that the Trinity cannot be true, Mormons also like to point to select Bible passages, including Genesis 1:26, Acts 7:55–56, and 1 Corinthians 8:6. They also refer to Jesus' praying to the Father in Gethsemane and to the three persons of God being involved in Jesus' baptism. While there are good resources available to explain individual passages,[12] it is important to understand that while there is one God and each of the three persons in the Trinity is fully God, they are not each other. Thus, the Father is not Jesus, and Jesus is not the Holy Spirit. Indeed, they are one in essence, but they are three in persons.

Another objection to the Trinity is that it was a later invention of the Christian church. Opponents like to aim their artillery at the Council of Nicaea in A.D. 325, though the Latin word *Trinity* apparently was formulated by the church father Tertullian (160–220) more than a century before the council. This gathering of bishops was convened to focus on the heretical view of a North African bishop named Arius who rejected the teaching that Jesus was God. Those opposed to the Trinity often bring up the name of the Roman emperor Constantine in an attempt to portray the Council of Nicaea as being used to promote a pagan concept of God. Actually, Constantine was not even involved in the debate and had nothing to do with the decision made at Nicaea.

Arius's teaching in the early fourth century that Jesus was just a created being led to a real possibility of a church split. The council was called to deal with this specific issue. The result was the Nicene Creed, which explained that Jesus was truly God in the flesh. Recited every Sunday by numerous Christians all over the world, the creed says in part, "I believe in one Lord Jesus Christ, the only-begotten Son of God, begotten of Him before all ages, God of God, Light of Light, Very God of Very God, Begotten, not made, being of one Substance with the Father, by whom all things were made." Christian pastor/theologian A. W. Tozer explained, "For more than sixteen hundred years this has stood as the final test of orthodoxy, as well it should, for it condenses in theological language the teaching of the New Testament concerning the position of the Son in the Godhead."[13]

Mormon apologist Gilbert Scharffs writes, "Both before and after the Nicean council in A.D. 325, most Christians favored the view of a man named Arius."[14] The facts do not support this view. Indeed, fewer than two dozen bishops (out of approximately three hundred) attending the council were ever in favor of Arianism; by the time the council concluded, only two continued to hold to Arius's position. Christian theologian Roger E. Olson writes,

> According to one account, soon after the council opened someone called for a reading of the Arian position so that all could know exactly what was to be debated. At that point the Arians—or at least

some of them—made a serious strategic error. Alexander and his bishops must have been delighted. Bishop Eusebius of Nicomedia stood before the council and read a clear and blatant denial of the deity of the Son of God, emphasizing that he is a creature and not equal with the Father in any sense. . . . Before Eusebius finished reading it, some of the bishops were holding their hands over their ears and shouting for someone to stop the blasphemies . . . Apparently, in spite of circulating letters written by Arius and Alexander before the council, most of the bishops were naïve about how clear-cut the issue really was. They had come to the council hoping to hear something moderate—a mediating position between these two opposite views. When one of their own expressed the Arian side in such stark terminology, making clear that they considered the Son of God a mere creature, they were convinced that this was heresy.[15]

Later, the doctrine of the Trinity was overwhelmingly confirmed in a fuller form at the Council of Constantinople in A.D. 381. That council dealt a final deathblow to Arianism while refuting the heresy of Macedonianism, which taught that the Holy Spirit was not God.

The Godhead in the Book of Mormon

On June 16, 1844, a week before his death, Joseph Smith gave his famous "Sermon in the Grove." In this message he stated, "I wish to declare I have always and in all congregations when I have preached on the subject of the Deity, it has been the plurality of Gods. It has been preached by the Elders for fifteen years."[16] However, the Book of Mormon tends to support a view of the Godhead that is in stark contrast to what Joseph Smith espoused toward the end of his life.

Though the Book of Mormon does speak of the Father, Son, and Holy Ghost, it gives the impression that the three are the same person, as opposed to three distinct persons. For example, Mosiah 13:34 says, "Have they not said that God himself should come down among the children of men, and take upon him the form of man, and go forth in mighty power upon the face of the earth?" Quoting the prophet Abinadi, Mosiah 15:1–4 declares, "I would that ye should understand that God himself shall come down among the children of men, and shall redeem his people. And because he dwelleth in flesh he shall be called the Son of God, and having subjected the flesh to the will of the Father, being the Father and the Son—The Father, because he was conceived by the power of God; and the Son, because of the flesh; thus becoming the Father and Son—And they are one God, yea, the very Eternal Father of heaven and of earth."

While not as explicit, there are a number of other Book of Mormon passages that speak of the Father, Son, and Holy Ghost as comprising the "one God."[17] Following are some examples:

- 1 Nephi 13:41: ". . . for there is one God and one Shepherd over all the earth."
- 2 Nephi 31:21: "There is none other way nor name given under heaven whereby man can be saved in the kingdom of God. And now, behold, this is the doctrine of Christ, and the only and true doctrine of the Father, and of the Son, and of the Holy Ghost, which is one God, without end. Amen."
- Alma 11:28–29: "Now Zeezrom said: Is there more than one God? And he [Amulek] answered, No."[18]
- Alma 11:44: ". . . and shall be brought and be arraigned before the bar of Christ the Son, and God the Father, and the Holy Spirit, which is one Eternal God, to be judged according to their works, whether they be good or whether they be evil."

If the people mentioned in the Book of Mormon really existed, it seems odd that their description of the Godhead points more toward a monotheistic view. Instead of advocating the existence of more than one God, as Joseph Smith did, their words suggest they would have considered such teaching to be unorthodox.

Questions for Discussion

- How would you respond to this statement: "The Trinity cannot be logically explained. Therefore, the Trinity cannot be true."

- Many people argue that the Trinity was an invention of the later Christian church. Explain why this is not the case and how the Trinity is presented in the pages of the Bible.

- Mormons have said they believe in three gods but one Godhead. Why should this be rejected as a form of monotheism?

─────────────────── Evangelism Tip ───────────────────

The Council of Nicaea is often cited as invalidating the doctrine of the Trinity. Ask your Mormon acquaintance, "Why do you think church leaders gathered in Nicaea in the first place? Who were the advocates for the positions? And do you believe this is where the word *Trinity* was created?" Often Mormons do not know that the principal players were Alexander and Athanasius versus Arius. Tertullian formulated the term *Trinity* more than a century earlier. In addition, the Council of Nicaea was not called to deal with the triune nature of God but rather the deity of Christ. This council affirmed, rather than rejected, biblical teaching.

Chapter 16

If God is a spirit, why did Moses say he saw God face-to-face?

Response Questions

- If Moses literally saw God's face, why did this same Moses also say this was impossible?
- If the Bible is meant to be taken literally in all cases, what do you do with the passages that say you are to cut off your hands and pluck out your eyes if they cause you to sin?

· · · · · · · · · · · · · · · · ·

"We read in the first chapter of Moses that God talked to Moses face to face, taught him that he was a son of God, and showed him the earth from its beginning to the end."[1]

—Michaelene P. Grassli, former Primary General President

Summary

In order to support Joseph Smith's First Vision account, Mormons often quote Exodus 33:11, which says the Lord spoke to Moses "face to face." This is taken to mean that it is possible to see the actual body of God the Father, even though John 4:24 says that God is a spirit and Exodus 33:20 says that nobody can see God's face and live. Understanding that the Bible uses figurative language to describe how Old Testament figures personally experienced the presence of deity can help us correctly interpret passages that were not meant to be taken literally.

SEVERAL PASSAGES IN THE Old Testament refer to men "seeing" God "face to face." These "theophanies" (visible forms of God) are sometimes pointed to as evidence that it is possible to see God. Genesis 32:30, for instance, states, "And Jacob called the name of the place Peniel: for I have seen God face to face, and my life is preserved."[2] In another verse, Deuteronomy 5:4, Moses reminds the Israelites, "The LORD talked with you face to face in the mount out of the midst of the fire."

Probably the passage most often cited to support people's ability to see God is Exodus 33:11, which says, "And the LORD spake unto Moses face to face, as a man speaketh unto his friend." Yet verse 20 reads, "And he [God] said, Thou canst not see my face: for there shall no man see me, and live." Certainly Moses would not have contradicted himself just a few verses after saying he saw God face-to-face. So what does this mean? God spoke with Moses face-to-face just as He spoke face-to-face with the children of Israel. Moses was indeed in the presence of God, but he never actually saw God's person, for God is invisible. As Hebrews 11:27 says, "By faith he [Moses] forsook Egypt, not fearing the wrath of the king: for he endured, as seeing him who is invisible."

This interpretation should seem plausible to a Latter-day Saint, especially if he or she considers the book of Moses, found in the LDS scripture Pearl of Great Price (which Joseph Smith said he translated between June 1830 and the end of February 1831). The first chapter of that book says that Moses could "endure" God's presence (v. 2). In verse 11, Moses is quoted as saying, "But now mine own eyes have beheld God; but not my natural but my spiritual eyes, for my natural eyes could not have beheld for I should have withered and died in his presence; but his glory was upon me; and I beheld his face, for I was transfigured before him." Despite this, many Latter-day Saints cite Exodus 33:11 to explain how it's possible that their founder, Joseph Smith, "*saw* two Personages," which were God the Father and Jesus Christ.[3]

Regarding the usage of "face to face," Christian theologians Norman Geisler and Ron Rhodes explain, "The phrase *face to face* in Hebrew usage means personally, directly, or intimately. Moses had this kind of unmediated relationship with God. But he, like all other mortals, never saw the 'face' (essence) of God directly."[4] In Exodus 33:22, the invisible God said He would take on a visible form and allow His "glory" to pass by Moses. To protect Moses, God would cover him with His "hand" as He passed by. God told Moses that he would see God's "back parts: but my face shall not be seen" (v. 23). To understand this phenomenon, imagine talking to someone in the dark. You can't actually see the person to whom you are speaking, but there is no doubt by the sound of the voice that you are speaking with the person face-to-face.

Exodus 33:20 becomes especially problematic for the LDS position since Joseph Smith altered the text in his "translation" of the Bible, thus preventing the possibility of any human seeing the face of God. It reads, "And no sinful man hath at any time, neither shall there be any sinful man at any time, that shall see my face and live." But after citing Exodus 33:20, John 1:18, 1 Timothy 6:14–16, and 1 John 4:12 and saying that these passages "seem to contradict other Bible verses," one LDS Church magazine explained it this way: "Fortunately, we have the Joseph Smith Translation of the Bible, which clarifies the four scriptures that say that man can't see God. The Prophet's inspired revisions of those verses explain that sinful people can't see God—only those who believe. And even then, a righteous person must be changed—transfigured—to see God."[5] While no ancient Hebrew manuscript, including the Dead Sea Scrolls, supports Smith's rendering, a Mormon who wants to believe that God inspired their founder to correct the text cannot simultaneously say that Smith—a sinful man without any priesthood authority—literally could have seen God.[6] After all, according to Doctrine and Covenants 84:22, "no man can see the face of God, even the Father, and live" without the "authority of the priesthood."

It is a daunting task for biblical writers to describe God in a way humans can understand. Therefore, anthropomorphism—applying human descriptions to God—is frequently utilized in the Old Testament (especially by the prophets and the poets) to give readers a better grasp of almighty God. An encyclopedia provides some examples of such language used to describe God:

> In Gen. 1, God is represented as speaking (v. 3), then as seeing (v. 4). He walks in the garden in the cool of the day (3:8). Elsewhere we read of the human form of God (Nu. 12:8), of the feet of God (Ex. 24:10), of the hand of God (Isa. 50:11), of the heart of God (Hos. 11:8). In addition to physical characteristics, emotional qualities appropriate to man are also ascribed to God. Thus He is jealous (Ex. 20:5), angry (Ps. 77:9), merciful (Jonah 4:2), mighty (Ps. 147:5), gracious and loving (Ps. 103:8). The Lord can resolve and He can also repent (1 S. 15:11). He is a shepherd (Ps. 23:1), a bridegroom (Isa. 62:5), and a warrior (Ex. 15:3). . . .
>
> That the Bible itself is very conscious of the limitation of anthropomorphism may be seen from the many verses that emphasize the

transcendence of God in relation to man or to the cosmos at large. Thus Deut. 4:12 states categorically that when God met with Israel at Sinai they heard the voice of the words but saw no form. Again, when Moses sought the vision of God in Exod. 33, he asked only to be shown God's way of glory, and even the glory of God was seen only in passing. . . . God alone has immortality "and dwells in unapproachable light, whom no man has ever seen or can see" (1 Tim. 6:16). Even the ways and thoughts of God are not as man's ways and thoughts (Isa. 55:8), and the natural man does not receive the things of the Spirit of God (1 Cor. 2:14).[7]

While the Bible does speak of the "hand of God" and describes Him as "repenting," it must be understood that these expressions are used in an anthropomorphic manner of speaking. It is nonsensical to say the Father has physical hands or that He has need of repentance, as if He could violate His own commandments. Taken to such an extreme, we would have to assume that God is made of stone because Psalm 18:31 says God is a rock or that He is to be thought of as a bird since Psalm 91:4 says He has wings and feathers. When all things are considered, it is impossible for a human being—whether Moses or Joseph Smith—to see God the Father with literal, physical eyes and live.

Questions for Discussion

- Why do you think anthropomorphisms were used in the Bible?

- What would you consider some commonsense rules for determining whether a particular verse should be taken literally or figuratively?

—————————————— Evangelism Tip ——————————————

Explain to your Mormon acquaintance that it is possible to read the Bible but misinterpret its intended meaning by failing to comprehend the language being used. Just as in any other type of literature, the author's purpose and the genre of the writing must be understood. While the Bible generally should be taken literally, there are figures of speech that if taken literally will result in faulty interpretations. Thus, we should not conclude that all children raised by righteous parents automatically turn out to be good (see Prov. 22:6) or that we should literally cut off our hands and pluck out our eyes (see Matt. 5:29–30) if they cause us to sin.

Chapter 17

Why do you emphasize the cross? Why highlight Christ's suffering and death?

Response Questions

- Why do you think Christians have used the symbol of the cross?
- From the very early years, Christians have used this symbol. If the LDS Church is Christian, why is this not a part of its tradition?

• • • • • • • • • • • • • • •

"The cross is used in many Christian churches as a symbol of the Savior's death and Resurrection and as a sincere expression of faith. As members of The Church of Jesus Christ of Latter-day Saints, we also remember with reverence the suffering of the Savior. But because the Savior lives, we do not use the symbol of His death as the symbol of our faith."[1]

—LDS Church manual *True to the Faith: A Gospel Reference*

Summary

Christians today hold the symbol of the cross in high esteem, for the cross is where Jesus died to atone for the sins of those who would believe in Him. To Mormons, however, the cross is a symbol of death and despair that represents a dying Christ rather than a living Christ. The New Testament, however, presents the cross as a very powerful reminder of God's victory over death. In fact, the Bible encourages believers to "glory in the cross."

Symbols can be very powerful. Consider your immediate reaction upon seeing the Nazi swastika or a white dress on a wedding day. Because LDS leaders have said the symbol of the cross is an unpleasant reminder of the pain suffered by Jesus during His passion, Mormon people have been discouraged from using this symbol. Perhaps this lack of enthusiasm for the cross is based not so much on the suffering Christ bore there as it is on the Mormon belief that the atonement took place someplace else. Mormon authors Monte S. Nyman and Charles D. Tate surmise, "It is probably the case that if one hundred Protestants were asked where the atonement of Christ took place, those one hundred persons would answer: At Golgotha, on the cross. It is also no doubt true that if one hundred Latter-day Saints were asked the same question, a large percentage would respond: In Gethsemane, in the garden."[2]

Brigham Young University professor Robert J. Matthews certainly minimized the role of Golgotha when he wrote, "It was in Gethsemane, on the slopes of the Mount of Olives, that Jesus made his perfect atonement by the shedding of his blood—more so than on the cross."[3] Andrew Skinner, also a BYU professor, wrote, "All of our Heavenly Father's planning and preparation, all of his interest in his children and all of his desires for them, all of his aims and goals for the entire universe came down to a singular moment in a specific time and place on this earth in a garden called Gethsemane. Without Gethsemane in God's eternal plan, everything else would have been a colossal waste—*everything*."[4] In a 2004 general conference message, Apostle M. Russell Ballard said, "Thankfully, Jesus Christ courageously fulfilled this sacrifice in ancient Jerusalem. There in the quiet isolation of the Garden of Gethsemane, He knelt among the gnarled olive trees, and in some incredible way that none of us can fully comprehend, the Savior took upon Himself the sins of the world."[5]

This is not to say that the cross is completely ignored in Mormon tradition. President Gordon B. Hinckley (1910–2008) noted, "It was the redemption which He worked out in the Garden of Gethsemane and upon the cross of Calvary which made His gift immortal, universal, and everlasting. His was a great atonement for the sins of all mankind."[6] However, in an article published in the *Ensign* magazine, author Joseph C. Winther wrote, "As terrible as Christ's suffering on the cross was, perhaps it was not as great as His suffering in Gethsemane. When He sweat drops of blood as He bore the weight of all the sins of mankind, the great agony of the Atonement took place."[7] Winther's conclusion raises an interesting question. If Christ actually bore (past tense) "all" of the sins of mankind in Gethsemane, what was left for Him to bear on the cross?

Traditionally, Mormon leaders have placed more emphasis on Jesus' suffering at Gethsemane than at Golgotha.

There are several reasons Christians must reject the notion that Christ's work of atonement had anything to do with His agony in Gethsemane. One of them lies in the prophetic passages of the Old Testament. Psalm 22, for example, contains several verses that speak to events taking place while Christ was hanging on the cross.[8] It should be noted that the Book of Mormon also points to an atonement that took place on a cross. First Nephi 11:33 says that Christ "was lifted up upon the cross and slain for the sins of the world," while 3 Nephi 27:14 says this allowed Jesus to "draw all men" unto Himself. As with the Bible, there is no mention of a garden atonement in the Book of Mormon.

Consider also Christ's prayer at Gethsemane. It could easily be summarized that Jesus agonized for Himself in the garden, as opposed to the cross, where He agonized for mankind. In Luke 22:42, Jesus prayed to the Father to "remove this cup." Mormons often see this as a reference to the "bitter cup" in Doctrine and Convenants 19:18 and conclude that Jesus partook of this cup by suffering for the sins of mankind while in the garden. However, Matthew 26 provides some interesting details that rule out this assumption. In verse 39, Matthew records how Jesus pleads with the Father that, if it be possible, "let this cup pass from me." Three times in a relatively short period of time, Jesus petitioned the Father to remove the cup. Then when Peter attempted to prevent Jesus' arrest by cutting off the ear of the high priest's servant, Jesus rebuked him, saying, "The cup which my Father hath given me, shall I not drink it?" (John 18:11). Jesus was arrested immediately after He asked this question of Peter. His time in the garden was already over. Thus it makes more sense to conclude that Jesus' metaphoric drinking of the cup was still future at this point, after He left the garden.

When it comes to the atonement, it could be said that Mormons emphasize Jesus' perspiration, whereas the New Testament emphasizes Christ's expiration. For example, Paul reminded the believers in Romans 5:6–8 that "when we were yet without strength, in due time Christ died for the ungodly. For scarcely for a righteous man will one die: yet peradventure for a good man some would even dare to die. But God commendeth his love toward us, in that, while we were yet sinners, Christ died for us." In 1 Corinthians 15:3, Paul reminds believers that he delivered "first of all" the message that "Christ died for our sins according to the scriptures." Since Jesus didn't die in Gethsemane, the Mormon notion must be rejected. Peter left no room for doubt as to where Christ took upon Himself our sins. He wrote in 1 Peter 2:24 that Christ bore our sins "in his own body on the tree," an obvious reference to the cross.

President Hinckley related the account of how he answered the question of a Protestant minister who had been invited to attend the open house of the newly renovated Mesa, Arizona, temple. "I've been all through this building, this temple which carries on its face the name of Jesus Christ," the minister said, "but nowhere have I seen any representation of the cross, the symbol of Christianity. I have noted your buildings elsewhere and likewise find an absence of the cross. Why is this when you say you believe in Jesus Christ?" Hinckley's answer was very typical. "For us," he responded, "the cross is a symbol of the dying Christ, while our message is a declaration of the Living Christ."[9]

This response is problematic. The comparison makes it seem as if Christians who see a great deal of significance in the cross fail, in some degree, to grasp the significance of Christ's resurrection. This historical event is indeed a vital aspect of the Christian faith since it validates Christ's role as Messiah. Paul wrote in 1 Corinthians 1:18, "For the preaching of the cross is to them that perish foolishness; but unto us which are saved it is the power of God." He later added in 1 Corinthians 15:14 that if Christ were not raised, then the Christian's faith is worthless.

Nowhere is there any indication in the New Testament that the cross should somehow be minimized because Christ rose from the dead. There is certainly room to remember the importance of both. These two events, in fact, go hand in hand since there can't be a resurrection without a death. Why Mormons such as Hinckley hold that the memory of the cross must be given a backseat in order to draw attention to the resurrection is puzzling since the cross clearly is a major New Testament theme. This response also overlooks the fact that, every Sunday throughout the world, members of the LDS Church participate in the sacrament service in Mormon chapels, a ritual meant to remind members of the death and sacrifice of Christ.[10]

It is common for Mormons to misunderstand the meaning of the cross, erroneously suspecting that Christians worship the symbol itself. The truth is, the cross is the most powerful symbol in the Christian world because it embodies God's love for us. It is a reminder of all that was accomplished through Christ's suffering. What exactly did His suffering and death on the cross accomplish? Consider these biblical passages:

- Romans 5:9—The shedding of His blood on the cross makes justification before an all-holy God a present reality. Christians need not wonder whether they will be "good enough."
- Romans 8:34—Christ's death resulted in Christians having One who intercedes on their behalf.
- 1 Corinthians 5:7–8—As the sacrificed Passover Lamb, Christ enables believers to rid themselves of the contamination of malice and wickedness and to embrace sincerity and truth.
- Galatians 3:13—Christ's death on the cross redeemed believers from the curse of the law, a system by which no sinful human could ever be justified.
- Colossians 1:21–22—Through the physical death of Christ, those who were at one time alienated and enemies of God are now reconciled and made holy in His sight.
- Colossians 2:13–15—The written code of regulations that condemned all people was nailed to the cross, resulting in the forgiveness of all the believer's sins.
- Hebrews 2:14—By His death Jesus removes the sting of death and frees those who were once held in slavery by the fear of death.
- Hebrews 9:13–14—Whereas the regular sacrifices of bulls and goats

had no power to take away sins or clear a worshipper's conscience, Christ's once-for-all death cleanses the conscience of the believer and takes away sin, enabling the believer to serve the living God.

• Hebrews 10:14—It is Christ, through His sacrifice, who perfects the believer, meaning that the anxiety of striving to be "good enough" has been taken away.

Pastor/theologian John Piper correctly notes that, without the cross, a believer's sins could not be blotted out.

> There is no salvation by balancing the records. There is only salvation by canceling records. The record of our bad deeds (including our defective good deeds), along with the just penalties that each deserves, must be blotted out—not balanced. This is what Christ suffered and died to accomplish. The cancellation happened when the record of our deeds was "nailed to the cross" (Colossians 2:13).[11]

In John 15:13, Jesus foreshadowed what would happen at the cross: "Greater love hath no man than this, that a man lay down his life for his friends." Nowhere did the apostle Paul avoid an association with the cross. In Galatians 6:14, he exclaimed, "But God forbid that I should glory, save in the cross of our Lord Jesus Christ, by whom the world is crucified unto me, and I unto the world." Despite what the world thinks, Christians feel no shame when they emphasize the cross. In his tract titled "Calvary!," John Charles Ryle (1816–1900), a well-respected bishop in the Church of England during the nineteenth century, summed it up well:

> Would I know the fullness and completeness of the salvation God has provided for sinners? Where shall I see it most distinctly? Shall I go to the general declarations in the Bible about God's mercy? Shall I rest in the general truth that God is a God of love? Oh, no! I will look at the crucifixion at Calvary. I find no evidence like that: I find no balm for a sore conscience and a troubled heart like the sight of Jesus dying for me on the accursed tree. There I see that a full payment has been made for all my enormous debts. The curse of that law which I have broken, has come down on One who there suffered in my stead; the demands of that law are all satisfied: payment has been made for me even to the uttermost farthing. It will

not be required twice over. Ah, I might sometimes imagine I was too bad to be forgiven; my own heart sometimes whispers that I am too wicked to be saved. But I know in my better moments this is all my foolish unbelief; I read an answer to my doubts in the blood shed on Calvary. I feel sure that there is a way to heaven for the very vilest of men, when I look at the cross.[12]

It also should be pointed out that the reverence Christians show the cross is no different than the respect Mormons might give to their symbols. For instance, Mormons wear symbols of temples on jewelry such as necklaces. And anybody who has visited Salt Lake City will quickly notice that Mormon symbolism is found throughout the downtown area. Probably the religion's best-known symbol is the angel Moroni, represented on the top of the majority of LDS temples in the world. Beehives, moonstones, sun stones, the all-seeing eye, and Masonic "grips" are in abundance on the physical temple in Salt Lake City. While Mormons are quick to distance themselves from the cross, some have no problem defending the numerous five-pointed pentagrams that decorate both the Salt Lake City and Nauvoo temples.

Not all Christians choose to wear a cross, but is the wearing of a cross wrong? Christian theologian Paul Copan responds to this common question:

> Once a Muslim expressed to me his disbelief and even scorn at the idea of Christians wearing crosses: "How can Christians wear with pride the instrument of torture and humiliation? If your brother were killed in an electric chair, would you wear an electric chair around your neck?" I replied that it depends: "If my brother happened to be Jesus of Nazareth and his death in an electric chair brought about my salvation and was the means by which evil was defeated and creation renewed, then he would have transformed a symbol of shame and punishment into something glorious."[13]

If the LDS Church is really a restoration of true Christianity, why don't the leaders emulate the apostolic emphasis of the New Testament? Neither Jesus nor any author of the New Testament claims Gethsemane had anything to do with the atonement of mankind. Instead, there are an abundant number of references to the cross and Christ's death. It was on the cross that Jesus paid the debt for sin, something Christians never could have done themselves.

Questions for Discussion

- Suppose a Mormon told you that it is sacrilegious to use the cross and perhaps even insinuated that Christians physically worship the cross, whether it's a large replica made of wood or an emblem worn around the neck. How can this argument be answered while also presenting the gospel message of Christianity?

- While Christians celebrate Jesus' resurrection, the Friday preceding this event, the day Jesus died on the cross, is known as "Good Friday." Is this morbid? Why or why not? In what ways can we as Christians better mentally prepare for resurrection day?

- In a Christian hymnal or on the Internet, look up the hymn "The Old Rugged Cross" by George Bennard (1873–1958) and read the words. (The chorus reads, "So I'll cherish the old rugged cross, till my trophies at last I lay down; I will cling to the old rugged cross, and exchange it some day for a crown.") What significance does the symbol of the cross hold for you in your life?

-------------------------------- Evangelism Tip --------------------------------

There is nothing more important than the death and resurrection of Jesus Christ. If Jesus was raised from the dead, as He promised in John 2:19, then there can be no greater miracle and proof of His deity. So when this subject comes up, use the opportunity to give a quick gospel presentation. While Mormons may not grasp the huge significance the cross has for Christians, make it known how Christ's death has changed your life and the potential it has to change anyone who comes to faith in Christ and receives the forgiveness He purchased on Calvary.

Chapter 18

How can you believe in a God who would send His children to an eternal hell?

Response Questions

- What is your definition of "hell"?
- Do you think it is fair that a third of your brothers and sisters from the preexistence didn't have the chance to progress merely because of one sin?
- How do you interpret the passages in the Book of Mormon that teach a traditional hell?

• • • • • • • • • • • • • • • •

"We reject the unscriptural doctrine that there are two places or states of eternal existence—heaven and hell—and that all men will go to one or the other."[1]
—Hugh B. Brown (1883–1975), member of the First Presidency

—————————— Summary ——————————

Hell. Just saying the word can cause a variety of emotions, including fear, anger, and disbelief. Some people think everyone has a divine right to heaven. According to Mormon theology, because of their previous obedience in premortality, almost all humans will enter one of three levels of heaven. Outer darkness, a place very similar to the Christian concept of hell, is reserved only for Satan and his demons, along with a few others called sons of perdition. This is a much different picture from what is portrayed in the Bible.

THE TRADITIONAL VIEW OF eternal punishment in hell is rejected in Mormon theology. Apostle John A. Widtsoe (1872–1952) said, "In the Church of Jesus Christ of Latter-day Saints, there is no hell. All will find a measure of salvation. . . . The gospel of Jesus Christ has no hell in the old proverbial sense."[2] Apostle Bruce R. McConkie (1915–1985) added, "To believe that in eternity all men will go either to a heaven of eternal bliss or a hell of eternal torment is a doctrine that offends the sense of justice of every reasonable man."[3]

While Mormonism denies its existence, there is a redefined concept of hell that is a part of LDS theology: "Latter-day scriptures describe at least three senses of hell: (1) that condition of misery which may attend a person in mortality due to disobedience to divine law; (2) the miserable, but temporary, state of disobedient spirits in the spirit world awaiting the resurrection; (3) the permanent habitation of the sons of perdition, who suffer the second spiritual death and remain in hell even after the resurrection."[4]

The first definition means that people can create their own hell on earth; that is, by willfully disobeying God's law, they suffer the consequences of committing such sins as adultery, cheating on taxes, or living a life of lies. However, since the worst "hell" possible in this temporal world is nothing compared to eternal separation from God, this cannot be what the Bible describes as *eternal* hell. The second definition refers to a spirit prison, where deceased, disobedient humans will be held in a temporary state. When living Mormons perform works in temples on behalf of the dead, an opportunity to accept the gospel is made available to them. The third aspect is outer darkness, which will be discussed later in this chapter.

A fourth possible meaning is the regret those relegated to lower kingdoms will have for eternity. President Joseph Fielding Smith (1876–1972) said, "Of course, those who enter the telestial kingdom, and those who enter the terrestrial kingdom will have the eternal punishment which will come to them in knowing that they might, if they had kept the commandments of the Lord, have returned to his presence as his sons and his daughters. This will be a torment to them, and in that sense it will be hell."[5] The *Encyclopedia of Mormonism* defines damnation as "falling short of what one might have enjoyed if one had received and been faithful to the whole law of the gospel. In this sense, all who do not achieve the highest degree of the Celestial Kingdom are damned, even though they are saved in some degree of glory. They are damned in the sense that they will not enjoy an eternal increase or the continuation of the family unit in eternity (D&C 132:4, 19)."[6]

Some Mormons hope that over time progression from a lower to a higher kingdom can be achieved. President Brigham Young (1801–1877) speculated that this could be possible.[7] However, presidents such as George Albert Smith (1870–1951) and Spencer W. Kimball (1895–1985) denied this possibility, as did Apostle Bruce R. McConkie (1915–1985).[8] Joseph Fielding Smith concluded that the idea of progressing from kingdom to kingdom "is *false reasoning, illogical,* and creates mischief in making people think they may procrastinate their repentance, but in course of time they will reach exaltation in celestial glory."[9]

Hell According to the Bible

While eternal punishment may not be a popular doctrine, it is necessary because God is holy (Isa. 6:3; Rev. 4:8) and just (2 Thess. 1:6). Indeed, sin has consequences, including eternal death (Rom. 6:23). The Bible is very clear that those who have spurned God's sacrifice and refused the gift of His Son will spend eternity in endless torment. It reveals only two options: heaven or hell. Jesus said in Matthew 18:8, "It is better for you to enter life crippled or lame than with two hands or two feet to be thrown into the eternal fire" (ESV). In Matthew 25:46 Jesus said, "And these shall go away into everlasting punishment: but the righteous into life eternal." And He said in Luke 13:28 that "there shall be weeping and gnashing of teeth" when those who thought they belonged in heaven based on their good works are sent away.

The Epistles tell the same story. Second Thessalonians 1:8–9 says that those who do not know God will "be punished with everlasting destruction from the presence of the Lord." Second Peter 2:9 says unforgiven sinners will have a "day of judgment to be punished." And Revelation 20:15 declares, "Whosoever was not found written in the book of life was cast into the lake of fire." This state will last throughout eternity (cf. Matt. 3:12; Mark 9:43; Jude 7, 12–13; Rev. 14:11).

Hell According to LDS Scriptures

This portrait of hell is not limited to the pages of the Bible. Consider some passages from the Book of Mormon:

- 2 Nephi 9:19: "O the greatness of the mercy of our God, the Holy One of Israel! For he delivereth his saints from that awful monster the devil, and death, and hell, and that lake of fire and brimstone, which is endless torment."

- 2 Nephi 9:26: "For the atonement satisfieth the demands of his justice upon all those who have not the law given to them, that they are delivered from that awful monster, death and hell, and the devil, and the lake of fire and brimstone, which is endless torment; and they are restored to that God who gave them breath, which is the Holy One of Israel."
- Jacob 6:10: "And according to the power of justice, for justice cannot be denied, ye must go away into that lake of fire and brimstone, whose flames are unquenchable, and whose smoke ascendeth up forever and ever, which lake of fire and brimstone is endless torment."

Alma 34:35 offers this stern warning to the "wicked" who put off repentance: "For behold, if ye have procrastinated the day of your repentance even until death, behold, ye have become subjected to the spirit of the devil, and he doth seal you his; therefore, the Spirit of the Lord hath withdrawn from you, and hath no place in you, and the devil hath all power over you; and this is the final state of the wicked."

What is this final state of the wicked? It seems very clear that this includes the Lord's Spirit being withdrawn from them so that the devil has all power over them and the ability to claim them as his own. Nowhere does this passage imply that this situation ever changes since it is considered "final." Referring to this passage, Marion G. Romney (1897–1988), a member of the First Presidency, said, "I have never found anything in the scriptures nor in the teachings of the prophets which encourages me to believe, that those who have the gospel taught to them here will be able to make up their loss if they choose to wait for the next life to obey it. I would not advise anyone to take that chance. As I understand the scriptures, taking such a hazard would be fatal."[10]

For those who deny the reality of hell, 2 Nephi 28:21–22 provides a warning: "And others will he pacify, and lull them away into carnal security, that they will say: All is well in Zion; yea, Zion prospereth, all is well—and thus the devil cheateth their souls, and leadeth them away carefully down to hell. And behold, others he flattereth away, and telleth them there is no hell; and he saith unto them: I am no devil, for there is none—and thus he whispereth in their ears, until he grasps them with his awful chains, from whence there is no deliverance."[11] Doctrine and Covenants 63:17 describes the "lake which burneth with fire and brimstone, which is the second death."

Outer Darkness

One LDS church manual reports that "the word hell is used to refer to outer darkness, which is the dwelling place of the devil, his angels, and the sons of perdition."[12] Doctrine and Covenants 133:73 says that this is a place of "weeping, and wailing, and gnashing of teeth." Joseph Fielding Smith wrote, "*Outer darkness* is something which cannot be described, except that we know that it is to be placed beyond the benign and comforting influence of the Spirit of God—banished entirely from his presence."[13] The punishment here is severe and, by all accounts, final and eternal in its length.

According to Mormon teaching, there are two classes of spirits who end up in outer darkness. The majority will be the one-third of the hosts of heaven who chose the side of Lucifer in the preexistence and fought against God in the war in heaven. That conflict arose when Lucifer objected to Jesus' appointment to be the Savior of the world. As punishment for their rebellion, they were denied physical bodies and became the demons, haunting the world with no hope of redemption. According to Doctrine and Covenants 29:38, they are destined for hell, which "is a place prepared for them from the beginning." The irony is that these hosts, who are literally spirit sons and daughters of the Mormon God, are doomed in eternity to outer darkness for what appears to be one sin in the preexistence. In an LDS context, this should not seem fair, since even the best of Mormons living today would have to admit that they have committed far more than one sin in their lifetimes.

Doctrine and Covenants 76:35–36 describes the sons of perdition as "having denied the Holy Spirit after having received it, and having denied the Only Begotten Son of the Father, having crucified him unto themselves and put him to an open shame. These are they who shall go away into the lake of fire and brimstone, with the devil and his angels." While it is not always clear in Mormon writings just who qualifies to be a "son of perdition," there seems to be some common characteristics. For one, the person had to have once been a member of the LDS Church. According to Joseph Smith, another trait is that such a person is stubborn because "he has got to say that the sun does not shine while he sees it; he has got to deny Jesus Christ when the heavens have been opened unto him, and to deny the plan of salvation with his eyes open to the truth of it."[14] Joseph Fielding Smith reiterated this concept when he said that a son of perdition "must first know and understand the truth with a clearness of vision wherein there is no doubt."[15]

In other words, a former member would still have to know the LDS Church was true but continue to fight against it. We have to wonder how many diabolical people there are in the world who (1) are former Mormons; (2) left the "one true church," even though they knew it was true; and (3) while believing it to be true, fight against it. The former members we know—whether atheist, Christian, or now an adherent of some other religion—all seem to be adamant in their denial of Mormonism. However, it is not uncommon for current LDS members to use the title "son of perdition" as an intimidation tactic to prevent struggling Latter-day Saints from leaving the faith.

It could be argued that the Bible's graphic descriptions of hell are mere metaphor. But then we must ask, "A metaphor for what?" If a metaphor is a figure of speech that uses a comparison between two things that have something in common, how is this supposed to put a person at ease? Such language hardly describes what many Mormons understand to be a "heavenly" existence.

Questions for Discussion

- Is the doctrine of hell an important issue? Explain your reasoning.

- Why do you think there is so much controversy over this doctrine, even within the Christian church?

- Do you agree with the assessment that if there is an outer darkness that will be inhabited mainly by spirit sons and daughters of God, this would be more unfair than the perceived unfairness of the biblical doctrine of hell? Why or why not?

Evangelism Tip

Just because we don't like something doesn't mean it's not true. After all, we might not like what would happen if we were to fall from a twenty-story building with no parachute, but regardless of our preferences, the result wouldn't be a pretty sight. In the same way, eternal punishment is not a pleasant topic, yet the Bible declares its reality. The gospel is good news, but it includes bad news for those who reject it. We have been commissioned to tell the truth to others about the consequences of dying in their sins, even when doing so may jeopardize a relationship.

Salvation

Chapter 19

Doesn't the book of James say that "faith without works is dead"?

Response Questions

- Do you think Christians like me don't believe in doing good works?
- How many good works are required to qualify for the best your religion has to offer?

• • • • • • • • • • • • • • • •

"Some Christians make the mistake of taking some of Paul's writing out of context, including the context of the whole Bible, and teaching that we are saved by grace, and not by works at all."[1]
—David Ridges, Church Educational System

—————————— Summary ——————————

Mormons are told by their church's leaders to do everything they can—including getting baptized, repenting, attending the temple, and enduring to the end—to qualify for the celestial kingdom. James 2:20 and 26 are often used as biblical support. Mormons need to know how contradictory the concept of earning one's right standing before God really is. Understanding the difference between justification and sanctification is crucial to grasping how Christians are saved by grace through faith, with works of sanctification following a true conversion to Christ.

MORMON LEADERS THROUGHOUT the years have stressed the importance of good works in order to become exalted and attain the celestial kingdom. Consider just a few quotes from General Authorities to support this idea:

- President Wilford Woodruff (1807–1898): "If I ever obtain a full salvation it will be by my keeping the laws of God."[2]
- President Joseph F. Smith (1838–1918): "Every man and woman will receive all that they are worthy of, and something thrown in perhaps on the score of the boundless charity of God. But who can justly expect to obtain more than they merit?"[3]
- President Heber J. Grant (1856–1945): "We ourselves are able to perform every duty and obligation that God has required of men. No commandment was ever given to us but that God has given us the power to keep the commandments. If we fail, we, and we alone, are responsible for the failure, because God endows His servants, from the Presidents of the Church down to the humblest member, with all the ability, all the knowledge, all the power that is necessary, faithfully, diligently, and properly to discharge every duty and every obligation that rests upon them, and we, and we alone, will have to answer if we fail in this regard."[4]
- Member of the First Presidency Henry D. Moyle (1889–1963): "Our Church is founded upon the premise that spiritual growth and exaltation must be earned by the efforts of the individual."[5]
- President Joseph Fielding Smith (1876–1972): "Very gladly would the Lord give to everyone eternal life, but since that blessing can come only on merit—through the faithful performance of duty—only those who are worthy shall receive it."[6]
- Apostle Bruce R. McConkie (1915–1985): "All must repent to be free. All must obey to gain gospel blessings. All must keep the commandments to merit mercy."[7]
- Apostle L. Tom Perry: "I bear witness of the power and comfort the gift of the Holy Ghost is to those who live worthy of it. What a reassurance it is for us to know that we are not left alone to find the course that we must follow to merit the eternal blessings of our Father in Heaven."[8]
- Apostle Neal A. Maxwell: "Thus, brothers and sisters, along with the great and free gift of the universal and personal resurrection there is also the personal possibility of meriting eternal life."[9]
- Member of the First Presidency James E. Faust: "Mercy will not rob

justice, and the sealing power of faithful parents will only claim wayward children upon the condition of their repentance and Christ's
Atonement. Repentant wayward children will enjoy salvation and all
the blessings that go with it, but exaltation is much more. It must be
fully earned. The question as to who will be exalted must be left to the
Lord in His mercy."[10]

Notice terms such as *earned* and *merit* used in the above quotes. This concept is taught in a church manual used by Mormon missionaries.

> Eternal life is a gift of God given only to those who obey His gospel.
> It is the highest state that we can achieve. . . . It is exaltation, which
> means living with God forever in eternal families. . . . However,
> Jesus did not eliminate our personal responsibility. He forgives
> our sins when we accept Him, repent, and obey His command-
> ments. . . . We must show that we accept Christ and that we have
> faith in Him by keeping His commandments and obeying the first
> principles and ordinances of the gospel. . . . We can return to live
> with God the Father only through Christ's mercy, and we receive
> Christ's mercy only on condition of repentance. . . . As we patiently,
> faithfully, and consistently follow this path throughout our lives, we
> will qualify for eternal life.[11]

In Mormonism, salvation is defined in two unique ways. Joseph Fielding
Smith explained, "Salvation is twofold: *General*—that which comes to all
men irrespective of a belief (in this life) in Christ—and, *Individual*—that
which man merits through his own acts through life and by obedience to
the laws and ordinances of the gospel."[12] General salvation, or resurrection
from the dead, is also called salvation by grace and is provided to all people.
It is synonymous with immortality, since the resurrected person lives forever.
The problem with this definition is that Jesus taught in John 5:29 that there
are two resurrections, one to life and one to damnation. It seems odd that a
resurrection to damnation is somehow made synonymous with a salvation
of any kind. In fact, even in Mormonism it has been taught that "all those
who do not gain eternal life, or exaltation in the highest heaven within the
celestial kingdom, are partakers of eternal damnation."[13]

Bruce R. McConkie stated that the "mere fact of resurrection" does not
give "a hope of eternal life, or any of the great spiritual blessings which flow

from gospel obedience. These blessings are not free gifts. Except for the free gift of immortality (which comes by grace alone and includes bodily or physical perfection), all rewards gained in the eternal worlds must be earned. That perfection sought by the saints is both temporal and spiritual and comes only as a result of full obedience."[14] Brigham Young University professor Clyde J. Williams also stressed the importance of obedience when he wrote, "The perfect relationship between the atoning grace of Christ and the obedient efforts of mankind is powerfully stated by Nephi: 'We know that it is by grace that we are saved, after all we can do' (2 Nephi 25:23). Furthermore, we are invited to 'come unto Christ, and be perfected in him.' When we deny ourselves 'of all ungodliness,' then and only 'then is his grace sufficient' for us (Moroni 10:32)."[15]

Naturally, the goal of a faithful Latter-day Saint is to achieve eternal life in the celestial kingdom. President Thomas S. Monson stated that it is "the celestial glory which we seek. It is in the presence of God we desire to dwell. It is a forever family in which we want membership. Such blessings must be earned."[16] In what appears to be a confusing maneuver of semantics, Brigham Young University professors Joseph Fielding McConkie (the son of Bruce R. McConkie) and Robert L. Millet claim that "people do not *earn* eternal life—there is no scriptural reference whatsoever to anyone earning the right to go where Gods and angels are. Rather, according to the words of the prophets—it is so attested in the scriptures almost a hundred times— people *inherit* eternal life." Proceeding to describe this "inheritance" by using a language of works, they write, "After we have done all that we can do, after we have denied ourselves of ungodliness and worldly lusts, then is the grace of God sufficient for us; then we are sanctified in Christ and eventually made perfect in Christ (see 2 Nephi 25:23; Moroni 10:32)."[17]

To do "all that we can do" and to deny "ourselves of ungodliness and worldly lusts" (see Matt. 16:26 JST) certainly sets an incredibly high bar for a Latter-day Saint to reach. In a later work, Millet attempted to tone down the perfectionist language found in his earlier commentary:

> This does not mean that we must do everything we can do *before* Christ can assist us. This is not about chronology. Further, who do you know who has or will ever do *all* they can do? Grace is not just that final boost into heaven that God provides at the end of a well-lived life, although we obviously will need all the help we can get. Rather, the Almighty assists us all along the way, every

second of every minute of every hour of every day, all through our lives. It does not mean that we will carry the bulk of the load to salvation and Jesus will fill in the gaps; he is not the God of the gaps. Our contribution to glory hereafter, when compared to his, is infinitesimal and miniscule. If I might be permitted a paraphrase of what the passage stated, "We are saved by grace, *above and beyond* all we can do, *notwithstanding* all we can do, *in spite of* all we can do."[18]

Millet's explanation of the Book of Mormon passage misses the mark. The context is not about when Christ offers His assistance or what percentage of the load is the responsibility of the individual, even if that contribution is "miniscule" compared to what Christ does. It is about what is required of Latter-day Saints should they hope to attain sufficient grace in order to achieve exaltation. In Mormonism, "the application of grace to personal sins is conditional because it is available only when an individual repents, which can be a demanding form of works. . . . God bestows these additional, perfecting expressions of grace conditionally, as he does the grace that allows forgiveness of sin. They are given 'after all we can do' (2 Ne. 25:23)—that is, in addition to our best efforts."[19]

Church leaders and correlated manuals have not supported the "*in spite of* all we can do" interpretation. The following examples would hardly make an exhaustive list:

- "The Lord will bless us to the degree to which we keep His commandments. Nephi put this principle in a tremendous orbit when he said: 'For we labor diligently to write, to persuade our children, and also our brethren, to believe in Christ, and to be reconciled to God; for we know that it is by grace that we are saved, after all we can do' (2 Nephi 25:23). The Savior's blood, His atonement, will save us, but only after we have done all we can to save ourselves by keeping His commandments."[20]
- "Because of what He accomplished by His atoning sacrifice, Jesus Christ has the power to prescribe the conditions we must fulfill to qualify for the blessings of His Atonement. That is why we have commandments and ordinances. That is why we make covenants. That is how we qualify for the promised blessings. They all come through the mercy and grace of the Holy One of Israel, 'after all we can do' (2 Nephi 25:23)."[21]

- "This grace is an enabling power that allows men and women to lay hold on eternal life and exaltation after they have expended their own best efforts. Divine grace is needed by every soul in consequence of the fall of Adam and also because of man's weaknesses and shortcomings. However, grace cannot suffice without total effort on the part of the recipient. Hence the explanation, 'It is by grace that we are saved, after all we can do' (2 Nephi 25:23)."[22]
- "Our sins make us unclean and unfit to dwell in God's presence, and we need His grace to purify and perfect us 'after all we can do' (2 Nephi 25:23). The phrase 'after all we can do' teaches that effort is required on our part to receive the fullness of the Lord's grace and be made worthy to dwell with him."[23]
- "We are saved by the power of the Atonement of Jesus Christ. We must, however, come unto Christ on His terms in order to obtain all the blessings that He freely offers us. We come unto Christ by doing 'all we can do' to remember Him, keep our covenants with Him, and obey His commandments (see D&C 20:77, 79; see also Abraham 3:25)."[24]

Salvation According to the Bible

When the subject of God's grace comes up in a conversation, it is not uncommon for a Mormon to reference James 2:20 and 26, both of which say that "faith without works is dead." Their implication is that Christians do not value good works in their theology. However, the immediate context names Abraham and Rahab as examples of how good works follow true faith in a believer's life. James is criticizing those who profess to have faith but whose actions do not support this claim. A living faith is not devoid of good works; instead, a living faith will produce good works. Pointing out the play on words in verse 20 (it literally means, "Faith without works does no work"), Christian theologian James White writes, "Deedless faith, being an anomaly by nature, is unproductive. It cannot, and will not, produce the fruit of *true* faith, that being salvation. . . . Faith that exists only in the realm of words (deedless faith) is useless."[25] Protestant theologians have long recognized the difference between what justifies sinful man before God and what sanctifies, or sets him apart for service unto God. The distinction between justification and sanctification is extremely important. According to Christian theologian J. I. Packer, justification "is thus a forensic term, denoting a judicial act of administering the law—in this case, by declaring a verdict of acquittal, and so excluding all possibility of condemnation. Justification thus settles the legal status of the person justified."[26]

Romans 6:23 says all people deserve death because the very best of sin-tainted works, in themselves, are, as Isaiah 64:6 says, like "filthy rags" in God's sight. Thus, the gift God bestows on His people is given by grace and received by faith. In Acts 13:39 Paul says, "And by him all that believe are justified from all things, from which ye could not be justified by the law of Moses." And in Romans 3:28 and 5:1, Paul adds, "Therefore we conclude that a man is justified by faith without the deeds of the law. . . . Therefore being justified by faith, we have peace with God through our Lord Jesus Christ." Legally, Christians are exonerated by God because Christ's atoning work has made them righteous in His sight.

Sanctification, on the other hand, is synonymous with holiness. Good works are the result of faith and a life lived out of love for God. Jesus said, "If ye love me, keep my commandments" (John 14:15). First John 3:23 explains what these commandments are: "That we should believe on the name of his Son Jesus Christ, and love one another." Performing good works outside of a relationship with the true God of the Bible does not result in salvation. As Jesus said in Matthew 7:21, "Not every one that saith unto me, Lord, Lord, shall enter into the kingdom of heaven; but he that doeth the will of my Father which is in heaven." The will of the Father, Jesus said in John 6:40, is to believe in Him. All who do, He declared, will "have everlasting life: and I will raise him up at the last day."

The claim that Christians believe they have the freedom to sin with passion after initially coming to faith in Christ is a straw man. Contrasting the "works of the flesh" with the "fruit of the spirit" in Galatians 5:19–23, Paul explained that good fruit should be evident in every believer's life. After all, believers are those who have "crucified the flesh with the affections and lusts" (v. 24). To believe that one could freely sin makes no sense. As Paul wrote in Romans 6:15, "What then? Shall we sin, because we are not under the law, but under grace? God forbid." Yet living a consistent Christian life will be a struggle because, as Romans 7:15 puts it, "what I hate, that do I." In verse 18 Paul wrote, "For I know that nothing good dwells in me, that is, in my flesh. For I have the desire to do what is right, but not the ability to carry it out" (ESV).

Ephesians 2:8–9 very succinctly packages the relationship between faith and salvation. It says, "For by grace are ye saved through faith; and that not of yourselves: it is the gift of God: Not of works, lest any man should boast." When this passage is considered in light of the "twofold" definition of salvation offered by Mormon leaders, it is clear there is no logical way the Mormon understanding can fit the passage. For instance, suppose Paul was talking about "general" salvation (resurrection of the dead). Substituting the word *resurrected* for the word *saved* would result in this rendering: "For by grace are ye resurrected through faith." But Mormonism says faith is not a requirement for general salvation, or resurrection. It is provided to all who have ever lived, regardless of their faith or actions. This, then, could not fit an LDS interpretation. Was Paul, then, referring to "individual" salvation, or exaltation? When the word *saved* is replaced with *exalted*, it says, "For by grace are ye exalted through faith; and that not of yourselves; it is the gift of God: not of works lest any man should boast." As the leaders and church manuals quoted above demonstrate, however, Mormonism teaches that many works are required for exaltation, which is inconsistent with Ephesians 2:8–9.

The following verse, Ephesians 2:10, needs to be considered as well. It says, "For we are his workmanship, created in Christ Jesus unto good works, which God hath before ordained that we should walk in them." It would be illogical to say that Paul was contradicting himself right after he said salvation is "not of works." He is certainly not advocating a sin-however-you-want mentality. Instead, he explains that Christians were created to do good works. Paul taught in 2 Corinthians 5:17 that a converted believer becomes "a new creature: old things are passed away; behold, all things are become new." In essence, the Christian possesses a different spiritual DNA.

Also crucial to properly understanding what James was talking about is grasping the context in which he was writing. Talking about passages that seem contradictory, New Testament scholar Mark Strauss explains,

> Paul says that a person is saved by faith alone, apart from works (Rom. 3:28). James insists that "faith without deeds is dead" (James 2:26), so that faith plus works saves you. These differences can be resolved when we recognize that Paul and James are addressing two different situations. Paul writes against legalists who are claiming that a person can earn salvation by doing good works, or who perhaps are claiming that salvation has come through the "works of the law"—the hallmarks of Judaism such as circumcision, dietary laws, and Sabbath observance. James, on the other

hand, is writing against those who are abusing the doctrine of free grace by claiming that once you are saved by faith, you can live any way you want. James rejects such libertarianism and insists that authentic faith will always result in actions, so that the two work hand in hand.[27]

A Christian who catches a glimpse of what Jesus Christ did on his or her behalf will quite naturally have a desire to serve God. Consider what your attitude would be if a kind couple gave you a gift of $10 million, an outrageous amount that most people will never earn in a lifetime. Would you naturally respond by wanting to spray-paint graffiti on your benefactors' house, throw lye in their grass, and kick their beloved family dog? Or, since you were given a gift that could never be repaid, would you be ever grateful? If you found out they needed someone to mow their grass and feed the dog while they were away on vacation, wouldn't you be the first to volunteer? The answers are obvious.

Jesus said, "Ye are my friends, if ye do whatsoever I command you" (John 15:14). He is a Friend who sticks closer than a brother and offers a life that benefits His people both temporally and spiritually. We value His friendship and willfully follow His directives, knowing they are for our good and not meant for harm. When it is understood that God justified His people freely through no act of their own and gave them a gift that can never be repaid, then the role of good works in the Christian's life becomes clear.

Questions for Discussion

- Why is it necessary to understand the difference between the Mormon concepts of general salvation (resurrection) and individual salvation (exaltation) if we hope to have an intelligent conversation with a Latter-day Saint?

- Suppose a Mormon tells you that justification really does come by grace through faith yet works are required too. How could you use Ephesians 2:8–10 to explain how Mormonism's definition of salvation differs from that taught in biblical Christianity?

- Any implication that works somehow "merit mercy" is akin to fingernails on a chalkboard. Do you agree or disagree with this assessment? Why?

—————————————— Evangelism Tip ——————————————

Mormons often have a wrong understanding about how Christians view the role of works in salvation, thinking that Christians believe they have freedom to live a life of debauchery once they have made a commitment to follow Christ. This is far from the truth! We have found that using illustrations (such as a person who receives a gift that can never be repaid) can help the Mormon better understand how righteousness is a vital part of sanctification. Emphasize how good works are a natural follow-through in a true conversion but do not justify us before an all-holy God.

Isn't it arrogant to think that you already have forgiveness of sins?

Response Questions

- If you were to die right now, do you have the assurance that all of your sins are forgiven?
- According to your faith, what must you do in order to have assurance that you will become exalted?
- From your perspective, are you doing all these things?

• • • • • • • • • • • • • • • •

"When we keep our covenants to take [Jesus'] name upon us, to remember Him always, and to keep all His commandments, we will receive the companionship of His Spirit. . . . The Holy Ghost remains with us only if we stay clean and free from the love of the things of the world. A choice to be unclean will repel the Holy Ghost. The Spirit only dwells with those who choose the Lord over the world."[1]

—Henry Eyring, member of the First Presidency

————————————— Summary —————————————

According to Mormonism, no one can ever be assured that God has forgiven all of his or her sins, for repentance brings forgiveness but repentance means never returning to the same sin again. Yet the Bible says we can "know" that we have eternal life. Once we are justified before God through faith, we understand that good works come as a response to God's free gift provided to us. Thus, it isn't arrogant to believe we have forgiveness of all our sins based on the work of Jesus Christ—it's just biblical.

WHEN SPEAKING TO AN LDS man on a street in central Utah, I (Bill) was addressing his lack of assurance when it came to forgiveness. When I explained that I knew I was forgiven of my sins, this gentleman shouted out in a mocking voice to those listening to our conversation, "This is the most arrogant man I have ever met." His response was very telling, since it showed that he believed human performance must be a part of the forgiveness equation. From his vantage point, my assurance was understood to be a sense of moral superiority. I assured him that this was not the case.

The mark of a true Christian revolves around this issue. Matthew 1:20–21 recounts how "the angel of the Lord" appeared to Joseph, Mary's espoused husband, and announced that the Child she was carrying, Jesus, would "save his people from their sins." The Bible states that all people have sinned and come short of God's glory, resulting in death (Rom. 3:23; 6:23). Left to ourselves, we are a hopeless people. But when Jesus came to this earth as the ultimate sacrifice for sin and rose from the dead on the third day, He provided a gift that could never be bought or repaid. As Christian theologian James White points out, "One who has been justified stands before God uncondemned *and uncondemnable*—not because of what he is in himself, but because of what Christ is in him."[2] This issue is of utmost importance, and, as we have discovered over the years, it effectively gets to the heart of the matter of salvation. If people do not know for sure that their sins are forgiven, how can it be known with confidence that they are God's "people"? Without this assurance, their claim to the title of "Christian" is merely presumptuous.

When dealing with the topic of forgiveness, start a conversation by asking your Mormon friend, "If you were to die right now, do you have the assurance that all of your sins are forgiven?" The following method using LDS scripture can help show the requirements necessary to qualify for salvation.

The Six-Verse Method

By using six verses from two of the standard works and asking a few questions, it's possible to show a Latter-day Saint how futile Mormonism's plan of salvation really is. Bear in mind that these questions are asked within a context that a Mormon will understand.

- 1 Nephi 3:7: ". . . for I know that the Lord giveth no commandments unto the children of men, save he shall prepare a way for them that they may accomplish the thing which he commandeth them."

Ask: Does this passage say that it's possible to keep all of God's commandments? How are you doing at this?

- Alma 11:37: "And I say unto you again that he [God] cannot save them [his people] in their sins; for I cannot deny his word, and he hath said that no unclean thing can inherit the kingdom of heaven; therefore, how can ye be saved, except ye inherit the kingdom of heaven? Therefore, ye cannot be saved in your sins."

  Ask: Do you struggle with sin? If so, doesn't this tend to prove that you, as a Mormon, are still "in your sins" and are "unclean"? If you are, doesn't this mean you are not saved?

- Moroni 10:32: "Yea, come unto Christ, and be perfected in him, and deny yourselves of all ungodliness; and if ye shall deny yourselves of all ungodliness, and love God with all your might, mind and strength, then is his grace sufficient for you."[3]

  Ask: Have you denied yourself of *all* ungodliness? If not, doesn't this verse tend to prove that you have yet to receive the grace that is sufficient to cleanse you of your sins? If you have not denied yourself of *all* ungodliness, when do you think you will eventually do so?

- D&C 25:15: "Keep my commandments continually, and a crown of righteousness thou shalt receive. And except thou do this, where I am you cannot come."[4]

  Ask: How many commandments must you keep continually? Some? Most? All?[5] If all, how are you doing at this?

- D&C 58:43: "By this ye may know if a man repenteth of his sins—behold, he will confess them and forsake them."

  Ask: As you understand it, doesn't forgiveness follow repentance? How many sins must you forsake?[6] Have you forsaken all of your sins? If not, doesn't that mean you have not truly repented?

- D&C 1:31: "For I the Lord cannot look upon in with the least degree of allowance."

  Ask: In light of the answers you've given to the above questions, do you think God will overlook the sins you struggle with and have yet to overcome?

Perfection: Now or Later?

When Latter-day Saints are presented with the above references, it is common for them to ask, "Are you saying we must be perfect?" Notice, however, that we never used that word. Why would a Mormon draw that conclusion?

Because when taken to its logical conclusion, perfection is most certainly implied, and their question proves this!

Mormon authors have tried hard to calm the fears of members who are overwhelmed by the implication that perfection is required. One example is a book written for Mormon youth by LDS apologist Anthony Sweat, titled *I'm Not Perfect. Can I Still Go to Heaven?* Citing a 2009 survey that polled 701 Mormon teens ranging from fourteen to eighteen years of age, the study showed that 53 percent believed they would go to the celestial kingdom if they died right then. But an astounding 40 percent believed they would end in the terrestrial kingdom, with the other 7 percent saying they were headed for the telestial kingdom, or outer darkness.

Sweat writes, "These numbers are disheartening to me because the youth who took these surveys appear to be actively engaged in the gospel: regularly attending church and Mutual, serving in Church callings, and enrolling in programs such as seminary and Especially for Youth. These teenagers are the kind of kids who consistently read their scriptures, pray, and try their best to keep the commandments and do what is right. Yet half don't think they are celestial material."[7] Sweat said that the most common answer he received from those thinking they wouldn't reach the celestial kingdom was, "I have sins and I'm not perfect." His book was written in an attempt to give the youth assurance that there is "the hope we can all have for the celestial kingdom because of the Atonement of Jesus Christ."[8]

The same lack of assurance is prevalent among Mormon college students as well. In a campus devotional, Brigham Young University president Cecil O. Samuelson told the student body that striving for perfectionism was "corrosive and destructive, and is the antithesis of the healthy quest for eventual perfection that the savior prescribes." In his talk, "Samuelson said a person can be deemed morally worthy while being imperfect."[9] Samuelson addressed Jesus' words recorded in Matthew 5:48, where He says in part, "Be ye therefore perfect." He correctly noted that the Koine Greek for the word *perfection* means "whole" or "complete," not "flawless."[10] If that is the way this passage has always been interpreted within LDS circles, one wonders why this topic needed to be addressed in the first place. The fact is, many Mormon leaders have used Jesus' words in Matthew 5 to impress upon members the need to overcome sin in order to earn their exaltation. No wonder the high school students felt unworthy for the celestial kingdom and the college students were struggling with perfectionism.

President Spencer W. Kimball (1895–1985) told of a man who wanted to make sure he had made final spiritual preparations before undergoing "radical surgery." Kimball wrote, "In the context of the spirit of forgiveness, one good brother asked me, 'Yes, that is what ought to be done, but how do you do it? Doesn't that take a superman?' 'Yes,' I said, 'but we are commanded to be supermen. Said the Lord, 'Be ye therefore perfect, even as your Father which is in heaven is perfect.' (Matt. 5:48.) We are gods in embryo, and the Lord demands perfection of us.'"[11]

Speaking in general conference, President Thomas S. Monson stated, "God our Father, and Jesus Christ, our Lord, have marked the way to perfection. They beckon us to follow eternal verities and to become perfect, as they are perfect (see Matthew 5:48; 3 Nephi 12:48)."[12] Latter-day Saints have been given conflicting counsel as to when they are supposed to reach this goal. President Heber J. Grant (1856–1945) gave the impression that this perfection finally could be reached sometime in the future eternities. Referring to the LDS doctrine of eternal progression, he encouraged members to build "upon the achievements of our first spirit-life, our first estate, and of our mortal life, or second estate, progressing through the endless eternities that follow, until we reach the goal the Lord set: 'Be ye perfect, even as your Father which is in heaven is perfect.' [Matthew 5:48.]."[13] Another church manual states, "Remind class members that while perfection cannot be entirely achieved in this life, we can make great progress toward it. The Lord expects us to do all we can toward giving up our sins and becoming perfect, and he has given us the gospel to help us do this."[14]

Some, like Kimball, have insisted that the "second estate," or this mortality, is the time to accomplish this perfection. "This Life Is the Time," Kimball titled chapter 1 in *The Miracle of Forgiveness*. In a section titled "Dangers of Delay," he warned church members: "Because men are prone to postpone action and ignore directions, the Lord has repeatedly given strict injunctions and issued solemn warnings. . . . And the burden of the prophetic warning has been that *the time to act is now, in this mortal life.* One cannot with impunity delay his compliance with God's commandments."[15]

Kimball warned, "This earth life is the time to repent. We cannot afford to take any chances of dying an enemy to God."[16] He criticized his people for their procrastination: "There are . . . many members of the Church who are lax and careless and who continually procrastinate. They live the gospel casually but not devoutly. They have complied with some requirements but are not valiant. They do no major crime but merely fail to do the things required—things like paying tithing, living the Word of Wisdom, having family prayers, fasting, attending meetings, service. . . . The Lord will not translate one's good hopes and desires and intentions into works. Each of us must do that for himself."[17]

There are many requirements that need to be fulfilled. When it comes to tithing, for example, the Mormon Church has emphasized its necessity in relation to repentance and forgiveness. President Kimball gave a First Presidency message in October 1982 where he said, "If one neglects his tithing, misses his meetings, breaks the Sabbath, or fails in his prayers and other responsibilities, he is not completely repentant. The Lord knows, as do we, the degree of full and sufficient compliance we make with these fundamental aspects of the law of repentance, which is really God's law of progress and fulfillment."[18] Referring to Kimball's final point in his "five essential elements of repentance" given in *The Miracle of Forgiveness*, Apostle Richard G. Scott told a general conference audience, "Full obedience brings the complete power of the gospel into your life with strength to focus on the abandonment of specific sins. It includes things you might not initially consider part of repentance, such as attending meetings, paying tithing, giving service, and forgiving others. The Lord said: "He that repents and *does the commands of the Lord shall be forgiven*."[19] Since tithing appears to be one of the essential ingredients for forgiveness, one must wonder what the Mormon should do with the following words from Mormon 8:32: "Yea, it shall come in a day when there shall be churches built up that shall say: Come unto me, and for your money you shall be forgiven of your sins."

Another Book of Mormon passage, 1 Nephi 3:7, affirms that God gives no commandments to the "children of men, save he shall prepare a way for them that they may accomplish the thing which he commandeth them." If this is true, then we must assume that those Mormons who fail to repent of all of their sins are guilty of squandering their mortal opportunity and indeed have procrastinated their repentance. This is a perilous situation since, as Kimball stated, "Incomplete repentance never brought complete forgiveness."[20]

In an article written to Mormon youth, Jay E. Jensen, a member of the Presidency of the Seventy, said, "Another prerequisite or condition to repentance is to know that no unclean thing can dwell with God (see 1 Ne. 10:21; 1 Ne. 15:34; Alma 7:21; Alma 40:26; and Hel. 8:25). You can hide sins from your bishop, you can hide them from your parents and friends, but if you continue and die with unresolved sins, you are unclean and no unclean thing can dwell with God. There are no exceptions."[21]

The Christian's Perfection

Referring to Matthew 5:48, Christian theologians Norman Geisler and Ron Rhodes write,

> This verse does not mean human beings can actually become perfect in this life. . . . The context of this verse is that the Jewish leaders had taught that we should love those near and dear to us (Lev. 19:18), but hate our enemies. Jesus, however, said we should love even our enemies. After all, Jesus said, God's love extends to all people (Matt. 5:45). And since God is our righteous standard, we should seek to be as he is in this regard. We are to be "perfect" (or "complete") in loving others as he is perfect. Furthermore, the Bible certainly does not give support to the idea that we can actually attain sinless perfection in this life, for all of us are fallen and sin continually (1 John 1:8). The good news is that by trusting in Jesus, his perfection becomes ours: "For by one offering He has perfected for all time those who are sanctified" (Heb. 10:14 NASB).[22]

In some ways there is a parallel between Mormons who think they only need more time to make things right and the servant in Jesus' story in Matthew 18:23–27. In this passage Jesus tells of a servant who owed the king an insurmountable debt of ten thousand talents. The servant pleaded with the king to have patience with him. Somehow, he thought having more time would solve his problem. Thankfully for him, the king had compassion and canceled the debt. In Luke 7:36–50, Jesus forgave a woman of her sins for no other reason than that she was worshipping Him. She was not required to go through a repentance process.

Understandably, some Mormons feel a great amount of anxiety in not knowing whether they have done enough to secure their forgiveness. This could be because they have blurred the lines between what justifies a person (or makes them right) with God and what sanctifies (or sets them apart) unto God.[23] This dilemma was explained in a sermon by Anglican bishop J. C. Ryle (1816–1900):

> I am persuaded that one great cause of the darkness and uncomfortable feelings of many well-meaning people in the matter of religion is their habit of confounding, and not distinguishing, justification and sanctification. It can never be too strongly impressed on our

minds that they are two separate things. No doubt they cannot be divided, and everyone that is a partaker of either is a partaker of both. But never, never ought they to be confounded, and never ought the distinction between them to be forgotten.[24]

Christians are justified, or made right with God, because of what Jesus did on the cross (cf. Rom. 9:16; Eph. 2:8–10; Titus 3:4–7). Princeton theologian Benjamin B. Warfield (1851–1921) succinctly summed up this incredible act when he said, "Justification by Faith, we see, is not to be set in contradiction to justification by Works. It is set in contradiction only to justification by our Own Works. It is justification by Christ's Works."[25] Christians can be confident of their forgiveness because it has nothing to do with their personal merit or performance.

Questions for Discussion

- Compare a person who believes he is forgiven and a person who is trying but isn't sure he is forgiven. How would their outlook on life differ? How would their attitudes toward works differ?

- Some Mormons might think it's arrogant for Christians to say they are a forgiven people. Why do you think Mormons look upon this as a prideful attitude? What are some possible responses to this complaint?

- How could 1 John 5:13 ("that ye may know that ye have eternal life") be used to show how the assurance of salvation for a true believer is something that can be known?

Evangelism Tip

The heart of the gospel can be found in these foundational truths: (1) Everyone is a sinner; (2) Jesus came to "save His people from their sins"; (3) forgiveness of sins is a free gift of God; and (4) Christians can know that they have eternal life. Asking Mormons about their ability to keep the requirements, as set forth by LDS scriptures and the General Authorities, is a gentle way of getting them to see the need to trust totally in God's mercy and grace. Thankfully, justification before an all-holy God is not based on our efforts.

Why don't you believe baptism is necessary for salvation when Acts 2:38 teaches this?

Response Questions

- Why do you believe baptism is necessary for salvation?
- If water baptism is required, what else must a person do to be saved?

• • • • • • • • • • • • • • • •

"We are, therefore, required to be baptized if we desire admittance into God's kingdom."[1]

—Seventy Spencer J. Condie

Summary

While Christians believe that baptism is a very important practice, they hold that it is by faith alone that a person is justified. At the same time, while this ordinance is not a requirement for salvation, the New Testament does give the impression that an unbaptized Christian is not to be the norm since the rite is a means of identifying with the death and resurrection of Christ. Every Christian ought to be water baptized as long as it's understood that this is not a work the person is doing to somehow qualify for justification in God's sight.

In Mormonism, water baptism is a requirement for both forgiveness and membership in the church. A church manual explains that "baptism is the gateway through which we enter the path to the celestial kingdom."[2] A missionary manual says, "Jesus taught that we must be baptized by immersion for the remission, or forgiveness, of our sins. Baptism is an essential ordinance of salvation. No person can enter the kingdom of God without being baptized. . . . We must be baptized to become members of the restored Church, The Church of Jesus Christ of Latter-day Saints, and to eventually enter the kingdom of heaven. This ordinance is a law of God and must be performed by His authority." In a note on this page in the manual, the missionary is reminded that "investigators should live the principles of moral worthiness, the Word of Wisdom, and commit to pay tithing" if they want to be water baptized.[3]

Generally, the Book of Mormon and Doctrine and Covenants teach that baptism is a necessary ordinance to achieving salvation.[4] This isn't surprising given that the teachings of Alexander Campbell (1788–1866) were popular during Joseph Smith's day. Campbell taught that baptism by the proper authority for the remission of sins was necessary for a person to be saved; baptism in other churches was considered insufficient, so a person had to be rebaptized in the right church to qualify for true salvation.[5]

The Meaning of Baptism

A common passage used to support the view of baptismal regeneration (the necessity to be baptized in order to be saved) is Acts 2:38. It reads, "Then Peter said unto them, Repent, and be baptized every one of you in the name of Jesus Christ for the remission of sins, and ye shall receive the gift of the Holy Ghost." The disagreement between Christian and LDS theology stems from the use of the word *for* in this verse. Those who accept baptismal regeneration argue that this means baptism grants remission of sins. However, the Bible emphasizes that it is the blood of Christ that cleanses a person from sin, not the water of baptism. For example, Colossians 1:14 says, "In whom we have redemption through his blood, even the forgiveness of sins." First John 1:7 adds, "But if we walk in the light, as he is in the light, we have fellowship one with another, and the blood of Jesus Christ his Son cleanseth us from all sin."

Because the meaning of a word is tied to its context, it can readily be seen how the Greek word translated "for" (*eis*) in Acts 2:38 cannot mean "in order to obtain" but rather "in view of" or "because of." The usage indicates "the ground or reason for the action. It answers the question, Why?"[6] Consider a similar usage found in Matthew 12:41: "The men of Nineveh shall rise in judgment with this generation, and shall condemn it: because they repented at [*eis*] the preaching of Jonas [Jonah]." Are we to assume that the people in Nineveh repented in order to *obtain* the preaching of Jonah? Or was their repentance in view of, or because of, Jonah's preaching? The latter interpretation makes more sense.

Explaining Acts 2:38, Christian commentator Richard N. Longenecker writes, "In trying to deal with the various elements in this passage, some interpreters have stressed the command to be baptized so as to link the forgiveness of sins exclusively with baptism. But it runs contrary to all biblical religion to assume that outward rites have any value apart from true repentance and an inward change."[7] Following his sermon in Acts 2, Peter stated in Acts 3:19, "Repent ye therefore, and be converted, that your sins may be blotted out, when the times of refreshing shall come from the presence of the Lord." No mention of baptism is made here. Longenecker noted, "This shows that for Luke at least, and probably also for Peter, while baptism with water was the expected symbol for conversion, it was not an indispensable criterion for salvation."[8]

Christian theologian G. R. Beasley-Murray explained, "At the close of his address on the same day, Peter calls for his hearers to repent and be baptized, with a view to receiving forgiveness and the Spirit."[9] The act of baptism is not something that saves a person but is an action that comes out of belief. Beasley-Murray wrote, "Baptism is an overt, public act that expresses inward decision and intent; since it is performed in the open, and not in secret, it becomes by its nature a confession of a faith and allegiance embraced."[10]

Another biblical passage that should be considered is Acts 16:30–31, where the Philippian jailor asked Paul and Silas what he had to do in order to be saved. They told the jailor simply, "Believe on the Lord Jesus Christ, and thou shalt be saved, and thy house" (v. 31). Paul and Silas eventually explained the "word of the Lord" to the jailor and "all that were in his house." As a result of their saving faith, they were baptized (vv. 32–33).

Consider Acts 10:44–48 as well. Here, Peter delivered the gospel of truth to the Gentiles, and before anyone from his audience was baptized in water, the "Holy Spirit fell on all who heard the word" (v. 44 ESV). Believing Jews who witnessed this event "were amazed, because the gift of the Holy

Spirit was poured out even on the Gentiles" (v. 45 ESV). As a result, Peter asked the crowd, "Can anyone withhold water for baptizing these people, who have received the Holy Spirit just as we have?" (v. 47 ESV). Peter obviously recognized the Spirit's coming upon them as God's confirmation that the Gentiles were a part of the church, just as the Jewish believers were part of the church.

It would be strange indeed for the Holy Spirit to fall on these Gentiles if they were not already believers. But as previously stated, it is not baptism but faith alone that justifies a person before God.[11] Mormons might argue that if this is the case, they too are qualified for salvation since they also "have faith." There is a difference, however. The Christian's faith is based on the fact that Jesus' sacrifice paid the entire debt of sin. Nothing more can be added to a debt that has been paid in full. Mormon leaders have argued that Christ's sacrifice was not all-sufficient. As James Faust (1920–2007), a member of the First Presidency, stated, "All of us have sinned and need to repent to fully pay *our* part of the debt. When we sincerely repent, the Savior's magnificent Atonement pays the *rest* of that debt."[12]

"Baptism is an essential principle," President Lorenzo Snow (1814–1901) said. "Some deem it wrong to number baptism among the essential principles ordained of God, to be attended to in obtaining remission of sins. In reply, we say that the Savior and Apostles have done so before us, therefore we feel obligated to follow their example."[13]As with many who believe in baptismal regeneration, Snow refers to 1 Peter 3:21, which reads, "The like figure whereunto even baptism doth also now save us (not the putting away of the filth of the flesh, but the answer of a good conscience toward God)." Adam Clarke (1762–1832), a Methodist theologian often cited by LDS leaders and apologists, rejects the interpretation Mormons have adopted. He wrote,

> 1 Peter 3:21 makes the ark a figure of baptism, and intimates that we
> are saved by this, as the eight souls were saved by the ark. But let us
> not mistake the apostle by supposing that the mere ceremony itself
> saves any person; he tells us that the salvation conveyed through
> this sacred rite is not the putting away the filth of the flesh, but the
> answer of a good conscience toward God; i.e. remission of sins and
> regeneration by the Holy Spirit, which are signified by this baptism.
> A good conscience never existed where remission of sins had not
> taken place; and every person knows that it is God's prerogative to

forgive sins, and that no ordinance can confer it, though ordinances may be the means to convey it when piously and believingly used.[14]

Like Clarke, Christian scholar Peter H. Davids also rejects the notion that Peter is implying that water baptism saves an individual. He writes, "The point in 1 Peter is that the outward washing is not the important part. That is simply 'the removal of dirt from the body.' Without something more one would go into the water a dirty sinner and come out a clean sinner. The water has no magic properties, nor does the ritual itself save. If it did, baptism would be like circumcision was for the Jew, and Christians would indeed be saved by works . . ." Davids interprets Peter's statement as it "parallels with Jewish rites and the use of the term 'pledge' in other literature. This sees the candidate for baptism being asked a series of questions, such as 'Do you pledge yourself to follow Jesus as Lord?' (perhaps reflected in Acts 8:37 and 1 Timothy 6:12). The response of commitment to God and identification with Christ is what saves, if it comes from a good conscience."[15]

Davids notes that "baptism in the name of Jesus was the first thing done to all converts in the New Testament period. The idea that a person would confess Christ and yet would not be baptized would be absurd to Peter . . . He would surely have admitted that the thief on the cross had been saved without being baptized (Luke 23:43), but why should that be the norm for people who are not on crosses or otherwise inhibited from baptism?"[16]

As these scholars have noted, baptism—while a very important ordinance in the life of the Christian believer—was never assumed to precede faith. Rather, candidates came to the waters of baptism already possessing the faith that purifies.

Questions for Discussion

- Should baptism play an important role in Christianity? What reasons can you give?

- How would you explain to a Mormon that Jesus' sacrifice on the cross was "all-sufficient"?

- A person who takes a wedding ring off her finger remains married. The ring simply serves as a symbol. Wearing it lets others know she is married. How could this analogy be related to baptism?

─────────────── **Evangelism Tip** ───────────────

When baptism is the topic of discussion, be aware that some Mormons will tend to think that Christians don't value baptism. It should be stressed that Christians take baptism very seriously since it lets others know that they are identified with Christ in His death and resurrection. Therefore, every Christian should be water baptized. But baptism is not a qualifier for justification before God. Ask the Mormon, "Do you consider baptism to be a 'righteous work'?" If so, then Titus 3:5 disqualifies this act, since Paul said we are saved by mercy, not by righteous works.

If there is no baptism for the dead, what about all those who have died without having heard the gospel?

Response Questions

- What biblical evidence (or Book of Mormon evidence, for that matter) is there to show the validity of baptism for the dead?
- Should something be considered true just because it appeals to our sense of fairness?

· · · · · · · · · · · · · · · · ·

"Furthermore, the dead are anxiously waiting for the Latter-day Saints to search out their names and then go into the temples to officiate in their behalf, that they may be liberated from their prison house in the spirit world."[1]
—President Howard W. Hunter (1907–1995)

—————————————— Summary ——————————————

Mormonism teaches that work can be performed in LDS temples on behalf of those already deceased. Vicarious baptisms for the dead allow the deceased a chance to receive the "restored gospel" in what has been called spirit prison. The proof text used is 1 Corinthians 15:29, which Mormons have interpreted to say something the apostle Paul never intended. While Mormons might like the idea that they can play a role in the salvation of the dead, the Bible and the Book of Mormon both strongly deny the possibility of a postmortem salvation.

Six days a week, Sundays excluded, faithful Mormons as young as twelve who are in good standing participate in proxy baptisms for those who are dead. Church leaders have taught that this work, performed in Mormon temples, allows the "restored gospel" to be presented to those residing in a temporary state called spirit prison. This is one of the reasons genealogy is considered so important by Latter-day Saints.

Robert Millet, a professor at Brigham Young University, explained, "Latter-day Saints believe that sometime during or just following the mortal ministry of Jesus, the doctrine of salvation for the dead was revealed to the first-century Church. . . . Joseph Smith called these events 'the fundamental principles of our religion,' to which all other doctrines are but appendages."[2] Smith said Latter-day Saints could "become saviors on Mount Zion" by "building their temples, erecting their baptismal fonts, and going forth and receiving all the ordinances and sealing powers upon their heads, in behalf of all their progenitors who are dead, and redeem them that they may come forth in the first resurrection and be exalted to thrones of glory with them. . . . The Saints have not too much time to save and redeem their dead."[3]

Under the heading that says Mormons "have a responsibility to be saviors on Mount Zion," a church manual quotes President John Taylor (1808–1887) as saying, "Saviors? Yes. Whom shall they save? In the first place themselves, then their families, then their neighbors, friends and associations, then their forefathers, then pour blessings on their prosperity. Is that so? Yes."[4] President Wilford Woodruff (1807–1898) taught, "This is a work that rests upon the Latter-day Saints. Do what you can in this respect, so that when you pass to the other side of the veil your fathers, mothers, relatives and friends will bless you for what you have done, and inasmuch as you have been instruments in the hands of God in procuring their redemption, you will be recognized as Saviors upon Mount Zion in fulfillment of prophecy."[5] Another manual tells church members, "Your effort approaches the spirit of the Savior's atoning sacrifice—you perform a saving work for others that they cannot do for themselves."[6]

Speaking about temple work, President Gordon B. Hinckley (1910–2008) said that "its primary purpose is to afford members of the Church the resources needed to identify their ancestors that they might extend to them the blessings that they themselves enjoy. They in effect say to themselves, 'If I love my wife and children so dearly that I want them for all eternity, then should not my deceased grandfather and great-grandfather and other forbears have opportunity to receive the same eternal blessings.'"[7] Henry Eyring, a member of the First Presidency, told a general conference crowd, "Many of your deceased ancestors will have received a testimony that the message of the missionaries is true. When you received that testimony you could ask the missionaries for baptism. But those who are in the spirit world cannot. The ordinances you so cherish are offered only in this world. Someone in this world must go to a holy temple and accept the covenants on behalf of the person in the spirit world. That is why we are under obligation to find the names of our ancestors and ensure that they are offered by us what they cannot receive there without our help."[8]

The freedom to choose whether or not to accept this gospel is provided to these spirits, according to Apostle James E. Talmage (1862–1933), who explained, "Let it not be assumed that this doctrine of vicarious labor for the dead implies even remotely, that the administration of ordinances in behalf of departed spirits operates in any manner to interfere with the right of choice and the exercise of free agency on their part. They are at liberty to accept or reject the ministrations in their behalf; and so they will accept or reject, in accordance with their converted or unregenerate state, even as is the case with mortals to whom the Gospel message may come."[9] Seventy Spencer J. Condie explained,

> We believe that everyone is free to choose, both in this life and in the spirit world. This freedom is essential to the plan of our Heavenly Father. No one will be coerced into accepting ordinances performed on his or her behalf by another. Baptism for the dead offers an opportunity, but it does not override a person's agency. . . . We simply do not know who among the dead will turn their hearts to the Lord and repent. We are not in a position to judge. We must do the work and leave the matter in the hands of the deceased person and the Lord.[10]

Thus, Mormons diligently do their temple work for the dead, with the hope that these spirits will choose to accept the message of salvation that will be presented to them.[11] It ought to be emphasized, though, that this doctrine was not originally intended to provide a "second chance" for salvation for those who knew about Mormonism in this mortal life. Rather, it was meant only for those who never heard a clear presentation of the Mormon view of the gospel. Consider the words of two important General Authorities:

- President Joseph Fielding Smith (1876–1972): "SOME NOT ELIGI-BLE FOR VICARIOUS SALVATION. There are too many people in this world, who have heard the message of the gospel, who think they can continue on to the end of this mortal life, living as they please, and then accept the gospel after death and friends will perform the ordinances that they neglect to perform for themselves, and eventually they will receive blessings in the kingdom of God. This is an error. It is the duty of men in this life to repent. *Every man who hears the gospel message is under obligation to receive it.* If he fails, then in the spirit world he will be called upon to receive it, but he will be *denied* the fulness that will come to those who in their faithfulness have been just and true, whether it be in this life or in the spirit world. SECOND CHANCE LEADS TO TERRESTRIAL KINGDOM. Moreover, we learn that those who *rejected* the gospel when it was offered them in ancient times, but afterward accepted the 'testimony of Jesus' in the spirit world when it was declared to them, and who were honorable men of the earth, are assigned to the terrestrial glory, *not* the celestial."[12]
- Apostle Bruce R. McConkie (1915–1985): "There are those who believe that the doctrine of salvation for the dead offers men a second chance for salvation. This is false, false, false. I know a man, now deceased, a non-member of the Church, who was a degenerate old reprobate who found pleasure, as he supposed, in living after the manner of the world. A cigarette dangled from his lips, alcohol stenched his breath, and profane and bawdy stories defiled his lips. His moral status left much to be desired. His wife was a member of the Church, as faithful as she could be under the circumstances. One day she said to him, 'You know the Church is true; why don't you be baptized?' He replied, 'Of course I know the Church is true, but I have no intention of changing my habits in order to join it. I prefer to live the way I do. But that doesn't worry me in the slightest. I know that as soon as I die, you will have someone go to the temple and do the work for me and everything will come out all right in the end anyway.' He died and she did and it was a total and complete waste of time."[13]

The Bible and the Book of Mormon are in agreement when they proclaim that there are no second chances for salvation. For example, 2 Corinthians 6:2 says, "Behold, now is the accepted time; behold, now is the day of salvation."

Hebrews 9:27 adds, "And as it is appointed unto men once to die, but after this the judgment." In the Book of Mormon, Alma 34:32–35 says,

> For behold, this life is the time for men to prepare to meet God; yea, behold the day of this life is the day for men to perform their labors. And now, as I said unto you before, as ye have had so many witnesses, therefore, I beseech of you that ye do not procrastinate the day of your repentance until the end; for after this day of life, which is given us to prepare for eternity, behold, if we do not improve our time while in this life, then cometh the night of darkness wherein there can be no labor performed. Ye cannot say, when ye are brought to that awful crisis, that I will repent, that I will return to my God. Nay, ye cannot say this; for that same spirit which doth possess your bodies at the time that ye go out of this life, that same spirit will have power to possess your body in that eternal world. For behold, if ye have procrastinated the day of your repentance even until death, behold, ye have become subjected to the spirit of the devil, and he doth seal you his; therefore, the Spirit of the Lord hath withdrawn from you, and hath no place in you, and the devil hath all power over you; and this is the final state of the wicked.

Mormons sometimes argue that this passage in Alma refers only to those who know better. This would include apostate Mormons or even so-called "anti-Mormons" who have done a great deal of study on Mormonism. But this passage does not support this premise. In fact, verse 32 says now "is the time for men (in general) to prepare to meet God." It does not specify that the time is now only for those who have understood the gospel fully and rejected it. If the warning here really is intended for those who know better, then it seems to be directed to every member of the LDS Church. Second Nephi 9:38 puts it clearly: "And, in fine, woe unto all those who die in their sins: for they shall return to God, and behold His face, and remain in their sins."[14]

Interpreting 1 Corinthians 15:29

In 1 Corinthians 15:29, the apostle Paul wrote, "Else what shall they do which are baptized for the dead, if the dead rise not at all? why are they then baptized for the dead?" President David O. McKay (1873–1970) wrote, "Not a few commentators have tried to explain away [this passage's] true significance; but its context proves plainly that in the days of the apostles there existed the practice of baptism for the dead; that is, living persons were immersed in water for and in behalf of those who were dead—not who were 'dead to sin' but who had 'passed to the other side.'"[15]

Brigham Young University professor Robert Millet said, "Many non-Latter-day Saint scholars believe that in 1 Corinthians Paul was denouncing or condemning the practice of baptism for the dead as heretical. This is a strange conclusion, since Paul uses the practice to support the doctrine of the resurrection. In essence, he says, 'Why are we performing baptism in behalf of our dead, if, as some propose, there will be no resurrection of the dead? If there is to be no resurrection, would not such baptisms be a waste of time?'"[16] Millet assumes that Paul was a participant in this rite. When verse 29 is dissected, though, it can be seen that Paul purposely did not use the first person *we* in this verse. Thus, Christian theologian D. A. Carson explained why this assumption is wrong:

> The most plausible interpretation is that some in Corinth were getting baptized vicariously for the dead. Several factors, however, put this into perspective. Although Paul does not explicitly condemn the practice, neither does he endorse it. Several writers have offered the following analogy. Imagine a Protestant writing, "Why do they then pray for the dead, if the dead do not rise at all?" No one would take this as an endorsement of the practice of praying for the dead; it is a criticism of the inconsistency of praying for the dead while holding that the dead do not rise. To make this rhetorical question an endorsement of the practice of praying for the dead, one would expect, "Why do *we* then pray for the dead?" Likewise, in 1 Corinthians 15:29 Paul preserves the more distant *they*. After all, his primary concern in 1 Corinthians 15 is the defense of the Christian doctrine of resurrection. His rhetorical question in verse 29 may simply be pointing out the inconsistency of those who deny the final resurrection, granted their rather strange baptismal practices. And they were strange. There is no good evidence for vicarious baptism anywhere in the New Testament or among the earliest apostolic fathers. By the same token, there is no hint that this vicarious baptism (if that is what it was) was intended by the Corinthian believers to cover as many deceased people as could be named. If the practice existed at all, it may have been tied to a few

people or special cases—for example, when a relative died after trusting the gospel but before being baptized. We really do not know. If it were something like that, one could understand why Paul does not make a federal case of it. In any case, Paul's clear emphasis is that people are justified by grace *through faith*, which demands a personal response. Christian baptism is part of that personal response, even as it is a covenantal pledge. In contrast, baptism on behalf of someone who has not exercised such faith sounds like magic—of something far from Pauline thought.[17]

Carson suggested that the reason the 1 Corinthians 15 passage is difficult to interpret is that this is the only passage in the Bible specifically mentioning "baptism for the dead." He wrote,

> The reason is not that God must say things more than once for them to be true or binding. The reason, rather, is that if something is said only once it is easily misunderstood or misapplied. When something is repeated on several occasions and in slightly different contexts, readers will enjoy a better grasp of what is meant and what is at stake. That is why the famous "baptism for the dead" passage (1 Cor. 15:29) is not unpacked at length and made a major plank in, say, the Heidelberg Catechism or the Westminster Confession. Over forty interpretations of that passage have been offered in the history of the church. Mormons are quite sure what it means, of course, but the reason why they are sure is because they are reading it in the context of other books that they claim are inspired and authoritative.[18]

The historical context also needs to be considered, and it reveals that baptism for the dead was not a regular practice of the Christian church. According to Christian theologian Geoffrey W. Bromiley, "apart from a possible reference in Tertullian (*De res*, 48c), there is evidence of such a practice only among heretical groups like the Cerinthians and the Marcionites," and neither of these groups existed when 1 Corinthians was written.[19] If Doctrine and Covenants 128:17 is true when it says that baptism for the dead is the most "glorious of all subjects belonging to the everlasting gospel," then it should be expected that the New Testament would have spoken much more about it.

What Does Peter Say?

President Joseph F. Smith (1838–1918) claimed he had a vision on October 3, 1918 that helped him understand two passages found in 1 Peter. He said, "As I pondered over these things which are written, the eyes of my understanding were opened, and the Spirit of the Lord rested upon me, and I saw the hosts of the dead, both small and great" (D&C 138:11). Smith reported that after Jesus' resurrection, Jesus appeared in the spirit world by "declaring liberty to the captives who had been faithful; And there he preached to them the everlasting gospel . . . And the saints rejoiced in their redemption, and bowed the knee and acknowledged the Son of God as their Redeemer and Deliverer from death and the chains of hell. But his ministry among those who were dead was limited to the brief time intervening between the crucifixion and his resurrection (D&C 138:18–19, 23, 27)."

Smith pointed to 1 Peter 3:19 to show that Jesus gave those who were already dead another chance to accept the gospel. That verse says that He "went and preached unto the spirits in prison." Because there is not much background information available to us, there are many interpretations of this verse. As New Testament scholar Mark Strauss says, "The verse is enormously difficult to interpret and we simply don't know what it means," adding that proposed interpretations "all are educated guesses."[20]

One possible interpretation given by Christian commentators is that the verse "refers to Christ's announcement to departed spirits of the triumph of his resurrection, declaring to them the victory he had achieved by his death and resurrection, as pointed out in the previous verse."[21] According to this view, the Greek word for "preached" means "proclaimed." Even those who rejected God in their earthly lives will acknowledge the lordship of Christ, for Philippians 2:10–11 says every knee shall bow and every tongue confess that Jesus Christ is Lord. However, not all who bow their knees will be able to call Him Savior. The people described in 1 Peter 3:19 are awaiting the final judgment in the same place as the rich man in Luke 16:19–31; they are not being invited to accept a postmortem salvation.

Another popular interpretation connects 1 Peter 3:19 with the reference to Noah in verse 20. Christian commentator Gleason Archer explained that this event "took place, not when Christ descended into Hades after His death on Calvary, but by the Spirit who spoke through the mouth of Noah during the years while the ark was under construction (v. 20). Therefore v. 19 holds out no hope whatever for a 'second chance' for those who reject Christ during their lifetime on earth."[22] Thus, according to this interpretation, the people in Noah's day had their chance to receive the truth while they were alive, but they rejected it and are now awaiting the final judgment.

Joseph Smith claimed his vision also gave him understanding of 1 Peter 4:6, another ambiguous passage. It says in part, "For this cause was the gospel preached also to them that are dead." The New International Version translates the last portion of this, "the gospel was preached even to those who are now dead." While the word *now* is not found in the original Greek, it was used by the translators because the context suggests that the preaching of the gospel had been delivered in the past to those who were now deceased. In order to support the Mormon view of a second chance to hear the gospel message and receive salvation after death, the first verb would need to be present tense (i.e., "for this cause *is* the gospel preached also to them that are dead"). It is not, which is a clear blow to the Mormon interpretation. To suggest that living people can become "saviors" of those already dead is not a Christian teaching and must therefore be rejected.[23]

Questions for Discussion

- Some Mormons believe baptism for the dead offers those who rejected the Mormon gospel in this life a chance to repent and spend eternity in the celestial kingdom. What do Mormon leaders like Joseph Fielding Smith and Bruce R. McConkie think of this view?

- How does the doctrine of baptism for the dead contradict biblical passages related to salvation?

- How does the Mormon view of baptism for the dead relate to the faith element of salvation? How much faith is really involved if this concept is true?

———————————— Evangelism Tip ————————————

Being able to do vicarious work on behalf of others is a comfort to many Mormons since their efforts allow the possibility for their relatives to accept the Mormon gospel in the next life. But instead of supporting the idea that the deceased are allowed to accept the gospel, the Bible says it is during this life that a decision must be made. One's salvation cannot depend on any person other than Jesus Christ Himself. What one does with Jesus in this life is what really matters.

Chapter 23

Wouldn't you like to have your marriage and family endure for all eternity?

Response Questions

- Does merely "liking" something to be true make it true?
- Where in the Bible does it say that earthly families were meant to be together forever?
- Is it logically possible for you to be with your children forever? After all, won't they be allowed to live in their own realms with their spouses if they too keep celestial law?

• • • • • • • • • • • • • • • • •

"I don't know how to speak about heaven in the traditional, lovely, paradisiacal beauty that we speak of heaven—I wouldn't know how to speak of heaven without my wife, my children. It would not be heaven for me."[1]

—Apostle Jeffrey R. Holland

—————————— Summary ——————————

According to Mormonism, one of the benefits of exaltation is the ability to live forever with one's earthly family. However, the idea of being together forever as a family unit is contingent on all family members qualifying for celestial exaltation. But which LDS family doesn't have at least one "black sheep" or rebel who doesn't follow Mormonism's straight and narrow road? While Mormons typically hope and expect to spend eternity with all of their loved ones, logic shows that this is an impossible goal.

A COMMON EXPRESSION WITHIN Mormonism is "Families are forever."
Mormons can get sentimental when talking about eternal families, for this is
a primary expectation in the next life. President George Albert Smith (1870–
1951) would have agreed with Holland's quote above. He said, "If I were to
think, as so many think, that now that my beloved wife and my beloved
parents are gone, that they have passed out of my life forever and that I shall
never see them again, it would deprive me of one of the greatest joys that I
have in life: the contemplation of meeting them again, and receiving their
welcome and their affection, and of thanking them from the depths of a
grateful heart for all they have done for me."[2]

Mormons believe that exaltation in the celestial kingdom will allow them
to be "united eternally with their righteous family members and [they] will be
able to have eternal increase."[3] Focusing on the meaning of "eternal increase"
within the exalted state, another church manual explains, "By definition,
exaltation includes the ability to procreate the family unit throughout eternity."[4] The idea of residing with one's family as a reward for a job well done on
earth has been a consistent theme throughout much of Mormonism's history.
Consider some of the following quotes in LDS Church publications:

- "Except a man and his wife enter into an everlasting covenant and be
  married for eternity, while in this probation, by the power and authority of the Holy Priesthood, they will cease to increase when they die;
  that is, they will not have any children after the resurrection. But those
  who are married by the power and authority of the priesthood in this
  life, and continue without committing the sin against the Holy Ghost,
  will continue to increase and have children in the celestial glory."[5]
- "Only in and through the family unit can we obtain eternal life."[6]
- "Families can be together forever. To enjoy this blessing we must be
  married in the temple. . . . If we keep our covenants with the Lord, our
  families will be united eternally as husband, wife, and children. Death
  cannot separate us."[7]
- "It is the celestial glory that we seek. It is in the presence of God that we
  desire to dwell. It is a forever family in which we want membership."[8]
- "The fullness of eternal salvation is a family affair. . . . The gospel plan
  originated in the council of an eternal family, it is implemented through
  our earthly families, and has its destiny in our eternal families."[9]
- "To be exalted in the highest degree and continue eternally in family
  relationships, we must enter into 'the new and everlasting covenant of

marriage' and be true to that covenant. In other words, temple marriage is a requirement for obtaining the highest degree of celestial glory."[10]

- "Under the great plan of the loving Creator, the mission of His Church is to help us achieve exaltation in the celestial kingdom, and that can be accomplished only through an eternal marriage between a man and a woman."[11]

The Family and Being Together Forever

Some Mormons have created a stereotype about the Christian's view of heaven, assuming it means sitting on a cloud, strumming a harp, and singing hymns to Jesus throughout eternity in a most boring fashion. While this is certainly not a completely accurate picture of heaven, perhaps the Latter-day Saint should consider Mormon 7:7 in the Book of Mormon. It reads, "And he [Jesus] have brought to pass the redemption of the world, whereby he that is found guiltless before him at the judgment day hath it given unto him to dwell in the presence of God in his kingdom, to sing ceaseless praises with the choirs above, unto the Father, and unto the Son, and unto the Holy Ghost, which are one God, in a state of happiness which hath no end."

In the mind of the Latter-day Saint, it makes sense that heaven includes the family unit. President Joseph F. Smith (1838–1918) explained, "I have the glorious promise of the association of my loved ones throughout all eternity. In obedience to this work, in the gospel of Jesus Christ, I shall gather around me my family, my children, my children's children, until they become as numerous as the seed of Abraham, or as countless as the sands upon the seashore. For this is my right and privilege, and the right and privilege of every member of the Church of Jesus Christ of Latter-day Saints who holds the Priesthood and will magnify it in the sight of God."[12] President Gordon B. Hinckley (1910–1995) wrote, "Can anyone believing in eternal life doubt that the God of heaven would grant His sons and daughters that most precious attribute of life, the love that finds its most meaningful expression in family relationships? No, reason demands that the family relationship shall continue after death. The human heart longs for it, and the God of heaven has revealed a way whereby it may be secured."[13]

Certainly Christians should invest heavily in their earthly families, but nowhere does the Bible teach that mom, dad, grandparents, children, or others will live together as a family unit in heaven. Jesus plainly explained the role of marriage and families in heaven in Matthew 22:23–30 and Mark 12:18–27.

Answering the question posed to Him by the Sadducees, Jesus answered them, "Ye do err, not knowing the scriptures, nor the power of God. For in the resurrection they neither marry, nor are given in marriage, but are as the angels of God in heaven" (Matt. 22:29–30). Mormon apologist Gilbert Scharffs complains about those who use this passage to reject eternal marriage when he writes, "This verse does not say there won't be any marriage in heaven, only that marriages will not be performed there."[14] This is nothing more than reading into a passage, as Scharffs provides no evidence to support his point.

In Mormonism, dwelling together as a family unit presupposes that each member of the family was able to follow the whole law during their mortal probation. As demonstrated in chapter 20, Mormonism teaches that only those who are truly obedient will qualify for the benefits of the celestial kingdom. According to President Joseph Fielding Smith (1876–1972), "To enter the *celestial* and obtain exaltation it is necessary that the *whole law be kept*."[15] For the sake of argument, suppose that keeping the whole law *is* possible. Where will all the billions and billions of family members from the beginning of time physically reside? Are we to assume that the God of Mormonism continues to reside with his extended earthly family? Does he worship the God who preceded him? And since Jesus is our spirit brother from the preexistence, will He become "Uncle Jesus" to the offspring of a Mormon who becomes a god? Will the heavenly Father be known as "Heavenly Grandfather" to these offspring?

What about those members of a Mormon family who do *not* qualify for celestial glory? Mormonism teaches that a person can't reach the celestial kingdom on the coattails of another faithful member; each person must individually qualify. Even if this concept ended up being true, the odds are that most LDS families will be incomplete because some of their loved ones will fail to live up to the proper standards during their mortal probation.

It is a misnomer to say that Christians don't believe in an eternal family structure since all forgiven humans are a part of God's family. As such, all redeemed believers will live in the presence of the Father, Son, and Holy Spirit. God will be the focus of our attention in eternity, not us. Sadly, Christians will not experience eternity with unforgiven loved ones. However, in Mormon teaching this same situation exists. Faithful Mormons will not be joined by family members who were unfaithful in mortality.

On the surface, the idea of eternal family units may sound very appealing to some, but once the LDS concept is carried to its logical conclusion, it breaks down quickly.

Questions for Discussion

- When Mormons say, "Families are forever," what thoughts come to your mind? What is the Mormon meaning of this phrase? How does this concept differ from the teaching of the Bible?

- Suppose a Mormon told you that he/she doesn't want to spend eternity strumming a harp and singing hymns in a heavenly choir. How could you more clearly explain what heaven is really like?

─────────────── Evangelism Tip ───────────────

Mormons might assume the Christian's idea of heaven is unappealing. If Mormons find the notion of making God the focal point of their eternity untenable, remind them that this could be because they don't share the same adoration and awe of God as you do. As sacred as marriage and family are in this life, Christians realize no institution could ever compare with the undeserved reward prepared for God's beloved bride. Those who value a relationship with their earthly families over a relationship with the eternal God of the Bible seem to have misplaced priorities.

Chapter 24

We'll just have to find out in the end who was right, won't we?

Response Questions

- Have you ever considered the possibility that you might be wrong about truth?
- If you are wrong and there really is such a place as hell, wouldn't you want to know before Judgment Day?

• • • • • • • • • • • • • • • •

"If there is any truth in heaven, earth, or hell, I want to embrace it. I care not what shape it comes in to me, who brings it, or who believes in it, whether it is popular or unpopular. Truth, eternal truth, I wish to float in and enjoy. . . . If any man under the heavens can show me one principle of error that I have entertained, I will lay it aside forthwith, and be thankful for the information."[1]

—President John Taylor (1808–1887)

Summary

When some Latter-day Saints find it difficult to respond to the evidence presented against their faith, they may become exasperated and attempt to shut down the conversation by saying it doesn't matter because "we'll all find out the truth in the end." If the Christian is right about faith, though, it does matter, for the difference is between heaven and hell. Using simple logic, it is possible to show the Mormon the importance of considering other possibilities instead of ignorantly falling back on a system that is in error.

WHEN A MORMON ASKS THE question posed in this chapter's title, it means he or she is seeking to abandon the conversation. Many Mormons have never seriously considered the possibility that their view could be in error. Because they have prayed about their faith and felt a comforting peace, they assume that the LDS Church must be true. Perhaps they have never been confronted with facts that could shake their faith.

While it is possible that Mormonism and biblical Christianity are both false—perhaps one of the thousands of other religions in the world best corresponds to reality—Mormonism and biblical Christianity cannot both be true. Logic demands that at least one of the two systems contradicting each other is wrong. But even if Mormonism is assumed to be the correct system, it leaves its followers typically unsure of their eternal destiny. When asked if they are headed to the top level of the celestial kingdom, Mormons often use words such as "I hope so" or "I think so." When asked if they are sufficiently following the commandments as required by the LDS Church, common responses are "I'm trying," "If I repent," "I'm doing the best I can," and "I'll do it when I get older." Rarely is an unqualified, "I *know* beyond a shadow of a doubt that I'm forgiven and am guaranteed the very best God has in store for me" offered in response.[2]

President Joseph Fielding Smith (1876–1972) did not hold out hope for at least half of his people, when he wrote,

> NOT HALF THE LATTER-DAY SAINTS TO BE SAVED. Those who receive the *fulness* [sic] will be privileged to view the face of our Father. *There will not be such an overwhelming number of the Latter-day Saints who will get there.* President Francis M. Lyman many times has declared, and he had reason to declare, I believe, that *if* we save one-half of the Latter-day Saints, that is, with an exaltation in the celestial kingdom of God, we will be doing well. Not that the Lord is partial, not that he will draw the line as some will say, to keep people out. He would have every one of us go in if we would; but there are laws and ordinances that we must keep; if we do not observe the law we cannot enter.[3]

Would Latter-day Saints today consider themselves that much better than the Latter-day Saints who lived more than half a century ago when Smith made the above comment? After all, if the commands for exaltation are that overwhelming, who could ever qualify? Because of this apparent impossibility, some Latter-day Saints have resigned themselves to the idea that they will never be good enough, and they claim they will be satisfied if they end up in the second heaven, called the terrestrial kingdom. When the tables are turned and they are asked what they think will happen to Bible-believing Christians in the end, they often explain that moral people will receive an opportunity to achieve the terrestrial kingdom if the "restored gospel" is embraced during a temporary stay in spirit prison. If this is a distinct possibility, why become a Mormon in the first place?

Sadly, many Mormons reject biblical Christianity based on a caricature of what it really is or because they do not like certain doctrines, such as the idea of an eternal hell.[4] A good question to ask is, "If there was a possibility you might be wrong, wouldn't you want to know now?" Christian pastor Timothy Keller made an excellent observation when it comes to Christianity clashing with cultural mind-sets. He wrote, "For the sake of argument, let's imagine that Christianity is not the product of any one culture but is actually the transcultural truth of God. If that were the case we would expect that it would contradict and offend every human culture at some point, because human cultures are ever-changing and imperfect. If Christianity were the truth it would have to be offending and correcting your thinking at some place. Maybe this is the place, the Christian doctrine of divine judgment."[5]

While a person cannot be forced to consider the claims of Christianity, the Mormon needs to know that rejecting something because of preconceived notions can be very dangerous. The goal is to get the Mormon to realize how important it is to research the topic at hand. Just as the Mormon would be quick to say Mormonism should not be rejected based on mischaracterizations of the religion, neither should biblical Christianity be rejected on the same basis. It also shouldn't be rejected just because people grew up in a Mormon family or community. Rather, Christianity should be rejected only if it is *not* true, and how can anyone determine this unless careful research is done? This is why the gospel ought to be presented clearly to nonbelievers who will listen, leaving the choice up to them.

Questions for Discussion

- In this chapter, it is proposed that rejecting biblical Christianity without having an accurate understanding of what it says is a dangerous outlook. Do you agree or disagree with this assessment? Provide specific reasons.

- Why should it not be dangerous for Christians to study other religions and philosophies? To whom could this be a threat, and what solution could you offer?

- Assurance of salvation is one of the great benefits of Christianity. How can this truth be used in a witnessing encounter with a Latter-day Saint?

───────────────── Evangelism Tip ─────────────────

Nobody can be forced to accept Christianity, of course, but we want to engage others in such a way as to let them see that Christianity does have truth claims that ought to be seriously considered. If Mormonism is true, it ought to be followed at all costs. If it's not true, then it ought to be abandoned and replaced. Because so many Mormons have not seriously considered any philosophies other than their own, it is important to challenge them to examine Christianity and its truth claims as objectively as possible. Blind rejection of anything can be dangerous.

Section 5

The Bible

Chapter 25

Why should a rational person trust in a Bible that has been corrupted?

Response Questions

- Can you tell me what you mean by "corrupted"?
- Isn't the Bible one of your scriptures? Are you absolutely sure that the criticisms your church leaders have had against the Bible are accurate?
- What if the Bible is trustworthy after all? Would this change your perspective on your faith? Would it change your perspective on my faith?

• • • • • • • • • • • • • • • • •

"[Regarding the lack of trust people should have in the Bible] Many insertions were made, some of them 'slanted' for selfish purposes, while at times deliberate falsifications were perpetrated."[1]
—Apostle Mark E. Petersen (1900–1984)

—————————————— Summary ——————————————

The Bible is probably the most maligned book on the face of the earth. Skeptics continually critique its history and attack its message. When the evidence is examined, however, the Bible stands as a trustworthy source despite its age. In fact, when compared with other ancient works, the evidence for the authenticity of the Bible is without compare. Shortly after the LDS Church began, Joseph Smith claimed he was commanded by God to fix the apparent corruptions in the Bible. The result was the Joseph Smith Translation, or Inspired Version of the Bible.

THE LDS CHURCH HAS HAD a history of sending mixed messages regarding the accuracy and importance of the Bible. At times, leaders claim to appreciate the Word of God, while at other times they minimize its reliability. For example, President Brigham Young (1801–1877) said, "We have a holy reverence for and a belief in the Bible."[2] However, referring to church founder Joseph Smith (1805–1844), one writer explained, "Yet the Prophet's reverence for the Bible was accompanied by his awareness of its incompleteness and of problems with the transmission of its texts. On one occasion he said, 'I believe the Bible as it read when it came from the pen of the original writers. Ignorant translators, careless transcribers, or designing and corrupt priests have committed many errors.'"[3] Of the four scriptures in the standard works of Mormonism, the Bible is the only one accepted with qualification. Article 8 in the LDS Articles of Faith, as written by Joseph Smith, states, "We believe the Bible to be the word of God as far as it is translated correctly."

According to a 1992 First Presidency Statement, "The Bible, as it has been transmitted over the centuries, has suffered the loss of many plain and precious parts."[4] Apostle Neil A. Maxwell (1926–2004) explained, "By faulty transmission, many 'plain and precious things' were 'taken away' or 'kept back' from reaching what later composed our precious Holy Bible."[5] Mormon apologist Gilbert Scharffs explains, "Books within the Bible have been added and subtracted in the early centuries after Christ's death at the whim of councils."[6]

These are strong accusations. If true, this would mean the Bible has suffered the most incredible acts of textual corruption ever imagined. One would have to assume that this corruption was completed very early in the life of the Christian church since no copies available support the LDS premise. In other words, there are no known early and authentic manuscripts containing these alleged "precious things" that Mormons assume were "taken away" or "kept back." By the time this supposed fraudulence began to take hold, hundreds, if not thousands, of biblical manuscripts, as well as many letters and writings of the early church fathers, already would have been circulating. In order to successfully suppress the truth, the conspirators (whoever they were) would have had to gather all the extant manuscripts dispersed over a huge geographical area and somehow erase (without detection) every "plain and precious" teaching from them. Since there is no evidence to support this elaborate conspiracy theory, it is nothing more than a monumental argument from silence.

While Article 8 uses the word *translated,* it is the "transmission" of the biblical text—the process of copying an ancient text—that is really being called into question. Mormon leaders argue that in the transmission of the text early on, portions were intentionally omitted. To bolster their claim that the Bible is unreliable, they have pointed out the many differences, or variants, among various ancient Bible manuscripts.

Regarding the Old Testament, Gleason Archer observed, "A careful study of the variants of the various earliest manuscripts reveals that none of them affects a single doctrine of Scripture. The system of spiritual truth contained in the standard Hebrew text of the Old Testament is not in the slightest altered or compromised by any of the variant readings found in the Hebrew manuscripts. . . . It is very evident that the vast majority of them are so inconsequential as to leave the meaning of each clause doctrinally unaffected."[7] The discovery of thousands of fragments and even some complete scrolls at Qumran near the Dead Sea beginning in 1947 helped scholars understand how accurate the Old Testament had been transmitted over a thousand-year time period.

The text of the New Testament is also very accurate. According to Christian scholar Bruce Metzger, there are more than 5,600 Greek manuscripts, with an additional 24,000 manuscripts in Latin, Ethiopic, Slavic, and Armenian. "We can have great confidence in the fidelity with which this material has come down to us, especially compared with any other ancient literary work," he said.[8]

When compared to other ancient historical sources, the Bible is rich in manuscript attestation. For example, works by writers such as Plato (*Tetralogies*), Caesar (*Gallic Wars*), and Tacitus (*Annals*) have just a few hundred manuscripts each, with the earliest copies generally hailing from about a thousand years after the original. Homer's *Iliad* is the next best attested ancient historical work. Though it was written in 800 B.C., the earliest copy in existence was produced four centuries after the original text, and there are only 1,757 copies. Biola University professor Clay Jones explains that this work is "dwarfed by the NT, which has more than three times the Greek manuscripts as the *Iliad.* When one adds the fifteen thousand manuscripts in other languages, and then considers that almost the entire NT could be reproduced by the quotations of the early church fathers. . . . The NT remains in a class by itself: it is by far the most attested ancient work. This troubles skeptics because if they reject the transmissional reliability of the NT, then they must also consider unreliable all other manuscripts of antiquity."[9]

On the accuracy of the New Testament, scholar F. F. Bruce comments:

> It is easily proved by experiment that it is difficult to copy out a passage of any considerable length without making one or two slips at least. When we have documents like our New Testament writings copied and recopied thousands of times, the scope for copyists' errors is so enormously increased that it is surprising there are no more than there actually are. Fortunately, if the great number of MSS increases the number of scribal errors, it increases proportionately the means of correcting such errors, so that the margin of doubt left in the process of recovering the exact original wording is not so large as might be feared; it is in truth remarkably small. The variant readings about which any doubt remains among textual critics of the New Testament affect no material question of historic fact or of Christian faith and practice.[10]

Should a Mormon doubt the trustworthiness of the above scholars, perhaps they would give heed to Brigham Young University professor Richard L. Anderson. Speaking on the accuracy of the New Testament at the Fourteenth Annual Symposium of the Archaeology of the Scriptures in 1963, he remarked, "For a book to undergo progressive uncovering of its manuscript history and come out with so little debatable in its text is a great tribute to its essential authenticity. First, no new manuscript discovery has produced serious differences in the essential story. This survey has disclosed the leading textual controversies, and together they would be well within one percent of the text. Stated differently, all manuscripts agree on the essential correctness of 99 percent of all the verses in the New Testament."[11]

The Joseph Smith Translation of the Bible

On the day that Joseph Smith's "Church of Christ"[12] was officially organized—April 6, 1830—Smith claimed to have received a revelation from God, telling him he was to be known as "a seer, a translator, a prophet, an apostle of Jesus Christ" (D&C 21:1). If Smith was indeed a "translator," it would seem only natural that he would use his ability to produce a trustworthy Bible.

Apostle John A. Widtsoe (1872–1952) said that the teaching of the Book of Mormon, along "with other new revelations from the Lord, convinced the Prophet that there were errors, unauthorized additions, and incomplete statements in the sacred volume of the Old and New Testaments. Such errors seemed to the Prophet, a devoted lover of the truth, out of keeping with the sacred nature of the Bible. Therefore, very soon after the organization of the Church, after placing the matter before the Lord, he began the 'inspired translation' of the holy scriptures."[13]

Nobody should confuse the Joseph Smith Translation (JST), also known as the Inspired Version, as being a traditional translation. David Rolph Seely, an associate professor of ancient scripture at church-owned Brigham Young University, wrote, "The prophet did not 'translate' the Bible in the traditional sense of the word—that is, go back to the earliest Hebrew and Greek manuscripts to make a new rendering into English. Rather, he went through the biblical text of the King James Version and made inspired corrections, revisions, and additions to the biblical text."[14] Even though the method of compiling the JST was certainly unorthodox, Seely said that "while it is not always possible to determine the exact nature of each of the Prophet's revisions, we accept them as being inspired."[15]

Comparing the "translation" process of the JST to the Book of Mormon, Brigham Young University professor Robert L. Millet wrote, "The Prophet translated the King James Bible by the same means he translated the Book of Mormon—through revelation. His knowledge of Hebrew or Greek or his acquaintance with ancient documents was no more essential in making the JST than a previous knowledge of Reformed Egyptian or an access to more primitive Nephite records was essential to the translation of the Book of Mormon."[16]

Quoting Robert J. Matthews, another Brigham Young University professor, Seely explained how the translation took place: "From the evidence it appears 'that the Prophet and a scribe would sit at a table, with the Prophet having the King James Version of the Bible open before him. Probably he would read from the King James Version and dictate the revisions, while the scribe recorded what he said.' Some of the corrections and revisions were small, including sometimes only vital punctuation changes. Other revisions were much more lengthy, restoring large passages of text."[17] Smith claimed he received the first part of the book of Moses in June 1830, and his "translation" appears in the JST as chapters 1 through 6 of the book of Genesis.[18]

A telltale mark of the JST is Smith's inclusion of a prophecy about himself in Genesis 50:33, which he added to the biblical text: "And his name shall be called Joseph, and it shall be after the name of his father;

and he shall be like unto you; for the thing which the Lord shall bring forth by his hand shall bring my people unto salvation." Seely explained, "While Joseph of Egypt, in the deliverance of his brethren from captivity, was a type of Jesus Christ, he is also a type of Joseph Smith, his descendant, who would open the work for salvation for the remnant of Israel."[19] Smith also wrote himself into the Book of Mormon narrative. LDS leaders and church manuals have often cited 2 Nephi 3:6–15 as containing "specific prophecies that Joseph of Egypt made regarding the Prophet Joseph Smith."[20]

Smith's theology evolved over time, as reflected in the JST, which he wrote between 1830 and 1833. Since much of his more heretical views appeared in his later years, it makes sense that these were not a part of his "translation." Just as the Book of Mormon holds to a more monotheistic view of the Godhead, Smith changed passages in the Bible that he thought could possibly be misconstrued as supporting polytheism. For example, Exodus 7:1 in the King James reads, "And the Lord said unto Moses, See, I have made thee a god to Pharaoh." In the JST, Smith changed this to say "a prophet to Pharaoh." In Exodus 22:28, the King James says, "Thou shalt not revile the gods"; Smith changed it to "revile against God." And "I saw gods ascending" in 1 Samuel 28:13 was changed to "I saw the words of Samuel ascending."

The alterations are hardly consistent. For example, in Romans 3:28 he says, "Man is justified by faith alone without the deeds of the law," yet in Romans 4:16 he writes, "Therefore, ye are justified of faith and works, through grace." The King James Version does not include the words *alone* or *works*. Often Smith makes a slight change to the text without changing the original meaning. In Ephesians 2:8, he keeps the basic King James rendition, only he adds the word *but* before "it is the gift of God." In Isaiah 44:6 and 8, he uses the word *besides* instead of *beside*.[21] Though this does not affect the meaning of the texts, it must be assumed that he was inspired to do so. The question is, what was the source of his inspiration?

According to Doctrine and Covenants 45:60–61, Smith was instructed in February 1831 to begin translating the New Testament "that ye may be prepared for the things to come." Later, in Doctrine and Covenants 73:4, Smith explained that on January 10, 1832, he was told by God "to continue the work of translation [of the Bible] until it be finished."[22] On July 2, 1833, a communication signed by Joseph Smith, Sidney Rigdon, and F. G. Williams announced, "We this day finished the translating of the Scriptures, for which we returned gratitude to our Heavenly Father."[23] In his 1899 *Church Chronology*, Mormon assistant church historian Andrew Jensen confirmed under the date of July 2, 1833, "Joseph the Prophet finished the translation of the Bible."[24] Since its 1993–1994 edition, the LDS *Church Almanac* had concurred with this statement;[25] however, for some reason beginning in the 2001–2002 edition, it began reporting that on July 2, 1833 "the Prophet Joseph Smith finished the translation of the New Testament."[26] This is not accurate since Smith claimed to have finished the New Testament on February 2, 1833.[27]

Because some LDS writers are claiming that Smith never finished his translation, doubt has been cast on whether or not this work should be considered complete. Seely reported, "But throughout his life the Prophet continued to work on the manuscripts, editing and making further changes, preparing them for publication virtually until the time of his death. . . . On many occasions the Prophet expressed his desire and hope that the new translation would eventually be made available to the Church in its entirety. The martyrdom of the Prophet prevented this in his lifetime."[28]

If the JST wasn't completed, a couple of problems arise. For one, if Smith really had been told by God that he was supposed to *finish* the translation (D&C 73:4), it would appear that Smith was either outright disobedient or a bad manager of his time since he lived for more than a decade after this commandment was given. Consider also that 1 Nephi 3:7 states, "The Lord giveth no commandments unto the children of men, save he shall prepare a way for them that they may accomplish the thing which he commandeth them." In addition, since Mormons like to use Doctrine and Covenants 107:91–92 to refer to their current prophet ("a seer, a revelator, a translator, and a prophet, having all the gifts of God which he bestows upon the head of the church"), it would seem that a new and inspired version of the Bible could (and should) be created by the current living prophet to once and for all solve this perceived dilemma.

As mentioned earlier, Smith claimed that "ignorant translators, careless transcribers, or designing and corrupt priests have committed many errors" in the Bible.[29] The irony is that it appears Smith was describing himself. When he commenced to revise the Bible in 1830, he had no expertise in ancient languages. Would this not make him an "ignorant translator"? And if there is a pattern of Smith making alterations that conflicted with ancient texts while at the same time supporting his presently held views, would that not also make him both "designing and corrupt"?

Questions for Discussion

- There is no question that Mormon leaders have been very critical of the Bible's transmission. Why do you think they have cast so much doubt on the accuracy of the biblical text?

- A number of manuscript discoveries in recent times have shown that the biblical text is very reliable when compared to other ancient texts. Why do you think the transcribers took such care in making copies of the Bible?

- F. F. Bruce says that no textual variant in the Bible affects any fact of Christian faith and practice. Why should this be reassuring to the Christian?

Evangelism Tip

Although it is one of their standard works, many Mormons doubt the reliability of the Bible. It is imperative to explain that the Bible is the most reliable ancient document in the world today. Despite the fact that it was written on three continents (Asia, Africa, and Europe) in three different languages (Hebrew, Aramaic, and Greek) by forty different authors in sixty-six different books over a fifteen-hundred-year time frame, the Bible still tells the one story about how God loves people and desires a relationship with them. Have confidence in the Word of God, for it never fails (Isa. 40:8).

Chapter 26

Why do you trust the Bible when it has so many contradictions?

Response Questions

- Could you show me a specific example so we can talk about it?
- If I could explain a perceived contradiction that you believe is in the Bible, would this change your perspective on the reliability of this Scripture?

• • • • • • • • • • • • • • • •

"Furthermore, we are not responsible for the Bible. We reverence it and accept it. Its general message is true, but we have some reservations concerning its accuracy. I think we would do well to acknowledge that there are problems and offer alternate points of understanding whenever possible, based on latter-day revelation or sound reasoning. But we should not feel obliged to assume the 'blame' for difficulties or errors or contradictions in the Bible."[1]

—Brigham Young University professor Robert J. Matthews

———— Summary ————

In their case against Christianity, critics often point to alleged contradictions in the Bible that they believe cannot be resolved. There are some important rules to remember to handle these supposed biblical discrepancies and properly interpret Scripture. When we consider context, the genre of the biblical book, and the use of literary devices, the Bible will be seen as completely consistent and will be properly understood so that the mind of God might be known, helping Christians know how they're supposed to believe and live.

BIBLICAL "CONTRADICTIONS" ARE often cited by skeptical Mormons as evidence that the Bible should not be considered trustworthy. While there are certainly a number of *apparent* difficulties, the problems generally dissipate once the facts are known and the evidence is considered. Instead of allowing anyone to discredit the entire Bible with the charge that it is filled with contradictions, ask for specific examples. The problem with most critics of the Bible is that they usually don't *want* to trust or believe its message, and therefore they do not take the time to carefully research the issue.

Although there are hundreds of possible passages that might be cited, there are several dozen used over and over again.[2] When a problem passage is introduced, turn to it in your Bible. Most of the time, the answer to the difficulty can be discovered by merely considering the context of the passage in question. Pulling a verse out of its original context often makes it look like it contradicts the rest of the Bible. Take, for instance, Ephesians 2:8–9, a passage even some Christians have improperly used to show that good works have no importance at all in the Christian's life. It says, "For by grace are ye saved through faith; and that not of yourselves: it is the gift of God: not of works, lest any man should boast." Reading just one more verse (v. 10) answers those who say works are optional in the Christian's life: "We are his workmanship, created in Christ Jesus unto good works, which God hath before ordained that we should walk in them." This idea that works are an important aspect of one's professed faith is consistent with James 2:14–26, which explains that "faith without works is dead." Again, good works is a part of *sanctification*, not *justification*, in a true believer's life.[3]

Recognizing the following points will help the Christian not only solve the majority of so-called discrepancies but also help clarify common interpretive mistakes as well.

- **Filling in the gaps with new information.** While full details may not always be available, sometimes history and archaeology bring to light issues that help the interpreter grasp the meaning of a passage. For example, the early Old Testament Hebrew texts of Psalm 22:16 were translated, "For dogs have encircled me, an evil congregation surrounded me; like a *lion* my hands and my feet." The Septuagint (a translation of the Hebrew Old Testament into Greek that was completed several centuries before Jesus) used the Greek word for "pierced" instead of "lion." However, before the middle of the twentieth century, the oldest texts available in Hebrew (the Masoretic Text), which dated only as far back as the tenth century A.D., contained the word *ka'ari* (lion), not *ka'aru* (dig or pierce). Even though "lion" doesn't make sense in the psalm's context, there was no evidence in the Hebrew manuscripts that the translation should have read "pierced." In the 1950s, an ancient Hebrew portion of Psalm 22:16 surfaced in a cave in Israel, showing that *ka'aru* was the right word and fitting perfectly with the prediction that the Messiah would suffer by being pierced.[4]

- **Giving the Bible the benefit of the doubt.** The Book of Mormon has had a number of changes to it—including changes in people's names to fit the chronology and the insertion of the word *not* to change the entire meaning of the text—yet rarely do Latter-day Saints say they believe this scripture is true only "as far as it is translated correctly." Just as a defendant is presumed innocent until proven guilty, all we ask is that the critics consider the possibility that the ancient Bible is truly God's Word without allowing bias to affect their consideration of a text.

- **Basing doctrine on more than just one verse.** A single verse often can be turned into a proof text when the original intent of the author is ignored. An improper interpretation is almost always the result. Hence, Mormons use 1 Corinthians 15:29 to argue that vicarious baptisms for those who have died can lead to salvation, even though Hebrews 9:27 and 2 Corinthians 6:2 explain that decisions for God must be made in this life.

- **Expecting different perspectives from eyewitness accounts.** Two news reports on the same incident often explain the events in a different way. In such cases reporters are generally given the benefit of the doubt because they focused on different aspects of the incident. This doesn't mean they were contradictory. The same approach needs to be taken when interpreting the Bible. For example, Matthew 28:5 says that there was an "angel" at the tomb of Christ, while John 20:12 reports that there were "two angels." How many angels were at the tomb? The answer is two, because the rule of thumb is wherever there are two angels, there will always be one. Read the Matthew passage closely, and you will see that he did not say there was "only" one angel. The apostle merely mentioned one because that angel was the focus of his writing.

- **Knowing the difference between what is and what should be.** The reader should never assume something is approved just because the

Bible reports the event. For example, the Old Testament describes polygamous relationships that depict one man being married to more than one wife. The mere reporting of it does not constitute tacit approval of this practice. Like divorce, God merely tolerated it. There is no instance where polygamy helped a man draw closer in his relationship with God. Another example of this is Genesis 3:4–5, where the serpent told Eve, "Ye shall not surely die" for breaking God's command and then added that Adam and Eve would "be as gods, knowing good and evil." While Mormons have considered the fall a necessary act that led to the positive outcome of becoming "as gods" (2 Nephi 2:25 says "Adam fell that men might be"), Jesus said in John 8:44 that Satan is the father of lies, who cannot be trusted. That his words are recorded in Scripture does not give approval to them. Original sin affects all (Rom. 5:17) in a negative way, for it is responsible for both physical and eternal death (Rom. 6:23).

- **Recognizing when language is meant to be figurative rather than literal.** Some have claimed that the Bible is a flat-earth book because Psalm 113:3 reports, "From the rising of the sun unto the going down of the same the Lord's name is to be praised." While it is a fact that the earth rotates as it revolves around the sun, even contemporary meteorologists use the terms *sunrise* and *sunset* in their daily reports. The Bible also should be allowed to use the ordinary language of appearance.

- **Allowing for numbers to be rounded.** Suppose you went to a ball game where 53,322 were in attendance, and someone asked you, "How many were at the game?" If you said 53,000, would it be fair for your friend to accuse you of lying since the number was 53,322? Even if you said 55,000, isn't it understood that rounding numbers up or down is a common occurrence? We find the same thing in the Old Testament books of Samuel, Kings, and Chronicles, which tell the same stories but sometime use different numbers for the same events. It should also be pointed out that the varying numbers do not change the meaning of the accounts or hinder essential doctrines.

- **Understanding the genre of a book.** There are different genres in the Bible, including poetry, parables, and allegory. This needs to be taken into consideration when determining the meaning of any passage. When God is mentioned as having a face, hands, and a side, that doesn't mean He is to be literally pictured as a glorified human being who has flesh and bone. These are simply poetic figures of speech.

Different approaches must be taken when interpreting the different poetical, historical, or doctrinal books.

- **Realizing copies of the Scriptures were made by hand and cannot be considered perfect reproductions of the original.** There is no doubt that there are imperfections in the copies (apographs) of the Bible we have today, and we do not have the original manuscripts (autographs). Through the practice of what is called "textual criticism," however, scholars have a good understanding about where these imperfections are located, and they clearly do not affect a single essential doctrine. Imagine picking up a bottle floating in the ocean with a note containing these letters: "Yuo mus# loook bot# ways be#ore cros#ing thee stret." It's not perfect, but the message can be deciphered and comes through loud and clear. The wealth of manuscript evidence is most helpful in determining the original wording of the Bible in those few places where there is any doubt.

- **Differentiating between a general statement and a prophecy.** Proverbs 22:6 says, "Train up a child in the way he should go: and when he is old, he will not depart from it." This verse is merely a truism and was never meant to say that B will result every time A is completed. Generally, a child who has been properly disciplined will turn into a godly adult, but there are many children who become embarrassments to their parents despite their godly upbringing.

- **Referencing the Old Testament with the New Testament.** Critics love to reference the Mosaic law and show how absurd (at least from the perspective of our modern world) some of its regulations sound, including dietary rules, clothing restrictions, and types of discipline in the theocracy of ancient Israel. Temporary theocratic standards must be separated from the more encompassing message of the New Testament. For example, Peter's vision of the unclean food in Acts 10 explains why Christians no longer follow the dietary laws of the Old Testament.[5]

There is no doubt that studying the Bible requires effort. This is why 2 Timothy 2:15 urges Christians to be diligent in always correctly handling "the word of truth." Whenever a Mormon points out an assumed discrepancy in the Bible and you don't have an immediate answer, don't stress. You might say, "I've never heard that passage explained like that before. Could I go home and look it up and get back to you?" And don't forget to do your homework so that you have an answer when you do get back to your Mormon friend.

In our zeal to defend the Bible, however, we must always be careful that we do not fall into the trap of misusing Scripture ourselves. For example, Revelation 22:18 says, "If any man shall add unto these things, God shall add unto him the plagues that are written in this book." Some Christians use this verse to show Mormons that other LDS scriptures (Pearl of Great Price, Doctrine and Covenants, and the Book of Mormon) should not be "added" to the Bible. But the books of the New Testament had not yet been compiled by this time, so this is not a fair use of this passage. John was referring to "this book," or the book of Revelation. We would agree that unique LDS scriptures are *not* authoritative, but we utilize other arguments to show this to be true. There is no benefit in "cheating" by improperly interpreting Scriptures, even when our interpretation may benefit our cause.

Questions for Discussion

- What is a good strategy for dealing with the argument that the Bible can't be trusted because it contains so many contradictions?

- Why is a verse's context so critical in determining its true meaning?

- What apparent biblical contradiction has recently been brought to your attention? Do some research to find how to answer the charge. One possibility is utilizing this chapter's recommended resources. Or you can go to www.carm.org and click on "Bible Difficulties" to view answers to some of the more common difficulties skeptics raise in their attempts to disprove the Bible.

Evangelism Tip

Bringing up supposed Bible contradictions is a common tactic used by some Latter-day Saints, and it is often utilized as a smoke screen to move a conversation to another topic. Don't allow your discussion to be hijacked in such a manner. Ask, "Isn't the Bible one of your standard works? Aren't you able to trust it?" Point out that the biblical proof texts often referenced in support of LDS doctrines are typically assumed by Mormons to be correct, yet whenever biblical passages conflict with their presuppositions, it is assumed that the Bible somehow can't be trusted. This double standard is called an unlevel playing field.

Chapter 27

Doesn't James 1:5 say we should pray for wisdom? Why won't you pray about the truth claims of Mormonism?

Response Questions

- Have you ever prayed about stealing someone's car or committing adultery? If not, why not?
- Is it possible that you might be sincere but be *sincerely wrong* about your beliefs?
- If praying about a religious book is the way to determine truth, have you prayed about the religious books of other religions such as Islam, Hinduism, and Jehovah's Witnesses? If not, why not?
- Would you leave the LDS Church if I prayed and believed that God told me that the claims of Mormonism weren't true?

● ● ● ● ● ● ● ● ● ● ● ● ● ● ● ● ●

"When people read the Book of Mormon, praying sincerely about its content and Moroni's promise, they will know it is true and the Spirit will move them to seek membership in The Church of Jesus Christ of Latter-day Saints, the church that Joseph Smith was commanded by God to organize."[1]
—Seventy Hugh Pinnock (1934–2000)

———————— Summary ————————

Using references from the Book of Mormon (Moroni 10:4) and the Bible (James 1:5), LDS missionaries encourage prospective converts to pray for guidance in seeking truth. They say that the person who takes their challenge can receive a personal confirmation about the Book of Mormon (and, ultimately, Mormonism), thus validating the prayer. While on the surface this advice sounds plausible, even spiritual, prospective converts in the New Testament were never commanded to pray about the truthfulness of Scripture or a particular religion. If a religion is true, it should withstand tests that go beyond such a subjective examination.

LATTER-DAY SAINTS GENERALLY BELIEVE their ability to discern doctrinal truth comes through a "personal testimony," which is also known as a "burning in the bosom." There are several passages Mormons reference, but most prominent is James 1:5 in the New Testament. This was a pivotal verse for Mormonism's founder Joseph Smith (1805–1844), who claimed that he prayed to God for wisdom when he was fourteen years old. James 1:5 says, "If any of you lack wisdom, let him ask of God, that giveth to all men liberally, and upbraideth not; and it shall be given him." The official First Vision account says that Smith's prayer was answered in 1820 as he knelt in the woods near his upstate New York home.[2]

Located in the last chapter of the Book of Mormon, Moroni 10:4 also is regularly referenced by Mormon missionaries. It says, "And when ye shall receive these things, I would exhort you that ye would ask God, the Eternal Father, in the name of Christ, if these things are not true; and if ye shall ask with a sincere heart, with real intent, having faith in Christ, he will manifest the truth of it unto you, by the power of the Holy Ghost." An investigator is told that, through prayer, God will help a person understand that Mormonism really is true. Doctrine and Covenants 9:8 reads, "But, behold, I say unto you, that you must study it out in your mind; then you must ask me if it be right, and if it is right I will cause that your bosom shall burn within you; therefore, you shall feel that it is right."

While Mormon testimonies will vary, they often sound very close to the following: "I testify to you that Joseph Smith was a prophet of God, that the Book of Mormon is a true history of ancient America, and that Christ's restored church is led by a true and living prophet." Even when confronted with information that is contrary to their belief system, many Mormons remain firm in their faith by clinging to their subjective feelings.

Tad R. Callister, a member of the Presidency of the Seventy, told this story at the end of a general conference address:

Some years ago I attended one of our worship services in Toronto, Canada. A 14-year-old girl was the speaker. She said that she had been discussing religion with one of her friends at school. Her friend said to her, "What religion do you belong to?" She replied, "The Church of Jesus Christ of Latter-day Saints, or Mormons." Her friend replied, "I know that church, and I know it's not true." "How do you know?" came the reply. "Because," said her friend, "I have researched it." "Have you read the Book of Mormon?" "No," came the answer. "I haven't." Then this sweet young girl responded, "Then you haven't researched my church, because I have read every page of the Book of Mormon and I know it's true."[3]

Notice how the Mormon girl's subjective feeling outweighed her friend's research. Did the Mormon girl in this story ask her friend to see what she found? Callister doesn't say. The conclusion is that it is somehow heroic to allow feelings to take precedence over investigation.

Setting the Test's Parameters

While it is important to be respectful to our Latter-day Saint friends and not minimize their experiences, we need to point out that the rules have been rigged since the prayer's request really has but one answer. After all, the investigator who declines the invitation to pray may be accused of not believing in prayer. On the other hand, those who agree to pray but don't receive the "right" answer will probably be thought of as not having a sincere heart, real intent, or adequate faith. In response to the question "Shouldn't Moroni's promise always work" with someone who "has not received a testimony of its truthfulness?" Daniel Ludlow, the director of LDS Church Correlation Review, confirms this suspicion:

God cannot and does not lie, and his promises made through his prophets are sure. Therefore, any person who claims to have followed the various requirements but says he has not gained a testimony should check to see which step he has not followed faithfully or completely:

1. He should read and ponder the Book of Mormon—all of it.
2. He should remember the methods God has used in working with the peoples of both the Book of Mormon and the Bible—and ponder these things in his heart.
3. He should put himself in a frame of mind where he would be willing

to accept (receive) all of "these things"—the Book of Mormon, the Bible, and the way God works with men.

4. "With a sincere heart, with real intent, having faith in Christ," he should ask God, the Eternal Father, in the name of Jesus Christ "if these things are not true."

5. He should be able to recognize the promptings and feelings which will be evidences to him of the truth of "these things" (including the Book of Mormon) as they are made manifest unto him "by the power of the Holy Ghost."[4]

There is a psychological edge that the Mormon missionaries have when someone agrees to their challenge. After all, the investigator may eventually get the "right" answer in an attempt to please the missionaries, close family members, or friends who have come to the same conclusion. In the end, one's good feelings may win the day, even if the object of the prayer is false. It should be noted that Joseph Smith disregarded the immediate context of James 1:5, which speaks of gaining wisdom, not knowledge. Wisdom is the proper application of knowledge. In this verse James tells his Christian audience to ask God for wisdom when they are undergoing trials and temptations, not for testing various truth claims.[5] First John 4:1 tells believers to "try [test] the spirits." Why? Because many false prophets have gone out into the world. The Bereans in Acts 17:11 were considered noble because they "searched the scriptures daily" and tested Paul's words against what God had already revealed. In other words, Christians are to test all truth claims with the Bible, not with subjective experiences, even if that experience involves a supernatural "vision."

When a Mormon friend brings up Moroni 10:4 in a conversation, you might ask your acquaintance whether his or her feelings have always been accurate. At one time or another, all of us have been fooled by our feelings, no matter how sincere we might have been. For example, Mormons believe that marriage is not only for life but also for eternity. Should it be assumed that the many Mormon couples who are divorced did not pray about their relationships beforehand? Surely knowing information about another person that could have exposed potential behavior problems—such as drug addiction, sex addiction, pornography issues, inward apathy to God, or repressed anger—would have helped with making a more informed decision. Yet how many Mormons must have "felt" God's approval in relationships that were tragically doomed from the beginning?

The Bible makes it very clear that subjective feelings can be deceptive. Jeremiah 17:9 says, "The heart is deceitful above all things, and desperately wicked: who can know it?" Proverbs 14:12 warns, "There is a way which seemeth right unto a man, but the end thereof are the ways of death," while Proverbs 28:26 adds that only fools trust in their heart. Because everyone is a fallen and sinful creature, it is possible to be swayed by emotions and desires. To *believe* something is true merely because one *feels* it to be true is no guarantee of truth. Jesus commanded His followers in Mark 12:30 to love God "with all thy heart, and with all thy soul, and with all thy *mind*, and with all thy strength."

Paul explained in 2 Timothy 2:15 that the believer must make the effort to study in order to correctly understand truth. In the next chapter (3:16–17), he added that all Scripture given by inspiration of God is "profitable for doctrine, for reproof, for correction, for instruction in righteousness" so that the man or woman of God might be competent and equipped to do good works. Christians are commanded in 1 Thessalonians 5:21 to "prove all things; hold fast that which is good." While it is true that faith does involve believing things that can't be proven, it is foolishness to believe something that has already been disproven. If the Bible disproves a spiritual truth claim, it must be rejected.

If praying about the Book of Mormon is the means for finding truth, shouldn't this test also apply to other religious books? It is curious how very few Mormons have taken the time and effort to read (and pray about) the scriptures of other religions. Using the rationale that people should pray about Mormonism's scripture, why shouldn't every religion's scriptures—such as the Qu'ran (Islam), the Vedas and the Bhagavad Gita (Hinduism), and the Tripitaka (Buddhism)—also be read and contemplated through prayer? How can the Mormon know the accuracy of Mormonism until he or she personally tests all religions in this way? Though we should most certainly use prayer to guide us in our search for truth, it should not be the only litmus test. Hopefully, prayer will lead us to the information we need in order to make an informed and proper decision.

Questions for Discussion

- Have you ever "felt" you were right about something only to find out later that you were wrong? Use a personal example to explain why feelings should not be trusted when it comes to a belief system.

- How did Joseph Smith take James 1:5 out of its context? What is a better explanation of this verse?

- Suppose a Mormon gives his or her testimony about why the LDS Church is true. What question could you ask that would show how a testimony alone is not a good indicator of whether or not something is true?

—————————— Evangelism Tip ——————————

Every faithful Mormon has a testimony, which is often shared with non-members at the end of spiritual conversations. When this testimony is told, be sure to let the person know you also have a testimony. You may want to tell your story about how you were once lost but now are saved and how grateful you are that God included you in His sovereign plan. Practice this testimony in front of a mirror, and then try it out with your friends. Your testimony demonstrates how God has personally worked in your life, showing that Mormons are not the only ones who have a spiritual story to tell.

Chapter 28

To whom is Jesus referring when He mentions the "other sheep" in John 10:16?

Response Questions

- What evidence is there that John 10:16 was referring to the Book of Mormon people?
- Why does the Bible seem to indicate in the New Testament Epistles that this was referring to the Gentiles?

• • • • • • • • • • • • • • • •

"The 'other sheep' here referred to constituted the separated flock or remnant of the house of Joseph, who, six centuries prior to the birth of Christ, had been miraculously detached from the Jewish fold in Palestine, and had been taken beyond the great deep to the American continent."[1]

—Apostle James E. Talmage (1862–1933)

Summary

Mormons use John 10:16 to show how the Book of Mormon was prophesied in the Bible. However, the New Testament indicates that Jesus was referring to the Gentiles, as prophesied in the Old Testament. Jesus' words were fulfilled, as indicated throughout the book of Acts and the Epistles. Those listening to Jesus would have had no understanding of a people existing on another continent. Because an interpretation should not be forced upon a passage, the most plausible meaning of the verse is that the Gentiles, not the Book of Mormon peoples, would be allowed to enter into God's fold.

MORMON LEADERS HAVE taught that the reference to "other sheep" in John 10:16 points to two groups of people known as the Nephites and the Lamanites. The verse reads, "And other sheep I have, which are not of this fold: them also I must bring, and they shall hear my voice; and there shall be one fold, and one shepherd." Third Nephi 15:12–24 in the Book of Mormon purportedly quotes Jesus speaking to the people in the Americas:

> Ye are my disciples . . . And behold, this is the land of your inheritance; and the Father hath given it unto you. And not at any time hath the Father given me commandment that I should tell it unto your brethren at Jerusalem . . . This much did the Father command me, that I should tell unto them: That other sheep I have which are not of this fold; them also I must bring, and they shall hear my voice; and there shall be one fold, and one shepherd. And they understood me not, for they supposed it had been the Gentiles; for they understood not that the Gentiles should be converted through their preaching. And they understood me not that I said they shall hear my voice; and they understood me not that the Gentiles should not at any time hear my voice—that I should not manifest myself unto them save it were by the Holy Ghost. But behold, ye have both heard my voice, and seen me; and ye are my sheep, and ye are numbered among those whom the Father hath given me.

Recounting his speaking to a group of Christian ministers, Apostle LeGrand Richards (1886–1983) said,

> I asked those men if they knew anything about those other sheep or the fulfillment of the promise of the Lord that he would visit them, and they would hear his voice, and there should be one fold and one shepherd. None of them could tell, and so I just turned to the Book of Mormon and showed them that when Jesus, following his crucifixion and resurrection and ascension, visited his people here in the land of America, he told them they were the other sheep of whom he spoke to his disciples in Jerusalem, and he said that never at any time did the Lord command him that he should tell his disciples in Jerusalem who the other sheep were; only that he had other sheep that were not of that fold, and them should he visit. He told them they were the other sheep. No one can answer intelligently

that statement in John 10:16 without the knowledge that the Book of Mormon has brought to us.[2]

Apostle Dallin H. Oaks addressed a 2006 general conference, saying,

> The Book of Mormon adds to our knowledge of how our Savior's earthly ministry reached out to all of His scattered flock. In addition to His ministry in what we now call the Middle East, the Book of Mormon records His appearance and teachings to the Nephites on the American continent (see 3 Nephi 11–28). There He repeated that the Father had commanded him to visit the other sheep which were not of the land of Jerusalem (see 3 Nephi 16:1; John 10:16). He also said that he would visit others "who [had] not as yet heard [His] voice" (see 3 Nephi 16:2–3). As prophesied centuries earlier (see 2 Nephi 29:12), the Savior told His followers in the Americas that He was going "to show [himself]" to these "lost tribes of Israel, for they are not lost unto the Father, for he knoweth whither he hath taken them" (3 Nephi 17:4).[3]

Gentiles or Book of Mormon people?

Mormons have insisted that the "other sheep" Jesus said would hear His voice (John 10:16) were people who would actually hear His literal voice. Since Jesus did not specifically address the Gentiles, they argue that He must have been speaking about the characters chronicled in the Book of Mormon. While this might seem like a plausible argument, the problem lies in the fact that the Bible often uses this type of language to describe a thought or message being transmitted by some means other than the actual speaking of a person. For instance, time and time again, the children of Israel were commanded to listen to "the voice" of the Lord.[4] Yet rarely do the children of Israel ever actually hear the voice of the Lord Himself. Instead, God used Moses and other prophets as His mouthpieces.

When it comes to John 10:16, the Christian church has traditionally understood the "other sheep" to mean the Gentiles. Protestant Reformer John Calvin wrote, "Though some refer this indiscriminately to all, both Jews and Gentiles, who were not yet disciples of Christ, yet I have no doubt that he had in his eye the calling of the Gentiles. For he gives the appellation *fold* to the assemblage of the ancient people, by which they were separated from the other nations of the world, and united into one body as the heritage of God."[5]

That John 10:16 is a reference to the Gentiles is by far the majority understanding of the text. For example, Edwin Blum says it "refers to Gentiles who would believe."[6] Merrill C. Tenney wrote, "The sheep 'not of this sheep pen' probably refers to the Gentiles whom Jesus sent his disciples to (Matt 28:19) and whom he wished to include in his salvation. He stresses this idea of unity later in his farewell prayer (17:20)."[7] F. F. Bruce explained, "These words of Jesus, then, point to the Gentile mission and to the formation of the community, comprising believing Jews and believing Gentiles, in which there is 'neither Jew nor Greek' (Gal. 3:28; Col. 3:11). The Jewish 'sheep' had to be let out of the 'fold' before they could be united with the 'other sheep' to form one new flock."[8]

Though Jesus' specific ministry was directed toward the Jews, Christ did not ignore the Gentile people living in Palestine during His mortal ministry. Consider the following verses:

- Matthew 12:9–21: Jesus healed a Jewish man's hand on the Sabbath. When challenged by the Pharisees for performing such a deed on the Sabbath, Jesus again spoke of ministering to His *sheep*. When the Pharisees made their rejection of Jesus clear, He quoted from Isaiah 42:1–4, a prophecy that speaks of God's servant who "shall bring forth judgment to the Gentiles" and in whose name they will trust.
- Matthew 15:22–28: A Canaanite woman whose daughter was "vexed with a devil" approached Jesus on behalf of her child. When Jesus tested her faith by explaining that He was "sent but unto the lost sheep of the house of Israel," she humbly replied that even lowly dogs "eat of the crumbs which fall from their masters' table." In response, Jesus granted her request. Jesus' use of the word *sheep* cannot be ignored since it is the same language He used in John 10. His actions in this account fulfills perfectly what was spoken of Him long before.
- John 4:5–26: Jesus conversed with the Samaritan woman at Jacob's well in Sychar.

Consider, as well, passages from the Old Testament book of Isaiah:

- Isaiah 11:1, 10: God's prophet predicts the day when the "root of Jesse" shall stand as a banner to the people and the Gentiles shall seek Him. In Romans 15:9–12, the apostle Paul refers to this passage as being fulfilled in Christ.

- Isaiah 55:5; 56:5–6: God calls unto all who are spiritually thirsty, including those who are not recognized as a nation, and the Lord promises to give them an everlasting name that is better than that given to "sons and . . . daughters." This name would be given to the "sons of the stranger," an expression used to speak of foreigners in Israel who did not have inherited rights.[9]
- Isaiah 60:2–3: It was predicted that there would be a day when a deep darkness would cover the people, while at the same time, "the Gentiles shall come to thy light, and kings to the brightness of thy rising." The prophet Malachi (1:11) also foretold of the day when God's name shall be "great among the Gentiles."

Following Christ's death and resurrection, the disciples carried on the tradition of taking the gospel to the house of Israel. However, when the Jews rejected Paul's message on his first missionary journey to Antioch of Pisidia, he declared in Acts 13:46 that he would direct his message to the Gentiles. In doing so, he quoted from Isaiah 49:6, which states that God would give a "light to the Gentiles" that would bring "salvation unto the end of the earth." This emphasis is further seen in Ephesians 2:14. Speaking of how the blood of Christ has brought together Jews and Gentiles, who were alienated from the commonwealth of Israel, Paul stated, "For he is our peace, who hath made both one, and hath broken down the middle wall of partition between us." It is difficult to ignore the similarity between this passage and John 10:16.

In his letter to the Roman Christians, Paul reiterated the fact that the nation of Israel had rejected the gospel message, thereby opening the prophetic door for the gospel to be preached to the Gentiles. In Romans 10:12, he pointed out that as far as God is concerned, "there is no difference between the Jew and the Greek: for the same Lord over all is rich unto all that call upon him." He then reminded his readers that Moses prophesied that God would "provoke [Israel] to jealousy by them that are no people . . . I was found of them that sought me not; I was made manifest unto them that asked not after me" (vv. 19–20). The pagan nations of the ancient world had no desire to seek after the God of Israel; yet God, in His mercy, was going to seek after them. Such a description seems to disqualify the people mentioned in the Book of Mormon since the so-called Nephites are portrayed as a people who had a history of seeking after the Lord.

In Romans 11:13, Paul spoke of himself as the "apostle of the Gentiles." He then warned his Gentile readers to be careful lest they allow pride to enter their hearts over the fact that Israel had been "broken off" of the tree while they themselves were "grafted in" (vv. 17–18). This distinction between Jews and Gentiles fits perfectly with what Jesus predicted in John 10:16. In Ephesians 3:3–6, Paul revealed a mystery that "in other ages was not made known unto the sons of men" but had only recently been revealed to God's people. This mystery is explained as the inclusion of the Gentiles as "fellowheirs" who would become "partakers of his [God's] promise in Christ by the gospel."

Though the Old Testament gave scattered hints to such a time, these references—like those to the ministry of Christ Himself—were not fully understood until that time actually arrived. It was only within the context of Christ's sacrifice that the references to the inclusion of the Gentiles along with Jews in God's plan became clear. The once-separated Gentiles were now on equal footing with their Jewish counterparts. Through the acceptance of the gospel, they too could experience the intimate love and personal relationship with their Creator. With all the evidence considered, it is a much more plausible interpretation that Jesus was referring to the Gentiles in John 10:16 and not the Book of Mormon people-groups.

Questions for Discussion

- Many Mormons will use John 10:16 as evidence in support of the Book of Mormon as scripture. Provide a good reason why this verse was talking about the Gentiles and not the Book of Mormon people groups.

- Mormons consider the Book of Mormon "another testament" of Jesus Christ. How could you demonstrate the falseness of this premise? If, in fact, there were no Book of Mormon people, how would that affect the Mormon position?

--- Evangelism Tip ---

Because the evidence for the Book of Mormon from outside sources is not very strong, many Mormons grasp at straws to support their view that the American continent was once the home of former Jews. When John 10:16 is raised, be sure to let your Mormon friend know that Old Testament prophecies overwhelmingly point to the Gentiles and not the Lamanites and/ or Nephites as the "other sheep" in this verse. Pointing to pertinent New Testament references that make this connection hopefully will expose the weak LDS position.

Chapter 29

Why doesn't your church build temples?

Response Questions

- Wasn't the main purpose of the temple in Jerusalem to sacrifice animals and atone for sin? If your temple ceremony is really a "restoration," why doesn't this practice take place in your temples?
- Is there any evidence from either the Bible or history to support marriages and work on behalf of the dead taking place in the Jerusalem temple?

• • • • • • • • • • • • • • • •

"Obedience to the sacred covenants made in temples qualifies us for eternal life—the greatest gift of God to man."[1]

—Apostle Russell M. Nelson

————————————— Summary ——————————————

The temple was a sacred place for biblical Jews. Once a year the high priest went into the Holy of Holies in the temple and made atonement for Israel. Worshippers also were called to bring blood sacrifices to the temple to be offered to God by Levite priests. In contrast, Mormon temples are used for marriages, sealings, and temple endowment ceremonies, as well as baptisms on behalf of the deceased. None of these have their origins in the biblical temple. There seem to be more differences than there are similarities between the Jewish and Mormon temples.

SPECIAL MORMON BUILDINGS called temples are located throughout the world, with secret ceremonies taking place inside that supposedly were initiated in biblical times. While some outside observers might assume that temples are similar in function to LDS chapel buildings, most of what takes place inside does not even closely resemble a traditional worship service or, for that matter, the temple worship from biblical times. Occultic symbolism also plays a role in Mormon temples.

The Purpose of Today's Mormon Temples

Unlike the temple of biblical times, LDS temples are used by worthy living members to perform proxy baptisms for the dead, to participate in the endowment, and to perform sealings for time and eternity. Vicarious baptisms on behalf of those who are deceased account for a great majority of the activity behind temple doors.[2] The endowment involves ceremonies in which the members learn about the plan of salvation while making covenants (promises), which Apostle Russell M. Nelson said "will qualify you and your family for the blessings of eternal life."[3] He also said, "The possibility of eternal life—even exaltation—is available to us through our obedience to covenants made and ordinances received in holy temples of God."[4] The endowment takes place shortly before a member goes on a mission (age nineteen for males, age twenty-one for females) or before they are married. "Single members in their late teens or early twenties who have not received a mission call and are not engaged to be married in the temple are generally not recommended to receive their own endowment."[5]

A sealing takes place only in the temple and allows a Mormon couple to be married for both time (this life) and eternity. Mormon couples are not encouraged to get married for time only in chapels outside the temple. President Harold B. Lee (1899–1973) wrote, "If Satan and his hosts can persuade you to take the broad highway of worldly marriage that ends with death, he has defeated you in your opportunity for the highest degree of eternal happiness through marriage and increase throughout eternity. It should now be clear to your reasoning why the Lord declared that in order to obtain the highest degree in the Celestial glory, a person must enter into the new and everlasting covenant of marriage. If he does not, he cannot obtain it."[6]

Children born to parents who were previously sealed in the temple are "born in the covenant" and are automatically sealed at birth. Parents who were not originally married in the temple can bring their children to be sealed in order to become an "eternal family." According to one church magazine,

The Salt Lake City temple, completed in 1893. The temple is a place where qualified Mormons perform works for themselves as well as their deceased ancestors.

"This means that if we are faithful to our covenants, our family relationships will continue for eternity."[7] Members are not allowed to talk about the covenants and ordinance ceremonies that take place in the temple. They "are too sacred to be discussed in detail outside the temple," and thus members are warned, "Do not be casual when talking about your experiences in the temple."[8]

Certain requirements must be met in order to attend the temple. One church manual says, "Before we can go to the temple, we must be active, worthy members of the Church for at least one year. Men must hold the Melchizedek Priesthood. We must be interviewed by the branch president or bishop. If he finds us worthy, he will give us a temple recommend. If we are not worthy, he will counsel with us and help us set goals to become worthy to go to the temple."[9]

Apostle Boyd K. Packer explains what takes place in the interview: "Here the member is asked searching questions about his or her conduct, worthiness, and loyalty to the Church and its officers. The person must certify that he or she is morally clean and is keeping the Word of Wisdom [including no alcohol, drugs, or hot drinks], paying a full tithing, living in harmony with the teachings of the Church, and not maintaining any affiliation or sympathy with apostate groups."[10] Nelson added, "The requirements are simple. Succinctly stated, an individual is required to keep the commandments of Him whose house it is. He has set standards. We enter the temple as His guests."[11] Those who do not meet these requirements are not given the all-important temple recommend card needed for entry. Even parents of a child getting married in the temple are not allowed to witness the wedding ceremony if the church does not consider them "temple worthy." President Thomas S. Monson told his people that obtaining this recommend is vital:

> If you have not yet been to the temple or if you *have* been but currently do not qualify for a recommend, there is no more important goal for you to work toward than being worthy to go to the temple. Your sacrifice may be bringing your life into compliance with what is required to receive a recommend, perhaps by forsaking long-held habits which disqualify you. It may be having the faith and the discipline to pay your tithing. Whatever it is, qualify to enter the temple of God. Secure a temple recommend and regard it as a precious possession, for such it is. Until you have entered the house of the Lord and have received all the blessings which await you there, you have not obtained everything the Church has to offer. The all-important and crowning blessings of membership in the Church are those blessings which we receive in the temples of God.[12]

Apostle Mark E. Petersen (1900–1984) claimed that the LDS ceremony actually follows an ancient model. He wrote, "In Biblical times sacred ordinances were administered in holy edifices for the spiritual salvation of ancient Israel. The buildings thus were not synagogues, nor any other ordinary places of worship. . . . Following the pattern of Biblical days, the Lord again in our day has provided these ordinances for the salvation of all who will believe, and directs that temples be built in which to perform those sacred rites."[13]

One church manual claims that "the Church today teaches the same principles and performs the same ordinances as were performed in the days of Jesus."[14] However, it also quotes the Book of Mormon (3 Nephi 19:19–20) to show that "sacrifice of blood was ended" after the destruction of the Jerusalem temple in A.D. 70 and that God now "requires a different kind of offering." So while the offering of blood sacrifices of animals was one of the main functions of biblical priests, the manual states that committed followers of God should become, as Paul said in Romans 12:1, "living sacrifices." And it adds, "If we are to be a living sacrifice, we must be willing to give everything we have for The Church of Jesus Christ of Latter-day Saints."[15]

If the LDS religion is truly a restoration of biblical Christianity, it would make sense that today's temple rites should be similar to what took place in ancient Israel. Yet there are many differences, including the following.

- The Jews recognized only one temple located in Jerusalem, while the LDS Church has dozens of temples scattered across the globe.
- The primary activity at the Jerusalem temple was the sacrifice of animals as atonement for the sins of the people. Worshippers in ancient Israel went to the temple with an attitude of unworthiness before an all-holy God. They approached His temple with humility as they looked to have their sins covered. In stark contrast, Mormons enter their temples with a positive sense of worthiness. A person cannot enter a Mormon temple (after it is dedicated) unless he or she is considered "worthy."
- The priests officiating in the Jerusalem temple had to be from the tribe of Levi and the family of Aaron. This was commanded in Numbers 3:6–10. The LDS Church ignores such commands and allows its "temple-worthy" members who have no such background to officiate in its temples.

- Wedding ceremonies did not take place in the Jerusalem temple, while this is a common practice in modern LDS temples.
- While there were no marriages performed in the Jerusalem temple, many Mormon families have been "sealed" for time and eternity in LDS temples.
- While it was not a practice ever performed in the Jerusalem temple, proxy baptism for the dead by living members of the LDS Church is the most common activity in Mormon temples.

Occultic Symbolism in the Temple?

The LDS Church has received much criticism regarding the many inverted pentagrams that are displayed on several of its temples, including both the exterior and interior of the temple in Nauvoo, Illinois. Several of these stars are located on the perimeter of the temple, and more than a hundred inverted stars can be found in the assembly room. Inverted pentagrams also can be found on the upper walls and embroidered into the curtains of the celestial room. Some have wondered why a church claiming to be Christian would blatantly use emblems currently associated with occultism as a temple decoration.

Mormon apologists come to their church's defense by insisting that pentagrams historically have been a positive symbol and only recently have become a symbol of evil. Therefore, they claim any connection between occultism and the Nauvoo pentagrams is nothing more than sensationalism. The five-pointed star is a simple design that has shown up in the artwork of several cultures. Determining when the inverted star actually came to be known as a symbol of evil can be confusing. There is no general consensus among historians, and even Wiccans and witches are not in full agreement. Some believe this happened around the time of the Inquisition, while others suggest it could have been as late as the nineteenth century.

At one time, Christians even used the pentagram, or pentacle, in their artwork. In fact, at one time the five-pointed star was commonly known as the "five wounds of Christ." However, the time frame in which Christians used this symbol tends to discount many LDS assertions. Today, the inverted pentagram is associated with evil. Of that there is little doubt. Consider the following.

- "The pentagram with one point upwards repels evil, but a reversed pentagram, with two points upwards, is a symbol of the Devil and attracts sinister forces because it is upside down and because it stands for the number 2. It represents the great Goat of the witches' sabbath and the two upward points are the Goat's horn."[16]

- "The spiritual knowledge of the Five-pointed Star is identical with its practical application. Let us beware that the figure is always well drawn, leaving no open space, through which the enemy can enter and disturb the harmony existing in the Pentagon. Let us keep the figure always upright, with the topmost triangle pointing to heaven, for it is the seat of Wisdom, and if the figure is reversed perversion and evil will be the result."[17]

- "*Inverted Pentacle.* The sacred symbol of Witchcraft often is misunderstood because of associations of the inverted pentacle, with single point down and double points up, with the infernal. If an upright five-pointed star represents God or the deity, then the reverse typically represents Satan . . . In Europe, some Witches have used the inverted pentacle to denote the second-degree rank. This use has declined, because of the association of the symbol with Satanism."[18]

Some Mormons argue that the artwork in the temple reconstructed in Nauvoo was based on its design from the nineteenth century, when the pentagram was considered a harmless symbol. When this temple was rebuilt and opened in 2002, the leaders decided to retain these symbols despite their current (and obvious) link to occultism The Mormon leadership was aware of the controversial nature of the inverted pentagrams, but they chose to ignore it.

Charles W. Allen explained how he was commissioned by the LDS Church to build the leaded glass stars that encircle the outside of the Nauvoo temple. The plan was to remain faithful to the original design, so Allen commenced to put together stars that would be placed in an inverted fashion. However, Allen noted that on May 8, 2001, he was approached by three men from his church. He writes, "Ron Prince, Cory Karl and Keith Stepan were in the shop this morning to see how I was doing and to take a look at the colored glass in the star sash. They really liked what they saw. Keith asked me whether, if President Hinckley wanted to have the star pointed in an up position, that would be possible? I said yes, that all I had to do is to rotate the sash. He made a recorded note of that for his next meeting with President Hinckley. There is some concern by members of the Temple Committee that the upside down star would be interpreted as a Satanic symbol which some cults believe in today."[19]

This paragraph is very telling since even some members of the temple committee were apprehensive as to how the stars would be interpreted. It also shows that President Hinckley had the final say as to which direction the stars would point. Allowing this symbol to be used in a modern context is akin to using the Nazi swastika today, with the rationalization that there is no harm with the symbol since it was not always associated with Adolph Hitler.

The Jewish Temple and Early Christianity

Following Jesus' death and resurrection, Jewish temple worship lost its significance with His followers, as a new covenant was established. Hebrews 8:12–13 states, "For I will be merciful toward their iniquities, and I will remember their sins no more. In speaking of a new covenant, he makes the first one obsolete. And what is becoming obsolete and growing old is ready to vanish away" (ESV).

The old system no longer is needed, as Hebrews 9:11–15 explains.

> But when Christ appeared as a high priest of the good things that have come, then through the greater and more perfect tent (not made with hands, that is, not of this creation) he entered once for all into the holy places, not by means of the blood of goats and calves but by means of his own blood, thus securing an eternal redemption. For if the blood of goats and bulls, and the sprinkling of defiled persons with the ashes of a heifer, sanctify for the purification of the flesh, how much more will the blood of Christ, who through the eternal Spirit offered himself without blemish to God, purify our conscience from dead works to serve the living God. Therefore he is the mediator of a new covenant, so that those who are called may receive the promised eternal inheritance, since a death has occurred that redeems them from the transgressions committed under the first covenant. (ESV)

According to the Bible, there is no need for further animal sacrifices. Temple work was fulfilled in the sacrifice of Jesus Christ. It is for these reasons that Christians do not participate in temple ceremonies. What takes place in Mormon temples has no historical precedent, for LDS leaders have turned the temple into something it was never intended to be.[20]

Questions for Discussion

- Why do you think attending the temple has such a strong appeal for many Latter-day Saints?

- If there are more differences than similarities between the biblical temple rituals and those performed in Mormon temples, why do you think Mormons continue to draw what seems to be a flawed parallel?

- Some argue that the pentagram hasn't always been an occultic symbol. Should this absolve the LDS Church of any and all criticism for its modern use of this symbol? Why or why not?

--------------------------- Evangelism Tip ---------------------------

Mormon leaders have claimed that what takes place in LDS temples is very similar to what took place during biblical times. However, the evidence for this is nonexistent. Ask your Mormon friend where the Bible—or, for that matter, the Book of Mormon—describes anything like the present activities in Mormon temples taking place in the Jewish temple in Jerusalem. Rather, the biblical temple was reserved for offerings and sacrifices carried out through priests of the tribe of Levi and the family of Aaron. Emphasize the work that Jesus has already done on the Christian's behalf, and explain why a physical temple is no longer needed today.

Chapter 30

Didn't the apostle Paul say there were three degrees of glory?

Response Questions

- How did you conclude from Paul's words that these were eternal destinations?
- Where in the Book of Mormon does it teach the idea that there are three degrees of glory?

• • • • • • • • • • • • • • • •

"There are, of course, three kingdoms of glory to which resurrected persons will go—the celestial, terrestrial, and telestial. (1 Cor. 15:39–42; D. C. 76.) Of these three, only the celestial is the kingdom of God; it is the kingdom reserved for the saints who obey the laws and ordinances of the gospel. Great hosts of persons will go to the other kingdoms and hence will not attain salvation in the full gospel sense."[1]

—Brigham Young University Professor Daniel H. Ludlow

—————— Summary ——————

Based primarily on a revelation Joseph Smith said he received from God, the idea that there are three heavens (or degrees)—the celestial, terrestrial, and telestial kingdoms—is very much a part of Mormon doctrine. Neither the Bible nor the Book of Mormon teaches that people go to one of three kingdoms based on belief and personal performance during their mortal probation on earth. Instead, the Bible teaches that there are only two eternal destinations—heaven or hell.

THE THREE HEAVENS DESCRIBED in Doctrine and Covenants section 76 are called the celestial, terrestrial, and telestial kingdoms. First Corinthians 15:40–41 is used to support this idea. It reads, "There are also celestial bodies, and bodies terrestrial: but the glory of the celestial is one, and the glory of the terrestrial is another. There is one glory of the sun, and another glory of the moon, and another glory of the stars: for one star differeth from another star in glory."

In appealing to this passage, a missionary manual explains,

> Because God rewards everyone according to deeds done in the body, there are different kingdoms of glory to which we may be assigned after the Judgment. Those who have repented of their sins and received the ordinances of the gospel and kept the associated covenants will be cleansed by the Atonement of Christ. They will receive exaltation in the highest kingdom, also known as the celestial kingdom. They will live in God's presence, become like Him, and receive a fullness of joy. They will live together for eternity with those of their family who qualify. In the scriptures this kingdom is compared to the glory or brightness of the sun. People who do not accept the fullness of the gospel of Jesus Christ but live honorable lives will receive a place in the terrestrial kingdom. This kingdom is compared to the glory of the moon. Those who continued in their sins and did not repent in this life will receive their reward in the lowest kingdom, which is called the telestial kingdom. This kingdom is compared to the glory of the stars.[2]

Another biblical passage used to support this teaching is 2 Corinthians 12:2, where Paul wrote, "I knew a man in Christ above fourteen years ago, (whether in the body, I cannot tell; or whether out of the body, I cannot tell: God knoweth;) such an one caught up to the third heaven." Is it possible the Bible teaches three separate levels of heaven?

The Biblical Meaning of the "Third Heaven"

While Paul certainly referred to a "third heaven" in 2 Corinthians 12:2, there is no reason to believe he was referring to one of three distinct eternal destinations of mankind. To properly interpret Scripture, the context of a passage must be grasped, including what the listeners of Paul's day would have understood it to mean. It is likely they would have interpreted Paul's three heavens as the atmospheric heaven, the celestial heaven, and the believer's heaven. Scripture supports this assertion. For example, Deuteronomy 11:11 refers to the atmospheric heaven, where rain and clouds are formed: "But the land, whither ye go to possess it, is a land of hills and valleys, and drinketh water of the rain of heaven." Psalm 147:8 likewise describes God as He "who covereth the heaven with clouds, who prepareth rain for the earth, who maketh grass to grow upon the mountains." Matthew 24:30 tells about Christ's return through this heaven: "And they shall see the Son of man coming in the clouds of heaven with power and great glory." Genesis 1:14 speaks of the celestial heaven, the abode of the sun, moon, and stars: "And God said, Let there be lights in the firmament of the heaven to divide the day from the night; and let them be for signs, and for seasons, and for days, and years."

Finally, there is the heaven the Bible calls the "dwelling place" of God, which is referenced many times in the Old Testament. Isaiah 63:15 says, "Look down from heaven, and behold from the habitation of thy holiness and of thy glory: where is thy zeal and thy strength, the sounding of thy bowels and of thy mercies toward me? are they restrained?" Psalm 102:19 says, "For he hath looked down from the height of his sanctuary; from heaven did the LORD behold the earth." And 2 Kings 2:11 says it was into this heaven that "Elijah went up by a whirlwind."

New Testament commentator Philip E. Hughes agrees with the above assessment, writing, "The probability is that Paul had in mind the conception of the heavens as threefold. Thus [Johann Albrecht] Bengel explains that the first heaven was that of the clouds, that is, of the earth's atmosphere, the second that of the stars (cf. the appearance of 'the lights in the firmament of heaven' on the fourth day of creation, Gen 1:14), and the third a heaven which is spiritual."[3]

Another passage Mormons use to support their view is John 14:2. Here Jesus says, "In my Father's house are many mansions: if it were not so, I would have told you. I go to prepare a place for you." Quoting this verse and then referring to revelations given to Mormonism's founder Joseph Smith, Area Authority B. Renato Maldonado said, "The Prophet Joseph Smith explained that 'mansions' may be understood to mean 'kingdoms'—those kingdoms in which we will dwell in the life after this. . . . The Lord has said that we will be blessed and will live in a degree of glory in the next life according to the eternal laws we obey in mortality."[4] A simple reading of chapters 13 and 14 of John can help the reader understand what Jesus meant. The Savior had just washed the disciples' feet (13:1–17) and foretold His betrayal (vv. 18–30). He then told Peter he was going to deny his Lord three times (13:31–14:4). Thomas asked Jesus how His followers could know the way to truth (14:5–7), and Philip asked Jesus to show them the Father (vv. 8–14). In light of this context, John 14:2 describes the encouragement Jesus was giving to Peter and the others as He promised His friends He would not abandon them, even after His death. In John 14:2, the Greek word rendered "mansions" by the seventeenth-century King James Version translators might suggest that there are separate locations, or levels, involved. However, the word is better translated "rooms," as it is used in modern versions such as the New International Version and the English Standard Version. Commentator Merrill C. Tenney writes, "The imagery of a dwelling place ('rooms') is taken from the oriental house in which the sons and daughters have apartments under the same roof as their parents."[5]

"Dwelling places" ("rooms") is a very different concept from what is offered by LDS leaders, who insist that humans who achieve godhood will rule their own worlds, just as they believe Elohim, or Heavenly Father, rules this one.[6] In the words of Jesus and Paul, there is no implication at all that there are three degrees of heavenly glory. The interpretation of three levels of heaven as separate eternal destinations has been forced upon biblical passages that were never intended to support such an idea.

Questions for Discussion

- Mormons generally have to utilize sources outside the Bible to support a "three-levels-of-glory" doctrine. Why is this problematic?

- When interpreted properly, the Bible gives answers; when wrongly interpreted, error creeps in. How can Christians best get their LDS friends to see the problem with creating doctrines that are not biblically based?

- What is the danger of inferring a teaching from passages that are taken out of context? Can sincere Christians be guilty of such misuse of Scripture? If so, can you give some examples? What are some ways to avoid such errors?

─────────────── Evangelism Tip ───────────────

Much of what Mormons believe about the degrees of glory is based on "latter-day revelation." While it is not inherently wrong to use nonbiblical material to support a particular belief, it is wrong if that particular belief conflicts with clear biblical teaching. For example, the Bible emphasizes that only two destinations await mankind: heaven or hell. In order to get the Bible to support the Mormon view of the hereafter, a person must "force" upon the text of Scripture an unlikely interpretation that the author never intended. A good student should let the Bible speak for itself. Clear passages always trump vague passages.

Joseph Smith and the Book of Mormon

How do you account for Joseph Smith's "First Vision"?

Response Questions

- Do you believe Joseph Smith saw God's actual person, or was this a mental apparition?
- If Joseph Smith didn't really see God's person, how would that affect your faith?
- If this teaching is so important, why is there no mention of the First Vision in the early years of Mormonism?

• • • • • • • • • • • • • • • •

"The greatest event that has ever occurred in the world since the resurrection of the Son of God from the tomb and his ascension on high, was the coming of the Father and of the Son to that boy Joseph Smith."[1]

—President Joseph F. Smith (1838–1918)

———————————— Summary ————————————

The First Vision account given by Joseph Smith describes how he went into the woods as a fourteen-year-old boy after asking God which church was true. He was told that all the sects were wrong and that he was to join none of them. While this story is the cornerstone of the LDS religion, the details surrounding this event originate with Smith and him alone. The official version of this story did not surface until the late 1830s—almost two decades after it allegedly happened. The First Vision narrative needs to be carefully considered, because if it never occurred, Joseph Smith's claim to being a latter-day prophet becomes highly suspect.

WHEN MOST PEOPLE HEAR the word *vision*, they think of a person having a mystical experience, seeing something only in his or her mind. It is something seen by the imagination and not experienced empirically through any of the five senses. However, in what has been called the First Vision, it is assumed that the teenaged Joseph Smith (1805–1844) was allowed to see God in the actual body of flesh that Mormon leaders say He possesses. For instance, President Ezra Taft Benson (1899–1985) declared,

> The first vision of the Prophet Joseph Smith is bedrock theology to the Church. The adversary knows this and has attacked Joseph Smith's credibility from the day he announced the visitation of the Father and the Son. You should always bear testimony to the truth of the First Vision. Joseph Smith did see the Father and the Son. They conversed with him as he said they did. Any leader who, without reservation, cannot declare his testimony that God and Jesus Christ appeared to Joseph Smith can never be a true leader, a true shepherd. If we do not accept this truth—if we have not received a witness about this great revelation—we cannot inspire faith in those whom we lead . . . Some of our own members have attempted to interpret the experiences of Joseph Smith and his revelations. They say that it really is not important whether or not Joseph Smith actually saw God the Father and His Son Jesus Christ. What matters, they claim, is that he thought he did. That is preposterous![2]

For Christians, the historical, bodily resurrection of Jesus Christ as described in 1 Corinthians 15 is the cornerstone of the faith, for as verse 14 puts it, "If Christ be not risen, then is our preaching vain, and your faith is also vain." In a similar way, Joseph Smith's First Vision is a necessary foundation for the truth claims of Mormonism. President Gordon B. Hinckley (1910–2008) stated, "There's no other event in all recorded history that compares with it, not even at the baptism of the Savior."[3] According to one church manual, "For your testimony of the restored gospel to be complete, it must include a testimony of Joseph Smith's divine mission. The truthfulness of The Church of Jesus Christ of Latter-day Saints rests on the truthfulness of the First Vision and the other revelations the Lord gave to the Prophet Joseph."[4] Seventy F. Burton Howard wrote, "Our own personal salvation depends upon whether we accept and have a testimony of what Joseph Smith saw and heard in the spring of 1820."[5]

A stained glass window in the Museum of Church History and Art, across from Temple Square in Salt Lake City, Utah, depicts God the Father and Jesus visiting Joseph Smith in the "Sacred Grove."

The official story begins with what Smith called a "religious excitement" that took place in the Palmyra, New York, area where he lived. In the first chapter of Joseph Smith—History, found in the Pearl of Great Price, he gave several details regarding this revival:

- Great multitudes were added to the churches involved (v. 5).
- Participating denominations included the Baptist, Methodist, and Presbyterian churches (v. 5).
- The religious excitement resulted in "confusion and strife" among the groups involved (vv. 8–9).

Using the above information, it is possible to pinpoint the revival he described, though it did not take place in 1820 as emphasized by modern Mormon leaders and manuals. Rather, this particular religious excitement took place in 1824.[6] This may not seem too important, but if the revival mentioned by Smith actually did take place in 1824 and not 1820, the visitation by the angel Moroni in 1823 would become Smith's "first vision."

It was the "war of words and tumults of opinions" among the participating denominations that caused Smith to pray and ask God for a solution to his religious confusion. In verse 15 of the first chapter of Joseph Smith—History, Smith explained that he went out to some woods near his home. There, he says "I . . . began to offer up the desires of my heart to God" when "I was seized upon by some power which entirely overcame me, and had such an astonishing influence over me as to bind my tongue so that I could not speak. Thick darkness gathered around me." In verses 16–17, he continued, "I saw a pillar of light exactly over my head, above the brightness of the sun, which descended gradually until it fell upon me. It no sooner appeared than I found myself delivered from the enemy which held me bound. When the light rested upon me I saw two Personages, whose brightness and glory defy all description, standing above me in the air. One of them spake unto me, calling me by name and said, pointing to the other—*This is My Beloved Son. Hear Him!*" Smith was then told that the churches "were all wrong" and "their creeds were an abomination in his sight; that those professors were all corrupt; that: 'they draw near to me with their lips, but their hearts are far from me,' they teach for doctrines the commandments of men, having a form of godliness, but they deny the power thereof" (v. 19).

If this event plays such a major role in Mormonism's history, why is there no mention of it in the early years of the church among the writings of LDS leaders or members, including Joseph Smith himself? Mormon historian James B. Allen concedes that the First Vision narrative, as understood by modern LDS members, is suspiciously absent for much of Mormonism's early history. He wrote,

According to Joseph Smith, he told the story of the vision immediately after it happened in the early spring of 1820. As a result, he said, he received immediate criticism in the community. There is little if any evidence, however, that by the early 1830's Joseph Smith was telling the story in public. At least if he were telling it, no one seemed to consider it important enough to have recorded it *at the time*, and no one was criticizing him for it. Not even in his own history did Joseph Smith mention being criticized in this period for telling the story of the first vision. The interest, rather, was in the Book of Mormon and the various angelic visitations connected with its origin.[7]

Allen continued to say "that none of the available contemporary writings about Joseph Smith in the 1830s, none of the publications of the Church in that decade, and no contemporary journal or correspondence yet discovered mentions the story of the first vision is convincing evidence that at best it received only limited circulation in those early days."[8] If the First Vision story were actually being circulated, Smith's detractors would have found this to be a lightning rod for criticism. Yet Allen stated that "the earliest anti-Mormon literature attacked the Book of Mormon and the character of Joseph Smith but never mentioned the first Vision."[9]

Smith's critics included Alexander Campbell, E. D. Howe, Ezra Booth, John Corrill, and J. B. Turner. Allen went on to say, "Not until 1843, when the *New York Spectator* printed a reporter's account of an interview with Joseph Smith, did a *non-Mormon* source publish any reference to the story of the first vision. In 1844 I. Daniel Rupp published *An Original History of the Religious Denominations at Present Existing in the United States*, and this work contained an account of the vision provided by Joseph Smith himself. It seems probable; however, that as far as non-Mormons were concerned there was little, if any, awareness of it in the 1830's."[10]

Allen says that it was not until 1842 that a detailed account of the First Vision was printed in a Mormon publication. "The *Times and Seasons* began publication in 1839, but, as indicated above, the story of the vision was not told in its pages until 1842. From all this it would appear that the general church membership did not receive information about the first vision until the 1840's and that the story certainly did not hold the prominent place in Mormon thought that it does today."[11] As an explanation for why this story is missing, Allen suggests that Smith may have felt "experiences such as these should be kept from the general public because of their extremely sacred nature."[12] If so, should it be assumed that everyone who allegedly knew of this story had the will to set aside its evangelistic capabilities when speaking to a skeptical prospective convert? Is this even remotely reasonable when one considers that Smith's encounter has profound importance in bolstering Mormonism's current view of the Godhead? Consider also that such "sacredness" didn't seem to prohibit the LDS Church from eventually using this narrative as a missionary tool.

This missing portion of early Mormon history may explain why several LDS General Authorities have given conflicting views regarding the First Vision. Note these examples:

- Brigham Young (1801–1877): "The Lord did not come with the armies of heaven . . . But He did send His angel to this same obscure person, Joseph Smith jun., . . . and informed him that he should not join any of the religious sects of the day, for they were all wrong."[13]

- John Taylor (1808–1887): "How did this state of things called Mormonism originate? We read that an angel came down and revealed himself to Joseph Smith and manifested unto him in vision the true position of the world in a religious point of view . . . None of them was right, just as it was when the Prophet Joseph asked the angel which of the sects was right that he might join it. The answer was that none of them are right. What, none of them? No."[14]

- George A. Smith (1817–1875): "Joseph Smith had attended these meetings, and when this result was reached he saw clearly that something was wrong. He had read the Bible and had found that passage in James which says 'If any of you lack wisdom let him ask of God that giveth to all men liberally and upbraideth not,' and taking this literally, he went humbly before the Lord and inquired of Him, and the Lord answered his prayer, and revealed to Joseph, by the ministration of angels, the true condition of the religious world. When the holy angel appeared, Joseph inquired which of all these denominations was right and which he should join, and was told they were all wrong,—they had all gone astray, transgressed the laws, changed the ordinances and broken the everlasting covenant, and that the Lord was about to restore the priesthood and establish His Church, which would be the only true and living Church on the face of the whole earth."[15]

Joseph Smith himself recorded a conflicting view in his 1832 diary, when he claimed he saw only "the Lord" in the "16th year of my age." Instead of being told by two personages that all the churches were wrong, in this account he claimed to have already known that the churches "had apostatized from the true and living faith and there was no society or denomination that built upon the Gospel of Jesus Christ as recorded in the new testament."[16] Keep in mind that there were no other witnesses to this event. In essence, in order to accept this account, one must put complete faith and trust in Joseph Smith and him alone.

Even if it were possible for Smith to see God, Doctrine and Covenants 84:21–22 explains that the priesthood would have been needed in order for Smith to see Him: "And without the ordinances thereof, and the authority of the priesthood, the power of godliness is not manifest unto men in the flesh; For without this no man can see the face of God, even the Father, and live."[17] Melvin J. Petersen, who taught church history and doctrine at Brigham Young University, acknowledged that Smith had no such priesthood in 1820, the year he claimed to have seen God. However, he pointed to John 1:18 of the Joseph Smith Translation of the Bible to support the idea that Smith saw God, which reads, "No man hath seen God at any time, *except he hath bourne record of the Son.*"[18]

In noting this dilemma, Brigham Young University professor Charles R. Harrell states, "Explanations about how Joseph could have seen God before being ordained to the Melchizedek Priesthood or having received its ordinances have been varied. Early Mormon brethren who confronted this issue concluded that Joseph did hold the priesthood having, in some sense, brought it with him from the preexistence." Harrell goes on to say, "According to Joseph Fielding Smith, since the priesthood wasn't yet on the earth, young Joseph was exempt from this requirement."[19]

If the First Vision never happened and Joseph Smith later conjured up the notion in an attempt to give his story some credibility, it creates a major problem because it calls into question his calling as a prophet and his integrity as a whole. As Gordon B. Hinckley stated in a 1961 general conference message, "I would like to say that this cause is either true or false. Either this is the kingdom of God, or it is a sham and a delusion. Either Joseph talked with the Father and the Son, or he did not. If he did not, we are engaged in blasphemy."[20] Therefore, the Latter-day Saint needs to refrain from accepting the story based merely on faith and take a closer look at the history of Smith's crucial claim.

Questions for Discussion

- Missionaries are encouraged to "memorize Joseph Smith's description of seeing the Father and the Son (Joseph Smith—History 1:16–17), and always be ready to describe the First Vision using his [Smith's] own words. Do not rush through it. Bear sincere testimony that you know it is true. Do not hesitate to explain how you came to know of its truth."[21] Why do you think such emphasis is put on the First Vision?

- What do you think are the most perplexing problems with the official First Vision account?

- Gordon B. Hinckley said that if the First Vision is not based in fact, Mormons are engaged in a great blasphemy. Why do you think he would draw such a conclusion?

─────────────────── Evangelism Tip ───────────────────

Mormons can be extremely bothered when they learn about troubling aspects of their church's beginnings. Because they might not be familiar with their history, they might assume the Christian who raises these issues is making things up or embellishing facts. Should your Mormon acquaintance not believe what you are saying, ask, "If I supplied you with the reference(s) for this, could you show me how I have misunderstood the issue?" Being willing to support your point(s) is vital because nobody should expect to be taken at his or her word without proper documentation.

What about the witnesses who claimed they saw the gold plates?

Response Questions

- Would it change your perspective regarding the Book of Mormon if the witnesses did not actually see tangible plates?
- Do you personally believe the plates were made of actual gold? How heavy do you think they would have been?

• • • • • • • • • • • • • • • •

"To consider that everything of saving significance in the Church stands or falls on the truthfulness of the Book of Mormon and, by implication, the Prophet Joseph Smith's account of how it came forth is as sobering as it is true. It is a 'sudden death' proposition. Either the Book of Mormon is what the Prophet Joseph said it is, or this Church and its founder are false, a deception from the first instance onward."[1]

— Apostle Jeffrey R. Holland

———————————————— Summary ————————————

As with the story of the First Vision, Joseph Smith's account of how he translated the Book of Mormon from gold plates is a nonnegotiable truth claim. Mormon leaders have made it very clear that the book was not only produced from an ancient record kept by the early inhabitants on the American continent but also speaks of real people and real events. If the book is nothing more than a nineteenth-century novel containing fiction, it undermines Smith's credibility as a latter-day prophet and, in essence, negates the very foundation of the Church of Jesus Christ of Latter-day Saints.

JOSEPH SMITH (1805–1844) claimed that he was visited by an angel named Moroni in 1823 and that this angel told him of an ancient record buried not far from the Smith family home in Palmyra, New York. Centuries earlier as a mortal, Moroni was responsible for burying the plates before his people, the Nephites, were obliterated by their dark-skinned Lamanite counterparts.[2] The angel told Smith that the record "was written upon gold plates" and included an account of "the former inhabitants of this continent, and the source from whence they sprang."[3] Smith claimed he annually visited the spot where Moroni buried the plates, though he was not allowed to retrieve them from their hiding place until September 21, 1827. His mother, Lucy Mack Smith (1775–1856), related the story:

> Joseph, on coming to them, took them from their secret place, and, wrapping them in his linen frock, placed them under his arm and started for home. After proceeding a short distance, he thought it would be more safe to leave the road and go through the woods. Traveling some distance after he left the road, he came to a large windfall, and as he was jumping over a log, a man sprang up from behind it and gave him a heavy blow with a gun. Joseph turned around and knocked him down, then ran at the top of his speed. About half a mile farther he was attacked again in the same manner as before; he knocked this man down in like manner as the former and ran on again; and before he reached home he was assaulted the third time. In striking the last one, he dislocated his thumb, which, however, he did not notice until he came within sight of the house, when he threw himself down in the corner of the fence in order to recover his breath. As soon as he was able, he arose and came to the house. He was still altogether speechless from fright and the fatigue of running.[4]

Joseph Smith claimed that the record he received from Moroni was "engraven on plates which had the appearance of gold, each plate was six inches wide and eight inches long, and not quite so thick as common tin. They were filled with engravings, in Egyptian characters, and bound together in a volume as the leaves of a book, with three rings running through the whole. The volume was something near six inches in thickness, a part of which was sealed."[5] As recorded in the *Kingston Sentinel*, Book of Mormon witness John Whitmer (1802–1878) spoke at a public Sunday

A replica set of Joseph Smith's "Gold Plates" on display in the Temple Square North Visitor's Center, Salt Lake City, Utah.

service, where he said the plates "he had often handled" were made "of pure gold."[6] Given Smith's reported dimensions, the plates were approximately one-sixth of a cubic foot. Gold weighs 1,204 pounds per cubic foot, so if these plates were really made of gold, their weight would have been two hundred pounds![7]

Recognizing that this is a very heavy load for any human to carry, Mormon apologists have tried to minimize the problem by insisting that handmade plates would not have been perfectly flat, causing an air gap between each plate and making the record much lighter. This overlooks the fact that gold is not only very dense but also extremely soft. Its own weight would cause uneven plates to eventually flatten out, especially near the bottom of the stack. When faced with this dilemma, a Mormon might argue that God gave Smith supernatural strength to carry (and run with) the plates. Mormons who use this argument are basically conceding that not even "a buff farm boy" like Smith could carry such weight over any distance while running.

The supernatural strength theory falls apart in light of the incredible efforts of Mormon apologists to reduce the weight of the plates. Such pains would not be necessary if they really believed God supernaturally intervened and gave Smith the strength of a Samson.[8] Some Mormon apologists have abandoned the traditionally understood narrative and offer instead the theory that the plates were made of a lighter, stronger alloy, probably composed of copper and gold. Often cited as the metal of choice is a Central American alloy called tumbaga. They argue that Smith never actually said the plates were made of gold but rather that they had the "appearance of gold." Though technically true, this rebuttal fails to take into consideration that Smith himself records Moroni proclaiming the existence of "gold plates," not merely golden-colored plates.[9]

Apostle John A. Widtsoe (1872–1952) argued that if "enough copper had been added to make the alloy an eight carat gold, the plates would be hard and stiff enough to preserve inscriptions made upon them. If the plates were of such an alloy, and if about ten per cent were allowed for the spaces between the leaves, the weight of the plates would be in the neighborhood of one hundred pounds. This would not be an excessive weight for a young man of the strength of Joseph Smith."[10] Elsewhere, Widtsoe was more specific with the weight, saying it "would not be above one hundred and seventeen pounds."[11] Contrary to any hopeful expectations Mormons might have, human beings cannot carry such a weight and reenact the events that took place between the time Smith allegedly retrieved the plates and arrived at his home three miles away.[12]

Many LDS apologists like to quote Mormon metallurgist Reed C. Putnam, who also assumed the plates were not perfectly flat. Instead of a capricious 10 percent air gap, as Widtsoe insisted, Putnam gave them an amazing 50 percent air gap! By doing so, he estimated that the plates probably weighed fifty-three pounds. Using the same arbitrary estimate of a 50 percent air gap, he concluded that the heavier twelve-carat plates would weigh 86.83 pounds.[13] This naturally assumes there was a 50 percent air gap between each of the plates, which bound together were six inches thick. Though tumbaga is generally stronger than pure gold, it is likely that the plates at the bottom of the stack would have flattened out due to the weight of six inches worth of plates, thus increasing the overall weight of the plates.[14]

Translation of the Plates

Artists' renditions of Smith translating the plates give the impression that he was merely looking at the metal record as one reads a book. However, eyewitness accounts say Smith actually spent considerable time translating them by way of a "seer stone" placed in a hat. Smith's wife Emma, one of several scribes during the translation process, stated that she "frequently wrote day after day, often sitting at the table close by him, he sitting with his face buried in his hat, with the stone in it, and dictating hour after hour with nothing between us."[15] When interviewed for Helen Whitney's 2007 Public Broadcasting Service documentary titled "The Mormons," Brigham Young University professor Daniel C. Peterson noted, "We know that Joseph didn't translate the way that a scholar would translate . . . Actually most of the translation was done using something called a seer stone. He would put the stone in the bottom of a hat, presumably to exclude surrounding light. And then he would put his face into the hat, it's a kind of a strange image for us."[16]

Many Latter-day Saints do not feel the need to reasonably explain how Smith was able to carry the extremely heavy and awkward plates under his arm while jumping over a log, fighting off attackers, and running away at the "top of his speed." These seemingly herculean exploits become largely irrelevant to the faithful because they can cite eleven witnesses who said they actually saw the plates. Their testimonies can be found at the beginning of every modern edition of the Book of Mormon and are divided into two groups: The Testimony of the Three Witnesses and The Testimony of the Eight Witnesses. The three witnesses were Oliver Cowdery, Martin Harris, and David Whitmer. Among the eight witnesses were Joseph Smith's father and two brothers, Hyrum and Samuel. Also included were four of David Whitmer's brothers, Christian, Jacob, Peter, and John. The eighth witness was Hiram Page, a brother-in-law to the aforementioned Whitmer brothers, as was Oliver Cowdery.[17] In their testimony, Cowdery, David Whitmer, and Harris state, "We have seen the engravings which are upon the plates; and they have been shown unto us by the power of God, and not of man. And we declare with words of soberness, that an angel of God came down from heaven, and he brought and laid before our eyes, that we beheld and saw the plates, and the engravings thereon."

At first this sounds quite impressive; however, further details about this angelic encounter give a different perspective. While Smith was translating the plates, he discovered that "three special witnesses were to be provided by the Lord, to whom He would grant that they should see the plates from which this work (the Book of Mormon) should be translated."[18] Doctrine and Covenants 17:1 tells of a revelation allegedly given in June 1829. Cowdery, Whitmer, and Harris were told, "Behold, I say unto you, that you must rely upon my word, which if you do with full purpose of heart, you shall have a view of the plates." The three were told they would be allowed to see other historical artifacts mentioned in the Book of Mormon, such as the Sword of Laban and the Urim and Thummim. According to Doctrine and Covenants 17:2 they were told, "It is by your faith that you shall obtain a view of them." One could assume that this faith condition was something like a loyalty test. In other words, God chose these three because they trusted Smith and believed the plates existed. However, it becomes readily apparent that all three would have to exercise faith in order to see the plates at all. It seems odd that faith was necessary to see plates that Mormons believe were tangible and physical.

This event did not take place in the room where Smith was supposedly translating the plates; instead, it happened in the woods, where Smith and the three men tried "to obtain, by fervent and humble prayer" the fulfillment of that revelation. (But again, why was something like prayer needed in order to see a tangible object purportedly in the possession of Joseph Smith?) When praying did not result in a "manifestation of divine favor," Martin Harris excused himself, thinking he was the hindrance. Once he left, the remaining three men prayed again; it was then that they beheld an angel standing before them holding the plates. After this experience, Smith went to find Harris, who was a "considerable distance" away. The two men prayed and the "same vision" was opened to their view.[19]

To better understand this story, it is important to grasp the cultural environment of Smith and his appointed witnesses. Folk magic and treasure digging were very common, and the Smith family, including young Joseph, was no exception to the rule. In a paper presented at a meeting of the Mormon History Association, LDS historian Ronald W. Walker noted,

> From Greek, Semite, and even earlier times, men and women had spoken of troves hidden in caves or elsewhere in the bowels of the earth, of guardian spirits who sought to preserve or protect them, and of specially gifted seers, who by using their divining rods and revelatory stones, could find the treasure (Walker 1984). Such ideas clearly were current in the folk culture of upstate New York at the time. James Fenimore Cooper, who had spent his youth at the Susquehanna River's headwaters, found "such superstition was frequent in the new settlements" (1899, 415). The *Palmyra Reflector* located the practice even closer to Harris's neighborhood. "Men and

women without distinction of age or sex became marvellous[ly] wise in the occult sciences," the newspaper reported. "Many dreamed, and others saw visions disclosing to them, deep in the bowels of the earth, rich and shining treasures" (1 Feb. 1831, 92–93; Cooper 1899, 415). Harris himself was not immune to such beliefs. In addition to crediting the Palmyra diggers with actual discoveries, he accepted the reality of seers, seer stones, and the gift of "second sight," which allowed its possessor to "see" beyond the limitations of time and space.[20]

Second sight has been described as the ability to see things that are not perceived by the five senses. A person who claims to possess second sight can see, in vision form, things that cannot normally be seen. Walker's description needs to be considered carefully since Joseph Smith's handpicked witnesses were all influenced by the folk magic of their day. Historian D. Michael Quinn writes,

> The Three Witnesses to the *Book of Mormon* were likewise involved in folk magic. Oliver Cowdery was a rodsman before his 1829 meeting with Smith, who soon announced a revelation authorizing Cowdery to continue the revelatory use of his "rod of nature." David Whitmer revered Smith's use of a seer stone and may have possessed one of his own. Whitmer authorized a later spokesman for his own religious organization to obtain revelations through a stone. Martin Harris endorsed Smith's use of a seer stone for divination and treasure-seeking. Before and after the discovery of the gold plates, Harris himself participated in treasure-digging and identified the Smith brothers Joseph and Hyrum as co-participants. Of the remaining Eight Witnesses, Jacob Whitmer (b. 1800) had a seer stone which his descendants preserved. His brother-in-law Hiram Page (b.1800) definitely had a stone of his own that he used for revelations. Christian, John, and Peter Whitmer Jr. were included in their pastor's accusation of magic belief.[21]

The ability of the eight witnesses to actually see physical plates is also clouded in contradiction. Mormon historian Marvin S. Hill noted that "William Smith said his father never saw the plates except under a frock. And Stephen Burnett quotes Martin Harris that 'the eight witnesses never saw them & hesitated to sign that instrument [their testimony published in the Book of Mormon] for that reason, but were persuaded to do it.' Yet John Whitmer told Wilhelm Poulson of Ovid, Idaho, in 1878 that he saw the plates when they were not covered, and he turned the leaves."[22] Hill states that Hiram Page gave only a "veiled reference" to what he saw, explaining that Page did not clearly "say he saw the plates but that angels confirmed him in his faith."[23] Hill seems to express his own frustrations when he writes,

> Despite Page's inconsistencies, it is difficult to know what to make of Harris' affirmation that the eight saw no plates in the face of John Whitmer's testimony. The original testimony of these eight men in the Book of Mormon reads somewhat ambiguously, not making clear whether they handled the plates or the "leaves" of the translated manuscript. Thus there are some puzzling aspects to the testimonies of the witnesses. If Burnett's statement is given credence it would appear that Joseph Smith extorted a deceptive testimony from the eight witnesses. But why should John Whitmer and Hiram Page adhere to Mormonism and the Book of Mormon so long if they only gave their testimony reluctantly? It may be that like the three witnesses they expressed a genuine religious conviction. The particulars may not have seemed as important as the ultimate truth of the work.[24]

When all the conflicting details surrounding the story of the gold plates and the origin of the Book of Mormon are examined, it becomes clear that Joseph Smith's claims are dangerously tenuous. If the discovery of the plates and their translation did not take place, then as Apostle Holland said in the introductory quote, "This Church and its founder are false, a deception from the first instance onward."

Questions for Discussion

- Why do you think it is important for Mormons to insist that the eleven "witnesses" actually saw tangible plates?

- If these witnesses testified in a court of law that they saw the plates only in a vision, how do you think this would affect the jurors?

- What explanations can you give for the strong influence Smith obviously had over these men?

——————————————— Evangelism Tip ———————————————

Many Latter-day Saints tend to discount or ignore troubling aspects of their history because they are so devoted to Joseph Smith. Their preconceived notions of Smith outweigh any facts that might appear to place their founder in a negative light. Sometimes it helps to challenge Mormons to look at LDS history as unbiased outsiders. Asking them to convince you by using actual evidence rather than their subjective experience can sometimes expose the problems surrounding the history of their church.

Chapter 33

If the Book of Mormon is just a novel, then why do Isaiah and Ezekiel predict its forthcoming?

Response Questions

- Could it be possible that Isaiah was referring to Jerusalem's spiritual condition at that time rather than to the Book of Mormon?
- What if the word *sticks* in Ezekiel refers to the two Israelite kingdoms and not to the Book of Mormon?
- If these passages do not actually refer to the Book of Mormon, how does this reflect on the credibility of LDS prophets and apostles who apparently misuse these Scriptures?

● ● ● ● ● ● ● ● ● ● ● ● ● ● ● ● ●

"In Old Testament times the prophets Isaiah and Ezekiel foresaw the coming of the Book of Mormon (see Isaiah 29:4–18; Ezekiel 37:16–20). These prophecies are now being fulfilled. The Book of Mormon has been brought forth and is being taken to all the world."[1]

—*Gospel Principles*

—————————————— Summary ——————————————

Several LDS leaders have pointed to the Old Testament books of Isaiah and Ezekiel as proof that God intended to clarify the Bible through the Book of Mormon. But Isaiah 29 concerns the city of Jerusalem and Israel's spiritual condition at that time, and Ezekiel 37 predicts the future coming together again of the separated northern and southern tribes of Israel. The prophets certainly were not referring to a book that would be written by Jewish people living on another continent.

In a 2007 general conference address, Apostle Russell M. Nelson insisted that the Bible predicted the coming forth of the Book of Mormon:

> How do scriptures of the Restoration clarify the Bible? Many examples exist. I will cite but a few, beginning with the Old Testament. Isaiah wrote, "Thou shalt . . . speak out of the ground, and thy speech shall be low out of the dust, and thy voice shall be, as of one that hath a familiar spirit, out of the ground, and thy speech shall whisper out of the dust." Could any words be more descriptive of the Book of Mormon, coming as it did "out of the ground" to "whisper out of the dust" to people of our day? But Isaiah was not the only Old Testament prophet who foretold the Book of Mormon. Ezekiel wrote: "Take thee one stick, and write upon it, For Judah, and for the children of Israel . . . : then take another stick, and write upon it, For Joseph, the stick of Ephraim, and for all the house of Israel . . . : And join them one to another into one stick; and they shall become one in thine hand." Today, Saints living in many nations of the earth gratefully hold the Bible (the stick of Judah) and the Book of Mormon (the stick of Ephraim) bound as one in their hands.[2]

If Nelson's analysis is correct, it would appear that God expected the Book of Mormon to be a scriptural companion to the Bible in these latter days. But is this a proper understanding of the Isaiah and Ezekiel passages?

Isaiah 29

Those who were listening to Nelson's talk would have been at a disadvantage had they not had their Bibles opened to Isaiah 29. Since Mormons are taught that Joseph Smith retrieved the gold plates from a stone box hidden in the ground, Nelson assumes that the "voice" whispering from the dust or out of the ground must be a reference to the Book of Mormon. According to Brigham Young University professor Charles R. Harrell,

> Latter-day Saints go beyond the traditionally accepted allegorical meaning of this passage and its fulfillment in ancient Israel to see a literal book that came to light in the latter days through the "unlearned" prophet Joseph Smith. "The vision of all" is spoken of in the Book of Mormon as a literal vision of all things—"a revelation from God, from the beginning of the world to the ending

thereof" (2 Ne. 27:7)—that would be recorded in a sealed book (i.e., the sealed portion of the gold plates) to come forth in the latter days. The "learned" individual is interpreted as being Charles Anthon, a professor of Greek and Latin languages at Columbia College (later Columbia University), who reportedly said he could not read the book "for it is sealed" (2 Ne. 27:15–20; Isa. 29:11).[3]

Harrell disagrees with the traditional LDS understanding of these passages and concedes that "Isaiah isn't talking about a literal book, much less one that would come forth in the future."[4] Nelson, like many LDS leaders before him, ignores the key passages in Isaiah 29 that set the historical stage for what follows. While he began his conference message with verse 4, verses 1–3 state, "Woe to Ariel, to Ariel, the city where David dwelt! add ye year to year; let them kill sacrifices. Yet I will distress Ariel, and there shall be heaviness and sorrow: and it shall be unto me as Ariel. And I will camp against thee round about, and will lay siege against thee with a mount, and I will raise forts against thee."

It can be readily seen that God is going to distress Ariel, which is another name for Jerusalem, or the City of David, where God had commanded sacrifices be made unto Him. Whether Isaiah had in mind an actual military assault on the city or was speaking metaphorically regarding Jerusalem's spiritual blindness has been a matter of debate. However, no non-Mormon scholar sees Isaiah's warning as a prediction regarding a future book.

Ezekiel 37

Citing Ezekiel 37:15–20, Apostle LeGrand Richards (1886–1983) concluded,

In ancient times it was the custom to write on parchment and roll it on a stick. Therefore, when this command was given, it was the equivalent of directing that two books or records should be kept . . . Now, granting that the Bible is the stick of Judah, where is the stick of Joseph? Can anyone answer? God commanded that it should be kept to record the fulfillment of his greater promises to Joseph. It would naturally be a record kept in another land, since Joseph was to be "separate from his brethren." It is plain from the reading of this scripture that the record of Judah, or the Holy Bible, would remain with this people, that the record of Joseph would be joined unto it, and that the two would become one. Should anyone object to God's doing exactly what he promised Ezekiel he would do? Could this promise be fulfilled in a simpler and more perfect manner than it was through the coming forth of the Book of Mormon? . . . The two records have now been joined together, constituting a complete fulfillment of another great prophecy. Again, who could object to God's doing the thing he promised to do? Until someone can explain where the record of Joseph is, the Book of Mormon stands unrefuted in its claim to be "the stick of Joseph."[5]

Understanding the Hebrew word for *stick* helps to clarify the message Ezekiel was trying to convey. The word used in these passages speaks of a literal piece of wood, not books or scrolls as Mormons often insist. Consider 1 Kings 17:10–12, when the prophet Elijah visits the Sidonian city of Zarephath:

So he arose and went to Zarephath. And when he came to the gate of the city, behold, a widow was there gathering sticks. And he called to her and said, "Bring me a little water in a vessel, that I may drink." And as she was going to bring it, he called to her and said, "Bring me a morsel of bread in your hand." And she said, "As the LORD your God lives, I have nothing baked, only a handful of flour in a jar and a little oil in a jug. And now I am gathering a couple of sticks that I may go in and prepare it for myself and my son, that we may eat it and die." (ESV)

The word for *sticks* in this passage is the same Hebrew word used in Ezekiel 37. Should it be assumed that the widow in this story was gathering books in preparation for what she thought was her final meal? There are other words for book or scroll that were available if a written document is what was meant.

Another passage to consider is 2 Kings 6:1–7. During the act of cutting down a tree, an axe head flew off its handle and landed in the water. Distressed because the tool was borrowed, the man who was using the axe sought the aid of Elisha the prophet. When he learned where the axe head landed, Elisha proceeded to "cut down a stick" and cast it into the water. Amazingly, the iron axe head floated to the top. Again, the Hebrew word used in this passage is the same one used in Ezekiel 37. It is unreasonable to assume that Elisha somehow cut a book off of a tree.

The problem this presents for the Mormon interpretation of Ezekiel 37 has not gone unnoticed by Mormon apologists. Brigham Young University professor Keith H. Meservy wrote two articles for *Ensign* magazine arguing that records were also made on "wooden tablets" and that this is what the "sticks" refer to in Ezekiel 37.[6] In 1990, Brian E. Keck challenged this assumption:

> The most recent additions to the debate are two articles by Keith Meservy, published in the September 1977 and the February 1987 issues of the *Ensign*. He provides evidence that the "sticks" referred to by Ezekiel were actually wooden writing boards—thin leaves of wood coated on one side with wax attached together with metal or leather hinges. These writing boards were fairly common in Babylonia in the first millennium B.C. The appearance of his arguments in the official Church magazine has given prestige to his ideas, which have subsequently appeared in modified form in both Sunday School and Institute manuals. . . . Even in the 1979 LDS edition of the Bible the word "stick" in the Ezekiel passage is identified in a marginal note as: "Wooden writing tablet," an interpretation most likely derived from Meservy's writings.[7]

Keck was not impressed with this LDS rebuttal.

> The basic problem for Mormon exegesis and the crux of the passage for Mormon and non-Mormon scholars alike is the meaning of the Hebrew word *es*, rendered by the King James translators as "stick." The word *es* spans the whole range of Semitic languages (Bergstrasser 1983, 217), yet its various meanings reveal extraordinary continuity between the different languages. The term generally refers to a tree, wood in general, firewood, and specific items made of wood. In Hebrew the traditional semantic range is correspondingly broad, but again the word basically means tree, wood, sticks, branches, firewood, and timber for building. Occasionally it can refer to objects made of wood, such as a pole, the handle of an axe, gallows, idols, and vessels (Brown, Driver, and Briggs 1980, 781–82). Moreover, in post-biblical Hebrew the term *es* again refers to trees, different types of wood, a pole, the gallows, and a wooden pot ladle (Jastrow 1971, 1101). Therefore, as far as our current lexical knowledge goes, the Hebrew *es* does not refer to a writing board or document.[8]

Keck interprets Ezekiel's prediction much as biblical scholars see it.

> The point of the whole passage is that just as Ezekiel brought two sticks together into one hand, so God will bring back the North and South Kingdoms into their homeland, to be ruled over by one leader, a Davidic descendant. . . . By placing the Ezekiel passage into the context of the sign-form, it becomes clear that Ezekiel's performance with the sticks was intended for the public and symbolized what God was planning to do—reunify the two kingdoms of Israel. . . . identifying the sticks of Ezekiel with Babylonian writing boards was a clever exegetical idea, but it does not hold up to a close inspection.[9]

Again, these passages have nothing to say about the Book of Mormon. Instead, Isaiah 29 speaks to a historical situation in Israel's past. Ezekiel 37 illustratively predicts the coming together of two nations, Judah and Israel, which had been separated since the time of King Rehoboam.

Questions for Discussion

- When context and history is considered, it becomes clear that neither Isaiah 29 nor Ezekiel 37 can possibly refer to the Book of Mormon. Why should LDS leaders care whether or not the Bible mentions the Book of Mormon?

- A common mistake in biblical interpretation is reading into a particular text and making it fit our presuppositions. How is this seen in the way Mormon leaders have tackled Isaiah 29 and Ezekiel 37?

──────────────────── Evangelism Tip ────────────────────

Allowing Mormons to fully explain why they think a certain verse supports their position is not only healthy for a positive, respectful discussion, but it also lets them describe in their own words why they see a connection to a particular verse. Listen to what they say and take careful mental notes. Avoid the temptation to unnecessarily interrupt before they can lay out their position. Not only is this common courtesy, but it also allows you to expect the same consideration when you give your view.

Chapter 34

What about the archaeology supporting the Book of Mormon?

Response Questions

- To which specific archaeological evidence(s) are you referring?
- Which do you think has more evidence in support of the places and people it talks about: the Bible or the Book of Mormon?
- Don't you think there should be at least some substantial evidence for the huge civilizations mentioned in the Book of Mormon?

• • • • • • • • • • • • • • • •

"It is the author's opinion that all the scriptures, including the Book of Mormon, will remain in the realm of faith. Science will not be able to prove or disprove holy writ. However, enough plausible evidence will come forth to prevent scoffers from having a field day, but not enough to remove the requirement of faith."[1]
—Apostle Neal A. Maxwell (1926–2004)

Summary

When compared to the evidence for the Bible, there is little to support the historicity of the Book of Mormon. Within Mormon ranks, debate rages as to where Book of Mormon lands are even located. Some faithful members look to the northern part of the North American continent, while others suggest the story took place in Central America. With so little to support this very important LDS scripture, it needs to be acknowledged that it requires much more faith to accept the Book of Mormon than to accept the Bible.

GO TO JERUSALEM, AND YOU will be able to photograph any number of biblical sites, including Hezekiah's Tunnel—built 2,700 years ago and mentioned in 2 Kings 20:20. Go to Caesarea, and see the place where a stone with an inscription to Tiberius Caesar from Pontius Pilate was found in the 1960s. Go to the Sea of Galilee, Jordan River, and Dead Sea, all bodies of water described in the pages of the Bible. Tells (the Arabic term for mounds) containing the ruins of towns from different eras of history are found throughout the country of Israel, just waiting for archaeologists to uncover what's below the surface.[2] While it is impossible to empirically prove the events of the Bible, the artifacts and sites, along with written history, make it clear these are stories of real places and people.[3] According to one Bible dictionary, "Instead of providing proof of specific events, archaeology is used to increase our knowledge of the everyday life, the history, and the customs of the people who appear in the Bible's long story. . . . Archaeological discoveries paint in the background of the Bible, helping to explain many of its events."[4]

Alfred Hoerth and John McRay explain that archaeology

> is by definition the "study of antiquity," and in its quest to recover and better understand earlier civilizations it embraces much more than excavation. Many relevant fields of study, such as language, geography, history, art, geology, biology, and chemistry, are utilized by archaeologists as they reach into the past. Archaeology is especially valuable in supplying information about objects, places, and activities for which no historical data exist. Sometimes historical records are clarified, or even corrected, by archaeological discoveries.[5]

Of course, the events described in the Bible still require an element of faith, such as the feeding of the five thousand, the resurrection of Jesus Christ, and Paul's conversion experience on the road to Damascus. It does not require faith, however, to believe that there really was a Jesus of Nazareth or that a man named Paul spread the Christian message throughout much of the Roman world. Quoting G. Ernest Wright, P. Kyle McCarter Jr. writes, "We shall probably never be able to prove that Abram really existed, that he did this or that, said thus and so, but what we can prove is that his life and times, as reflected in the stories about him, fit perfectly within the early second millennium, but imperfectly with any later period."[6]

Archaeology in the land of the Bible is a recent science, as there was little known before the early 1800s.[7] As of 1990, "only about two hundred of the

Unlike the Book of Mormon, there is plenty of evidence to support the history as documented by the Bible. For instance, archeologists have learned much about first-century Israel and Herod the Great by studying Caesarea, located in Israel on the Mediterranean Sea.

approximately five thousand sites in the Holy Land have been excavated," and there are about ten thousand sites in Mesopotamia that are listed as possibilities for excavation.[8] Proper archaeology requires a number of resources, including manpower, finances, favorable weather, and peaceful political conditions. When these conditions are met, there are plenty of places for the biblical archaeologist to excavate.

Searching Out Book of Mormon Lands

LDS scholars disagree about where the events recorded in the Book of Mormon took place. The controversy surrounding the actual location of Book of Mormon place-names was highlighted in a *Deseret News* article. It began by saying, "The discussion on Book of Mormon geography was getting heated. Scholars gathered in Provo, Utah, to discuss their theories about where the events described in the Book of Mormon took place. Some placed the Nephite capital city Zarahemla in Mesoamerica, others in South America. Others argued for a setting in the American heartland." This 2010 article noted, "The Book of Mormon geography conference was held at Brigham Young Academy on May 23–24, 1903. But the advice President Joseph F. Smith gave at that conference 107 years ago could apply equally to current disputes over Book of Mormon geography."[9]

Mormon John L. Lund wrote, "Many members of the Church are confused about the disagreements over where the primary events of the Book of Mormon took place. This confusion is the result of well-meaning members of the Church advocating three different geographical places. Adding to the confusion are contradictory statements made by some Church leaders."[10] The

Encyclopedia of Mormonism notes, "In early Church history, the most common opinion among members and Church leaders was that Book of Mormon lands encompassed all of North and South America, although at least one more limited alternative view was also held for a time by some. The official position of the Church is that the events narrated in the Book of Mormon occurred somewhere in the Americas, but that the specific location has not been revealed."[11] This theory is known in Mormon circles as the *hemispheric model*. President Joseph Fielding Smith held this view, explaining,

> When the Lord began to lead the family of Lehi to this land, he said to them: "And inasmuch as ye shall keep my commandments, ye shall prosper, and shall be led to *a land of promise*; yea, even a land which I have prepared for you; yea, *a land which is choice above all other lands*." It is generally understood that they landed in South America, and that their nations, the Nephites and Lamanites, dwelt in South and Central America during the greater part of their sojourn here. At any rate, the time of their civilization was principally spent in the south and not in the region now comprising the United States. This proves beyond the possibility of doubt that the choice land was South as well as North America, and while the City New Jerusalem, which the *Book of Mormon* tells us is to be built on this land that is choice above all other lands, will be in Jackson County, nevertheless, if one accepts the *Book of Mormon, one must accept the whole hemisphere as the land of Zion.*[12]

Despite Smith's strong admonition, the hemispheric model has generally been replaced with the *limited geography model*. This is espoused by many Brigham Young University professors, who point to Mayan and Aztec ruins in Central America as evidence for the Book of Mormon peoples. As many secular scholars have pointed out, these sites certainly provide plenty of evidence for ancient civilizations. However, the idea that these peoples were associated with the Book of Mormon is pure speculation.

A third viewpoint is called the *heartland model*, which has been popularized by Mormon apologists such as Rod L. Meldrum and Wayne N. May, as well as radio/television personality Glenn Beck.[13] This position holds that the Book of Mormon events took place on the same grounds as LDS Church history, which is the eastern portion of the United States. Proponents of the heartland model argue that they are more in line with what Joseph Smith taught, and they often point to Native American sites as evidence to support their view. For instance, Meldrum believes that the area around the Hopewell Indian mounds in Newark, Ohio, is the Land Bountiful mentioned in Alma 22:29.[14]

Mormon leaders have remained largely silent on the debate in recent years. In past years, however, many General Authorities have scoffed at any view that did not include North America. For example, President Ezra Taft Benson (1899–1994) wrote, "Consider how very fortunate we are to be living in this land of America. . . . This was the place of three former civilizations: that of Adam, that of the Jaredites, and that of the Nephites. This was also the place where our Heavenly Father and His Son, Jesus Christ, appeared to Joseph Smith, inaugurating the last dispensation."[15] Saying that "most LDS scholars and an increasing number of members and leaders believe that Book of Mormon events transpired in Mesoamerica" rather than North America, LDS apologist Michael Ash accuses fellow members like Meldrum and former LDS leaders like Smith and Benson of a shallow reading of the text. He wrote, "It's likely that Joseph Smith, most of his contemporaries, and probably most modern-day prophets assumed and even embraced this hemispheric view. It also seems likely that Joseph and his contemporaries believed that the Indian remnants of his local vicinity furnished evidence of the lives and wars of the Nephites and Lamanites. From where did such beliefs arise? A superficial reading of the Book of Mormon—in the context of cultural beliefs about the Indians in Joseph's day—plausibly suggests such a scenario."[16]

Regardless of which view a Mormon holds, one of the fundamental tenets taught to Mormon children and new converts is that the Book of Mormon is an account of real people and real events. Mormon leaders, apologists, and scholars alike typically have declared their allegiance to the Book of Mormon as actual history. Brigham Young University professor Robert L. Millet stated, "The historicity of the Book of Mormon record is crucial. We cannot exercise faith in that which is untrue, nor can 'doctrinal fiction' have normative value in our lives. . . . Only scripture—writings and events and descriptions from real people at a real point in time, people who were moved upon and directed by divine powers—can serve as a revelatory channel, enabling us to hear and feel the word of God."[17]

The LDS Museum of Church History and Art, which is located across the street from Temple Square in Salt Lake City, displays no artifact that can be proven to be of "Nephite" origin. For the LDS Church to produce archaeological evidence to support what is supposed to be a historical book but whose geography eludes them is understandably a monumental task. Without knowing where to dig, how is it possible to even produce archaeological evidence? This has not stopped faithful Mormons from pointing to historical objects they believe "parallels" the Book of Mormon narrative.[18] Even Old World locations that some Mormons see as evidence for the Book of Mormon are not without an incredible amount of controversy and disagreement.[19]

Just because Joseph Smith claimed that he translated a record of ancient Americans who had originally migrated from Israel doesn't mean this actually happened. While Christians have evidence from the Holy Land that supports the Bible and, ultimately, their beliefs, faithful Latter-day Saints are left remaining hopeful that perhaps a Book of Mormon site or relic will eventually be found.

Questions for Discussion

- It has been said that archaeology cannot "prove the Bible." What do you think this means? Do you agree?

- What archaeological discoveries do you know of that support the Bible's authenticity?

- Suppose you ran across a Mormon who believes the Book of Mormon is a story of good morals but does not accept it as a historical book. What problems do Mormons face if the Book of Mormon is nothing more than a fictional tale? How would your faith be affected if no historical evidence for the Bible existed?

Evangelism Tip

When the topic of Book of Mormon archaeology comes up in a conversation, it is best to ask your Mormon friends for specific evidence that supports the historicity of the Book of Mormon. It also may be good to ask for evidence from a non-LDS source that supports their premise. If the Book of Mormon recounts stories about real people and places, there should be at least some physical evidence that supports its historical claims. Explain to your Latter-day Saint friend that while faith is important, the lack of evidence to support the Book of Mormon requires *blind* faith, something Christians don't need in order to accept the Bible.

Chapter 35

Why do you have difficulty accepting Joseph Smith as a true prophet of God?

Response Questions

- In your opinion, what did Joseph Smith say or do that classifies him as a "true prophet"?
- How many erroneous predictions must a person give before he should be considered a false prophet?
- If a prophet taught doctrine that conflicts with the teachings of the Bible, could it rightly be said that he was not God's spokesman?

• • • • • • • • • • • • • • • •

"We must accept the divine mission of the Prophet Joseph Smith. . . . Each member of the Church, to be prepared for the millennial reign, must receive a testimony, each for himself, of the divinity of the work established by Joseph Smith."[1]
—President Harold B. Lee (1899–1973)

———————————————— Summary ————————————————

Joseph Smith certainly is adored and celebrated by members of the LDS Church. Unfortunately, many Latter-day Saints are unaware of the more controversial teachings and behavior of their founder. Either Smith was a true prophet of God, whose teachings should be heeded, or he was not, meaning he and his teachings should be rejected. Smith made crucial errors in his prophecies, including prophecies about war and a temple to be built in Missouri. According to the Bible, therefore, he ought to be rejected.

PRESIDENT JOSEPH FIELDING SMITH (1876–1972) firmly declared, "Mormonism, as it is called, must *stand or fall on the story of Joseph Smith*. He was either a prophet of God, divinely called, properly appointed and commissioned, or he was one of the biggest frauds this world has ever seen. *There is no middle ground*."[2] Smith's successor, Harold B. Lee (1899–1973), wrote, "Today the work of the kingdom of God in the earth is a monument to the name of the Prophet Joseph Smith. Millions have been caught up by the glory of his mission, as he has proclaimed it and directed it throughout the whole earth."[3]

While Mormons do not worship Joseph Smith (1805–1844), they certainly revere him and hold him in the highest esteem. President Brigham Young (1801–1877) stated, "I honor and revere the name of Joseph Smith. I delight to hear it; I love it. I love his doctrine."[4] President John Taylor (1808–1887) wrote in Doctrine and Covenants 135:3: "Joseph Smith, the Prophet and Seer of the Lord, has done more, save Jesus only, for the salvation of men in this world, than any other man that ever lived." Recognizing that Joseph Smith's birthday precedes Christmas by two days, President Gordon B. Hinckley (1910–2008) stated, "We stand in reverence before him. He is the great prophet of this dispensation. He stands as the head of this great and mighty work which is spreading across the earth. He is our prophet, our revelator, our seer, our friend. Let us not forget him. Let not his memory be forgotten in the celebration of Christmas. God be thanked for the Prophet Joseph."[5] The December 18, 2011 edition of the *Deseret News* contained an article titled "Two December Births to Celebrate: Jesus Christ and Joseph Smith." Kristine Frederickson wrote, "Jesus Christ, whose birth we commemorate on Dec. 25 is the Savior of the world. Joseph Smith is his prophet and how fitting that we remember both this time of year. Both lived humbly yet courageously, seeking to do the will of their father. We should remember Joseph Smith on his birthday, Dec. 23, and give worship on Dec. 25 for the author and finisher of faith, Jesus Christ."[6]

It is clear Mormons must avow complete allegiance to this man. One church manual puts it this way: "For your testimony of the restored gospel to be complete, it must include a testimony of Joseph Smith's divine mission."[7] One hymn that is sung regularly at the biannual general conference refers to Smith:

> Praise to the man who communed with Jehovah!
> Jesus anointed "that Prophet and Seer"—
> Blessed to open the last dispensation;
> Kings shall extol him and nations revere.[8]

Joseph Smith: A True Prophet?

Without the benefit of a complete written Scripture, the Israelites of the exodus were given two basic tests for evaluating the claims of a professed prophet. The first is found in Deuteronomy 13:1–5. Those who enticed God's people to follow "other gods" were to be rejected. Doctrinal purity was taken very seriously, so much so that under Mosaic law, false prophets faced the death penalty. Smith is fortunate he didn't live under such theocratic rule, for he most certainly would have been judged as a false prophet for introducing a view of God that does not fit the Old Testament model.[9]

The second test is found in Deuteronomy 18:21, which asks how one can know "the word which the LORD hath not spoken." The answer is given in verse 22: "When a prophet speaks in the name of the LORD, if the word does not come to pass or come true, that is a word that the LORD has not spoken; the prophet has spoken it presumptuously. You need not be afraid of him" (ESV). Even a false prophet sometimes could accurately forecast the future but never consistently so. Any failure of a prophecy to come to pass was a sure sign of a false prophet. Let's consider a couple of the many prophecies given by the Mormon founder.

The Prophecy on War

Gordon B. Hinckley wrote,

> Finally, what of Joseph Smith's prophecies? There were more than a few, and they were fulfilled. Among the most notable was the revelation on the Civil War. You are familiar with it; it was spoken on Christmas Day, 1832. There were many high-minded men and women who deplored the institution of slavery then common in the South, and there was much talk of abolition. But who but a prophet of God would have dared to say, thirty-nine years before it was to happen, that "war [would] be poured out upon all nations," beginning "at the rebellion of South Carolina," and that "the Southern States [would] be divided against the Northern States"? (D&C 87:1–3.) This remarkable prediction saw its fulfillment with the firing on Fort Sumter in Charleston Harbor in 1861. How could Joseph Smith have possibly foreseen with such accuracy the event that was to come thirty-nine years after he spoke of it? Only by the spirit of prophecy which was in him.[10]

The War Between the States, otherwise known as the Civil War, had its official beginning in the early morning hours of April 12, 1861, when batteries located on the perimeter of Charleston Harbor fired upon the island fort named after Revolutionary War hero Thomas Sumter. The following day Major Robert Anderson was forced to surrender, giving the newly formed Confederate States of America its first military victory. Three days after the attack, President Abraham Lincoln called for 75,000 men to enlist in what many people thought would be a very short conflict. Four years and hundreds of thousands of casualties later, the Civil War was over and President Lincoln had been assassinated. Many Latter-day Saints, like Hinckley, contend that Section 87 in Doctrine and Covenants authenticates Joseph Smith's prophetic calling since he supposedly foretold this national tragedy as far back as December 25, 1832.

It would be wrong to assume that difficulties between the northern and southern states could not have been sensed long before Fort Sumter. Civil War historian Bruce Catton stated, "There had been many woeful misunderstandings between North and South in the years that led up to the Civil War."[11] Joseph Smith was keenly aware of this discontent on that Christmas Day of 1832 when he wrote, "The people of South Carolina, in convention assembled (in November), passed ordinances, declaring their state a free and independent nation. . . . President Jackson issued his proclamation against this rebellion, called out a force sufficient to quell it, and implored the blessings of God to assist the nation to extricate itself from the horrors of the approaching and solemn crisis.[12]

Not far from Smith's Kirtland, Ohio, headquarters, a newspaper called the *Painesville Telegraph* printed a story from the *New York Courier and Enquirer* titled "The Crisis." The article spoke of the "probabilities of dismemberment" stemming from discontent in South Carolina and Georgia over states' rights. It is interesting to note that the date of this article is Friday, December 21, 1832, just four days before Smith received his alleged "prophecy." Since nothing came from this incident, some might argue that Joseph Smith either jumped the prophetical gun or was predicting the wrong rebellion. However, Mormons have insisted that Smith was a prophet because war eventually broke out almost three decades later. A close look at Smith's prophecy discloses many problems.

In Doctrine and Covenants 87:2–3, Smith predicted, "War will be poured out upon all nations, beginning at this place." In order to maintain the integrity of the Mormon prophet, some Latter-day Saints insist that this prophecy stretches beyond the Civil War and actually includes a number of military conflicts around the world. Commenting on this prediction, one church manual asks the question, "Has War Been Poured Out on All Nations?" In response, a 1958 talk by Presiding Bishop Joseph L. Wirthlin (1893–1963) is cited, in which he listed military conflicts that had taken place since the American Civil War, including the war between Denmark and Prussia in 1864, Italy and Austria in 1865, the Spanish-American War in 1898, World Wars I and II, and Korea. The manual also added post-1958 conflicts such as "the Vietnam War in Southeast Asia, the war in Angola, and the Six-Day and Yom Kippur wars in the Holy Land."[13]

Joseph Fielding Smith also is cited in the manual as saying, "I think the great world war commenced in April, 1861. At any rate, that was the beginning of the end . . . Based upon what the Lord says in this Section 87 of the Doctrine & Covenants—the Section on war which I read—I place the time of the beginning of the end at the rebellion of South Carolina. I say I place it there. I beg your pardon. The Lord places it there because it says beginning at this place these things would take place."[14] Wirthlin, Smith, and a host of other Mormons may wish to draw such a conclusion, but it is doubtful that any credible historian will agree that these military struggles had any connection whatsoever with the "rebellion of South Carolina."

In Doctrine and Covenants 87:4, Joseph Smith states that "slaves shall rise up against their masters, who shall be marshaled and disciplined for war." Though some slaves did flee north and fight for the Union, this portion of the prediction seems to be offset by the fact that many southern slaves also fought for the Confederacy. Wirthlin again gave an incredibly broad interpretation of this verse when he said it refers to "slaves all over the world, and I think of those, particularly in the land of Russia and other countries wherein they have been taken over by that great nation and where the people are actually the slaves of those individuals who guide and direct the affairs of Russia and China"[15]

In Doctrine and Covenants 87:6, Smith also predicted that there would be "famine, plague, and earthquake," and "chastening hand of an Almighty God, until the consumption decreed hath made full end of all nations." Again, in the aforementioned manual, this is given a generic fulfillment: "In the judgments that precede the Millennium, all earthly kingdoms will come to an end and the kingdom of God will triumph and become the one political power during the thousand years of peace and righteousness (see Revelation 11:15)."[16] By giving these predictions such far-reaching interpretations, the revelatory prowess of Smith becomes insignificant.

Certainly Smith's contemporaries believed this prophecy dealt with the Civil War. Two days after the shelling of Fort Sumter, Heber C. Kimball (1801–1868) said, "In this country the North and the South will exert themselves against each other, and ere long the whole face of the United States will be in commotion, fighting one against another, and they will destroy their nationality."[17] He then went on to blame this turmoil on the fact that the United States had not treated the Mormons properly. On July 28, 1861, Brigham Young said the Civil War would not end until the "land is emptied."[18] Smith prophesied that the South would call upon Great Britain for assistance and that it, in turn, would call upon other nations for help. Although England did provide some supplies, it did not involve itself in the actual fighting, and its leaders never called upon other nations for help in its defense.

In an April 1843 revelation recorded in Doctrine and Covenants 130:12–15, Smith connected South Carolina's discontent with the policies coming out of Washington, D.C., with Christ's second coming:

> I prophesy, in the name of the Lord God, that the commencement of the difficulties which will cause much bloodshed previous to the coming of the Son of Man will be in South Carolina. It may probably arise through the slave question. This a voice declared to me, while I was praying earnestly on the subject, December 25th, 1832. I was once praying very earnestly to know the time of the coming of the Son of Man, when I heard a voice repeat the following: Joseph, my son, if thou livest until thou art eighty-five years old, thou shalt see the face of the Son of Man; therefore let this suffice, and trouble me no more on this matter.

Smith would not live to be eighty-five, as he died at the hands of a mob in Carthage, Illinois, on June 27, 1844. He was thirty-eight.

The Prophecy About a Temple in Independence, Missouri

In September 1832, Joseph Smith claimed to have received a revelation regarding the building of the "city of New Jerusalem. Which city shall be built, beginning at the temple lot, which is appointed by the finger of the Lord, in the western boundaries of the State of Missouri, and dedicated by the hands of Joseph Smith, Jun., and others with whom the Lord was well pleased" (D&C 84:1–3). This temple would be "reared in this generation.

For verily, this generation shall not all pass away until an house shall be built unto the Lord, and a cloud shall rest upon it, which cloud shall be even the glory of the Lord, which shall fill this house" (vv. 4–5).

The Saints were driven from that area and eventually made their way to the Salt Lake valley in 1847. Joseph Fielding Smith cited Doctrine and Covenants 124:49–54 to explain why the Mormons were not allowed to complete the Missouri temple.[19] Here, God supposedly allowed a postponement of the temple's construction because the Saints were "hindered by the hands of their enemies, and by their oppression." Because Joseph Fielding Smith offered this explanation over a hundred years after the revelation was originally given, he gave the impression that this postponement somehow nullified the portion of the prophecy that speaks of the temple being built by the generation that was alive in 1832. However, Apostle Orson Pratt (1811–1881) certainly didn't understand this passage as allowing for an indefinite delay. Instead, he gave the impression that these hindrances were only a temporary glitch. As late as 1870, Pratt reminded his listeners that the City of Zion and the temple must still be built by the generation living in 1832:

> God has been with us from the time that we came to this land, and I hope that the days of our tribulation are past. I hope this, because God promised in the year 1832 that we should, before the generation then living had passed away, return and build up the City of Zion in Jackson County; that we should return and build up the temple of the Most High where we formerly laid the corner stone. He promised us that He would manifest Himself on that temple, that the glory of God should be upon it; and not only upon the temple, but within it, even a cloud by day and a flaming fire by night. We believe in these promises as much as we believe in any promise ever uttered by the mouth of Jehovah. The Latter-day Saints just as much expect to receive a fulfilment of that promise during the generation that was in existence in 1832 as they expect that the sun will rise and set to-morrow. Why? Because God cannot lie. He will fulfil all His promises. He has spoken, it must come to pass.[20]

If Pratt's enthusiasm was misplaced, it appears that no one felt compelled to correct him. A year later, in a general conference message on April 9, 1871, Pratt again expressed his hope of seeing this prophecy fulfilled:

We just as much expect that a city will be built, called Zion, in the place and on the land which has been appointed by the Lord our God, and that a temple will be reared on the spot that has been selected, and the corner-stone of which has been laid, in the generation when this revelation was given; we just as much expect this as we expect the sun to rise in the morning and set in the evening; or as much as we expect to see the fulfillment of any of the purposes of the Lord our God, pertaining to the works of his hands. But says the objector, "thirty-nine years have passed away." What of that? The generation has not passed away; all the people that were living thirty-nine years ago have not passed away; but before they do pass away this will be fulfilled.[21]

If this prophecy is to be understood as written, there is no hope of seeing it fulfilled. As Joseph Fielding Smith conceded, "It may be reasonable to assume that in giving this revelation to the Prophet the Lord did have in mind the generation of people who would still be living within the one hundred years from the time of the announcement of the revelation, and that they would enjoy the blessings of the temple, and a glorious cloud would rest upon it. It is also reasonable to believe that no soul living in 1832, is still living in mortality on the earth."[22]

Was Jonah a False Prophet?

After looking more closely at these supposed prophecies, some Mormons might acknowledge that Smith made a few "errors." But they do not see this as a serious problem, since they can point to prophets in the Bible whom they believe made similar mistakes. One common example used is the prophet Jonah. As recorded in the four-chapter Old Testament book named after him, Jonah was commanded by God to "go to Nineveh, that great city, and cry against it; for their wickedness is come up before me" (1:2). Instead of going to Nineveh to preach God's judgment upon the city, Jonah disobeyed and attempted to run from God.

It took near-death experiences, first on a storm-tossed ship and then inside a fish, before Jonah was persuaded to deliver the ultimatum (Jonah 3:3). When he finally proclaimed the city's destruction within forty days, "the people of Nineveh believed God, and proclaimed a fast, and put on sackcloth, from the greatest of them even to the least of them" (v. 5), including the king of Nineveh. Although God fully intended to inflict destruction upon the city,

Joseph Smith claimed the Garden of Eden was located in the area of Independence, MO. After their expulsion, Adam and Eve fled to what Smith called the Valley of Adam-ondi-Ahman, located about seventy miles north of Independence.

He relented based upon the humbled response of the Ninevites. Jonah 3:10 says, "And God saw their works, that they turned from their evil way; and God repented of the evil, that he had said that he would do unto them; and he did it not."

The righteous nature of God allows for pardon on the condition of repentance. Jeremiah 18:8 states, "If that nation, against whom I have pronounced, turn from their evil, I will repent of the evil that I thought to do unto them." There is little doubt that Nineveh would have been destroyed if its inhabitants had not responded to Jonah's message. Even Jonah himself understood that there was a possibility the destruction of Nineveh might not come to pass when he told God in Jonah 4:2, "O LORD, is not this what I said when I was yet in my country? That is why I made haste to flee to Tarshish; for I knew that you are a gracious God and merciful, slow to anger and abounding in steadfast love, and relenting from disaster" (ESV).

While some lay Mormons might attempt to use the "Jonah defense" to shield their faith's founder, it is not a common tactic used by LDS leaders.

Speaking of the Ninevites, Orson Pratt taught that "they all turned and repented of their sins, and the Lord had compassion and did not execute the judgment on them because of their repentance."[23] Apostle Orson Whitney told a general conference audience in 1919,

> All God's promises and prophecies are conditional. Who am I, saith the Lord, that have promised and have not fulfilled? I command, and a man obeys not; I revoke, and they receive not the blessing. There never was a time in the history of the world when a nation against which a divine prophecy, a prophecy of disaster, had been uttered, could not obtain a revocation of the edict, if they were willing to pursue the course that God desired them to take. He sent Jonah to Nineveh, to tell them that within forty days that great city should be destroyed; but Nineveh repented, and God revoked his decree. The judgment passed over, but it would surely have come if the king and nobles and people had not humbled themselves and done the thing that was required of them. There is always an alternative—no "dead-open-and-shut" business about God's dealings with men. He gives them a chance.[24]

The problem with equating Joseph with Jonah is that many of Smith's prophecies did not come to pass, even after all the proper conditions were met. With this being the case, according to Deuteronomy 18:22, there is no reason to fear Smith's pronouncements because he has been proven to be a false prophet.

Questions for Discussion

- Considering the two prophecies mentioned in this chapter, does it matter whether or not Smith was correct? Why or why not?

- Some Mormons like to point to Jonah as an example of a prophet who made a mistake yet was still called a prophet. Why is this not a good example?

- Joseph Smith taught a number of doctrines that contradict the Bible. Does this fact matter? If so, why? If not, then how is it possible to distinguish a true prophet from a false prophet?

————————————— Evangelism Tip —————————————

Whether or not Joseph Smith met the requirement of a true prophet of God is an extremely sensitive subject. Be aware that loyalty to Smith can bring a discussion to an abrupt halt if the Mormon feels that criticism of the LDS founder is presented in a sardonic tone. Though Smith's prophetic credentials most certainly need to be examined and discussed at some point, it pays to be perceptive when seeking the right opportunity to do so. Overt criticism of Smith is sometimes taken better after the Mormon has a chance to hear some of your other concerns.

Why would Joseph Smith be willing to die as a martyr if he didn't believe God spoke to him?

Response Questions

- How do you define *martyr*?
- Do you personally believe Smith gave his life willingly?
- Let's suppose Smith was a martyr for his faith. How would this guarantee the truthfulness of what he taught?

• • • • • • • • • • • • • • • •

"Praise to his memory, he died as a martyr; / Honored and blest be his ever great name! / Long shall his blood, which was shed by assassins, / Plead unto heaven while the earth lauds his fame. / Hail to the Prophet, ascended to heaven! / Traitors and tyrants now fight him in vain. / Mingling with Gods, he can plan for his brethren; / Death cannot conquer the hero again."[1]

—LDS Hymn "Praise to the Man"

Summary

There is no doubt that the killing of Joseph Smith at the Carthage Jail was an atrocious act. However, all the circumstances surrounding a religious figure's death should be considered before the label of martyr is attached to the person, no matter how tragic the situation. Latter-day Saints are free to venerate their founding prophet, but the controversy surrounding Smith's death goes far beyond that of mere religious conviction. Despite the fact that Smith allegedly said he was going to his death as a "lamb led to the slaughter," the facts tend to taint this claim.

In 1839, MORMONISM's founder Joseph Smith (1805–1844) and the majority of his followers moved to Commerce, Illinois, a swamp-ridden town on the Mississippi River that he later renamed Nauvoo. Under Smith's leadership, the city became a prosperous example of what happens with vision. During his five-year stay at Nauvoo, Smith wore a number of hats, including that of the lieutenant general of the Nauvoo Legion, a local militia made up of all Mormon males between the ages of sixteen and fifty. At its peak, the Legion numbered five thousand members, which equaled more than half of the standing U.S. Army of that day.[2]

Smith was also a politician who served as the city's mayor and, at the time of his death in 1844, was campaigning for the presidency of the United States. Today, many Mormons look to this man as literally sacrificing himself for the cause of truth. President Brigham Young (1801–1877) explained, "He holds the keys of that kingdom for the last dispensation—the keys to rule in the spirit-world; and he rules there triumphantly, for he gained full power and a glorious victory over the power of Satan while he was yet in the flesh, and was a martyr to his religion and to the name of Christ, which gives him a most perfect victory in the spirit-world."[3]

Some basic facts leading up to Smith's imprisonment and eventual death must not be overlooked. For example, Smith's plural marriages—including relationships with teenage girls and married women[4]—along with what some considered to be an abuse of political authority, upset many of the local citizens. Concerning the perception of Joseph Smith by outsiders, LaMar Petersen wrote,

> An English clergyman visited Smith at Nauvoo and saw him as a "coarse plebeian sensual person in aspect, his countenance exhibiting a curious mixture of the knave and the clown." A Mississippi riverman "felt a little abashed at being in the presence of a man who had been in company with an angel; but hearing him converse removed all qualms and convinced me he was but a man and one of the coursest sort too." The *New York Sun* (August 5, 1842) righteously editorialized: "He stands before us a swindler of his community, an impious dictator over free will, and now in his most glaring, and even hideous aspect—a libertine unequalled in civilized life—a Giovanni of some dozen of mistresses, and these acquired under the garb of prophetic zeal."[5]

While Smith was able to protect his image with many Latter-day Saints living in Nauvoo, his hypocritical lifestyle apparently was not hidden from some of his followers. Petersen wrote, "Was Joseph's conduct exemplary? Being so constantly exposed before his people how could he have fooled them? Apostle Amasa Lyman thought perhaps not all were fooled. He told fellow-Apostle Abraham H. Cannon: 'Joseph Smith tried the faith of the Saints many times by his peculiarities. At one time, he had preached a powerful sermon on the Word of Wisdom, and immediately there after, he rode through the streets of Nauvoo smoking a cigar. Some of the brethren were tried as was Abraham of old.'"[6]

On June 7, 1844, a group of disaffected Mormons published what turned out to be the only edition of the *Nauvoo Expositor*, which strongly criticized Smith for his behavior. According to historian D. Michael Quinn, "The first issue promised that details of all its allegations would appear in the next edition."[7] Accusing the publishers of forming "a conspiracy for the purpose of destroying my life, and scattering the Saints or driving them from the state," Smith and the Nauvoo city council took immediate action.[8] According to LDS historian Reed C. Durham Jr.,

> As mayor of Nauvoo, Joseph Smith summoned the city council. Following fourteen hours of deliberation in three different sessions, the council resolved on Monday, June 10, about 6:30 PM, that the newspaper and its printing office were "a public nuisance" and instructed the mayor "to remove it . . . without delay." Joseph Smith promptly ordered the city marshal to destroy the press and burn all copies of the paper. At 8:00 PM the marshal carried out the mayor's orders (HC 6:432–49). That action, justified or not, played into the hands of the opposition. It riled anti-Mormon sentiment throughout Hancock County and provided substance for the charges used by the opposition to hold Joseph Smith in Carthage Jail, where he was murdered on June 27, 1844.[9]

On June 10, 1844, Francis M. Higbee, one of the seven men responsible for printing the critical newspaper, filed a complaint. According to the warrant signed by Justice of the Peace Thomas Morrison, Smith and others involved were charged with committing "a riot at and within the county aforesaid, wherein they, with force and violence broke into the office of the *Nauvoo Expositor*, and unlawfully and with force burned and destroyed the printing press, type and fixtures of the same, being the property of William Law, Wilson Law, Charles Ivins, Francis M. Higbee, Chauncey L. Higbee, Robert D. Foster, and Charles A. Foster."[10]

Fearing that a mob was "organizing to come upon the city, and plunder and destroy said city, as well as murder the citizens," Joseph Smith declared martial law on June 18. While addressing the Nauvoo Legion that afternoon, he drew his sword, and "presenting it to heaven," said, "I call God and angels to witness that I have unsheathed my sword with a firm and unalterable determination that this people shall have their legal rights, and be protected from mob violence, or my blood shall be split upon the ground like water, and my body consigned to the silent tomb. While I live, I will never tamely submit to the dominion of cursed mobocracy. I would welcome death rather than submit to this oppression; and it would be sweet, oh, sweet, to rest in the grave rather than submit to this oppression, agitation, annoyance, confusion, and alarm upon alarm, any longer."[11]

Smith's actions were interpreted by the state of Illinois as an act of treason. When he and his brother Hyrum turned themselves in on June 25, they were arrested on that charge and placed in a minimum-security cell at the Carthage Jail, about twenty-two miles from Nauvoo. On the morning of June 27, Smith wrote a letter to his wife Emma, saying, "I am very much resigned to my lot, knowing I am justified and have done the best that could be done."[12] It wasn't until after he finished his note that Smith discovered the Illinois governor had departed for Nauvoo, leaving him vulnerable to his enemies. That same morning John S. Fullmer visited Smith in his cell and gave him a "single barrel pistol." Smith, in turn, gave the gun to Hyrum.[13] Later that day, Cyrus H. Wheelock visited the jail, and as he was leaving, he took out a pepperbox six-shooter. He asked the prisoners, "Would any of you like to have this?" As John Taylor wrote, "Brother Joseph immediately replied, 'YES, give it to me,' whereupon he took the pistol, and put it in his pantaloons pocket."[14] Toward the end of the day (5 P.M.), armed men with blackened faces stormed the two-story Carthage Jail, with the two Smiths and their two companions (Willard Richards and John Taylor) inside. Joseph "sprang to his coat for his six-shooter, Hyrum for his single barrel, Taylor for Markham's large hickory cane, and Dr. Richards for Taylor's cane."[15] Mormon historian Richard L. Bushman describes the scene:

> Hyrum was the first to fall. A ball through the door struck him on the left side of the nose, throwing him to the floor. Three more balls

entered his thigh, torso, and shin, killing him. John Taylor was hit in the thigh and fell against the windowsill, breaking his watch. Crawling toward the bed, he was struck again in the hip. Joseph pulled the trigger six times into the hall, dropped the pistol on the floor, and sprang to the window. With one leg over the sill, he raised his arms in the Masonic sign of distress. A ball from the doorway struck his hip, and a shot from the outside entered his chest. Another hit under the heart and a fourth his collarbone. He fell outward crying, *"O Lord my God!"* Landing on his left side, he struggled to sit up against the curb of a well and died within seconds.[16]

A Lamb Led to the Slaughter?

John Taylor described how Smith had declared prior to his incarceration, "I am going like a lamb to the slaughter; but I am calm as a summer's morning; I have a conscience void of offense toward God, and toward all men. I SHALL DIE INNOCENT, AND IT SHALL YET BE SAID OF ME—HE WAS MURDERED IN COLD BLOOD" (D&C 135:4). This statement has been repeated by numerous Mormons and in LDS manuals, but did Smith's words match his actions?

When Smith referenced Isaiah 53:7 ("He was oppressed, and he was afflicted, yet he opened not his mouth: he is brought as a lamb to the slaughter, and as a sheep before her shearers is dumb, so he openeth not his mouth"), he made a clear—but clearly inaccurate—comparison between himself and Jesus. Jesus gave His life willfully. He offered no struggle or resistance, not even verbally. In fact, when Peter used physical force in an attempt to protect his master from the mob, Jesus rebuked him (cf. John 18:11). How can Smith's use of a lethal weapon, purposely used to cause bodily harm to his attackers, be compared to this? It is not so much Smith's defending himself that is troubling and offensive to many Christians but rather his erroneous comparison to the Savior of the world.

When Smith said he would die "innocent," what exactly did that mean?

- Was he innocent of the charge of riot? Though Smith was not present when the press was destroyed, he was clearly responsible for giving the order.
- Was he innocent of the *Nauvoo Expositor* charge of secretly practicing polygamy? Smith's polygamous and polyandrous ways were common

knowledge among Smith's close circle of friends and are well documented today.[17]

- Was he innocent of abusing his political power? The fact that even
  Mormons can't be sure his order to destroy the press was within legal
  bounds tends to indicate that he was at least somewhat at fault.
- Was he innocent of the charge of treason? Smith didn't know he would
  be charged with treason until he arrived in Carthage, well *after* he
  made the above statement.

Another point to consider regarding Smith's claim of being "like a lamb
led to the slaughter" is his response when the clash took place, for Smith
took out his pistol and began firing. According to John Taylor, Smith pulled
"the six-shooter left by Brother Wheelock from his pocket, opened the door
slightly, and snapped the pistol six successive times; only three of the barrels,
however, were discharged. I afterward understood that two or three were
wounded by these discharges, two of whom, I am informed, died."[18] Who
fired the first shot in the midst of the noise and confusion probably will never
be known. Mormons have always insisted that Smith returned fire after his
brother Hyrum had been mortally wounded. However, an account given by
Governor Thomas Ford provided some different details:

> The conspirators came up, jumped the slight fence around the jail,
> were fired upon by the guard, which, according to arrangement,
> was overpowered immediately, and the assailants entered the prison,
> to the door of the room where the two prisoners were confined,
> with two of their friends, who voluntarily bore them company. An
> attempt was made to break open the door; but Joe Smith being
> armed with a six-barrelled pistol, furnished by his friends, fired sev-
> eral times as the door was bursted open, and wounded three of the
> assailants. At the same time several shots were fired into the room,
> by some of which John Taylor received four wounds, and Hiram
> Smith was instantly killed.[19]

The moral justification for Smith's attempt to defend himself in an unjusti-
fied attack upon him is not being questioned. However, such a scene hardly is
reminiscent of the final hours and moments of Jesus' earthly ministry. While
Smith could have chosen to fire a warning shot with the hope of scaring his
murderers away, he instead chose to fire directly into the crowd, knowing full

The Carthage jail, located in Carthage, Illinois, where Joseph Smith and his brother Hyrum were killed by a mob on June 27, 1844.

well that his aim at so close a range was going to cause bodily harm. Is this the behavior of someone who plans to *willingly* lay down his life?

Allow us to provide a hypothetical situation to illustrate our case. Suppose a journalist at the *Salt Lake Tribune* published an exposé on a well-known but controversial religious figure (for clarity, let's call him "Rev. Bob") in the Salt Lake City area. Knowing that another edition will follow with more unflattering details and accusations, Rev. Bob becomes deeply concerned that such a hit piece could ruin his credibility and possibly endanger himself and his followers. In order to preempt what he insists are libelous accusations, he directs some of his most zealous adherents to break into the *Tribune* offices, find the journalist's desk, hack into his computer, and reformat the hard drive, thereby preventing any further offensive information from being printed.

To add insult to injury, they smash the computer and monitor with baseball bats. In doing so, the perpetrators are caught on surveillance cameras. Rev. Bob is quickly connected to the crime and is summarily arrested at his home. As the police car transporting him arrives at the jail, an angry mob, furious that this religious leader would attempt to cover up his repugnant behavior, meets the entourage and threatens to do him bodily harm. As the mob moves closer, a shot rings out. Fearing for his life, Rev. Bob panics and grabs a gun from the holster of an officer standing nearby and fires on the crowd, shooting three people. In the confusion, he himself is killed by others in the mob who are also armed.

Though a wild and morbid story, the question remains: Would Rev. Bob's death be reported as a "martyrdom" because he was well known for his distinct religious beliefs? Remember, Joseph Smith was *not* arrested because he was performing any particular religious duty. He was *not* standing behind a pulpit preaching a sermon or sharing with an unbeliever on the sidewalk what he believed to be true. He was *not* arrested for taking food to the poor or repairing a widow's roof. As noted previously, he was considered by many in the community to be a scoundrel, and it was his disgusting behavior that created the conflict when the publishers of the newspaper exposed him. He was sent to jail because he was an assumed lawbreaker—charged with riot— and he died as a result of a brief firefight in which he participated, *willingly* using deadly force. Mormons are certainly free to insist that their founder perished as a martyr, but the facts lead a dispassionate observer to a different conclusion. He did not die as an innocent, helpless lamb. Mormons should be honest enough to admit that those who do not share their admiration for Smith at least have some good historical reasons for disagreeing with their claim that he died as a martyr in any traditional sense of that term.

Though Latter-day Saints often view Smith through rose-colored glasses, many of his contemporaries did not. As Ford's history recounts,

> Thus fell Joe Smith, the most successful impostor in modern times; a man who, though ignorant and coarse, had some great natural parts, which fitted him for temporary success, but which were so obscured and counteracted by the inherent corruption and vices of his nature, that he never could succeed in establishing a system of policy which looked to permanent success in the future. His lusts, his love of money and power, always set him to studying present gratification and convenience, rather than the remote consequences of his plans. It seems that no power of intellect can save a corrupt man from this error. The strong cravings of the animal nature will never give fair play to a fine understanding, the judgment is never allowed to choose that good which is far away, in preference to enticing evil near at hand. And this may be considered a wise ordinance

of Providence, by which the counsels of talented but corrupt men, are defeated in the very act which promised success. It must not be supposed that the pretended prophet practiced the tricks of a common impostor; that he was a dark and gloomy person, with a long beard, a grave and severe aspect, and a reserved and saintly carriage of his person; on the contrary, he was full of levity, even to boyism romping; dressed like a dandy, and at times drank like a sailor and swore like a pirate. He could, as occasion required, be exceedingly meek in his deportment; and then again rough and boisterous as a highway robber; being always able to satisfy his followers of the propriety of his conduct. He always quailed before power, and was arrogant to weakness. At times he could put on the air of a penitent, as if feeling the deepest humiliation for his sins, and suffering unutterable anguish, and indulging in the most gloomy forebodings of eternal woe. At such times he would call for the prayers of the brethren in his behalf, with a wild and fearful energy and earnestness.[20]

It can easily be said that the above depiction of the founder of Mormonism is tainted by bias, but the pendulum swings both ways. While Jesus' enemies also saw Him as an imposter, hindsight proves otherwise. The accusations against Him were unfounded. This is not true of Joseph Smith. Available evidence, even from LDS sources, exposes his questionable character. This is why many choose not to label Joseph Smith as a martyr in the traditional sense, any more than they would venerate religious figures like Jim Jones, David Koresh, and Marshall Applewhite. Call them fanatics or label them deluded and insane, but martyrs? No way.

With all this said, what if Smith *had* died for his beliefs, making his death in fact a traditional martyrdom? Would this have any bearing on his professed truth claims? To insist that this somehow legitimizes Mormonism would mean any religion with "martyrs" should be considered true. But would we want to make a case for the truthfulness of Islam because some of its adherents (believing it to be the will of Allah) perform suicidal acts and are called "martyrs" by other Muslims? Rather, the very essence of a religion, such as its teachings and its revelation of the God of this universe, needs to be understood in order to determine whether that faith is true. Based on our study, Joseph Smith's religion deviates from the very core essentials of the Christian faith; thus, regardless of how Smith died, neither he nor his teachings should be followed.

Questions for Discussion

- In what ways did Joseph Smith's death differ from the deaths of Jesus, John the Baptist, and Stephen, as recorded in the Gospels and the book of Acts?

- What criteria do you think should be considered when determining whether or not a person died as a martyr?

- Even if Joseph Smith was a martyr for his faith, why would his death not be good evidence for the authenticity and truthfulness of Smith's religion?

─────────────── Evangelism Tip ───────────────

While we don't recommend making this chapter's topic into a central argument, it does seem to come up in many conversations. The life of Joseph Smith stands in stark contrast to that of Jesus. This is why equating Smith's death to that of a "lamb to the slaughter," a description given to the Messiah in Isaiah 53:7 and explained in Acts 8:30–35 as a reference to Jesus, is so offensive to Christians. Since the prophecy in Isaiah is about the Savior Christians worship, Mormons need to understand how sacrilegious the comparison really is.

Appendix I

Ten questions for members of the Church of Jesus Christ of Latter-day Saints

HERE IS A SAMPLING OF possible questions a Christian can use to direct a conversation with a Mormon onto a topic of eternal significance:

1. **Keeping the commandments:** Doctrine and Covenants 25:15 in the standard works says that unless a person keeps the commandments "continually," he or she cannot go where God is. Do you keep the commandments continually? If not, where do Mormons like you go when they die?

2. **Mormonism's teachings not found in the Book of Mormon:** Joseph Smith once said that a person could get nearer to God by abiding by the precepts of the Book of Mormon than by following any other book. Where in the Book of Mormon does it say Nephites held the Melchizedek priesthood, Nephites practiced baptism for the dead, Nephites believed in the plurality of gods, God has a body of flesh and bones, Heavenly Mother exists, all humans existed as spirits in a previous existence, Jesus and Lucifer are brothers, marriage is necessary for exaltation, or three degrees of glory exist?

3. **Justified by faith alone:** Your leaders have taught that exaltation requires works, such as temple marriage and enduring to the end. If this is true, then why did Joseph Smith insert the word *alone*

into Romans 3:28 of his Inspired Version (also known as the Joseph Smith Translation) of the Bible? (It reads, "Therefore we conclude that a man is justified by faith alone without the deeds of the law.")

4. **An unchangeable God:** Joseph Smith once said, "We have imagined and supposed that God was God from all eternity. I will refute that idea, and take away the veil, so that you may see." But the Book of Mormon says in Moroni 8:18, "For I know that God is not a partial God, neither a changeable being; but he is unchangeable from all eternity to all eternity." Did God change, or has He always been God?

5. **No other true Gods:** Isaiah 44:6 and 8 says God knows of no other gods. Does your God know about the God he served when he was a human?

6. **Salvation:** Because 2 Nephi 25:23 says that people are saved by grace "after all we can do," have you done all you can do? How do you know when you have accomplished this?

7. **Assurance of salvation:** The apostle John stated in 1 John 5:13 that it is possible for believers to "know" that they have eternal life. If you were to die right now, do you know for certain you will have eternal life? If not, when will you finally know? Wouldn't you like to have this issue settled before you die?

8. **Nature of God:** If God is the offspring of another God and you found out that He has more knowledge and power than Heavenly Father, would you worship Him instead?

9. **Changing doctrines:** The doctrine of polygamy was abolished in 1890 with the Manifesto; the curse on those with African heritage was lifted in 1978. Why did the LDS Church change its position on these issues when Alma 41:8 says, "The decrees of God are unalterable"?

10. **Knowledge of truth:** As a person who values religious truth, have you ever considered the possibility that you might be wrong about truth? If there was the slightest possibility you could be wrong, would you want to know?

Appendix 2

Ready references for witnessing to Mormons

BELOW ARE HANDY REFERENCES that can be useful when having a conversation with a Latter-day Saint.

Witnessing
Proverbs 12:15; 28:26: Only fools trust in their feelings
Proverbs 14:12: What *seems* right can lead to death
John 7:24: We are to make righteous judgments
2 Corinthians 11:4: False Christs do exist
Galatians 1:8–9: False gospels do exist
Galatians 4:16: Discussing truth should not make us enemies
Ephesians 4:15: Speak the truth in love
Colossians 4:6: Let your speech be gracious
1 Thessalonians 5:21: Test everything
1 Peter 3:15–16: Share the truth in gentleness and with respect
1 John 4:1: Test the spirits to see whether they are from God
Jude 3: Contend for the Christian faith

Godhead
Numbers 23:19: God is not a man
Deuteronomy 6:4; Mark 12:29: God is one God
Psalm 90:2: God is God from all eternity to all eternity
Psalm 102:27: God is eternally the same
Isaiah 43:10: No God before or after God

Isaiah 44:6, 8: God knows of no other gods
Isaiah 45:5–6, 22: There is no God besides God
Malachi 3:6: God does not change
John 1:1, 14; 20:28; Romans 9:5; Philippians 2:5–11;
  Colossians 1:15–17; 2:9; Hebrews 1:8; Revelation 1:8: Jesus is God
John 4:24: God is Spirit
1 Corinthians 15:1–5: The resurrection of Jesus is true
Hebrews 7:24–25: Jesus has a permanent priesthood

Bible
Isaiah 40:8: God's Word stands forever
John 17:17: God's Word is Truth
Acts 17:11: Searching the Bible makes one noble
2 Timothy 3:16: God inspired the Bible
2 Peter 3:16: Paul's words were considered Scripture

Salvation
Psalm 103:12: God removes (forgives) sins as far as east is from the west
Isaiah 64:6: Our righteous acts are like filthy rags
Jeremiah 17:9: The heart is desperately wicked
Matthew 1:21: Jesus came to save His people from their sins
John 1:12; Romans 8:14; 9:8: We become children of God by faith
John 5:29: There are two resurrections: one to life and one to damnation
John 6:47: He who believes in Jesus has eternal life
John 14:6; Acts 4:12: Salvation is found only in Jesus
Romans 3:23: All are sinners and fall short of God's glory
Romans 3:28; Galatians 2:15–16: Man is justified by faith, not law
Romans 6:23: Sin's wages = death; God's gift = life
2 Corinthians 6:2: Today is the day of salvation
Galatians 2:21: Righteousness is not gained through the law
Ephesians 2:8–9: Salvation comes by grace
Philippians 2:12: Work out (not for) your salvation
Titus 3:5: We are saved through God's mercy
Hebrews 8:12–13: God mercifully forgets forgiven sins
Hebrews 9:27: After death comes judgment
James 2:10: Breaking one law makes one guilty of all
1 Peter 2:5: All Christians possess a royal priesthood
1 John 5:13: You can know if you have eternal life

Notes

Introduction

1. While technically a nickname that comes from a Book of Mormon character, the term *Mormon* is commonly used by those within the religion. We will follow the format used by one Mormon apologist, who says that "using the full title, The Church of Jesus Christ of Latter-day Saints, several times in each paragraph would be awkward, redundant and space consuming. Therefore, when appropriate, other commonly used names are substituted: Latter-day Saints, LDS Church, LDS members, Mormons and the Church" (Scharffs, *The Missionary's Little Book of Answers*, 7–8).
2. Joseph Smith—History 1:19 (PoGP). For further information on the First Vision, see chapter 31.
3. To someone not familiar with basic doctrinal differences between Christianity and Mormonism, we recommend another book we wrote called *Mormonism 101: Examining the Religion of the Latter-day Saints* (Grand Rapids: Baker, 2000).

Chapter 1

1. Stuy, *Collected Discourses*, 2:305. This was from a stake conference message on Nov. 2, 1891.
2. Gary J. Coleman, "Mom, Are We Christians?" *Ensign*, May 2007, 94.
3. Joseph Smith—History 1:19 (PoGP). For more information on the First Vision account, see chapter 31.
4. *Teachings of Presidents of the Church: David O. McKay*, 93.
5. *Doctrines of the Gospel Student Manual: Religion 430–431*, 59.
6. Neil Andersen, "Be Thou an Example to the Believers," *Ensign*, November 2010, 41.
7. *Preach My Gospel*, 65.
8. Scharffs, *The Missionary's Little Book of Answers*, 10.
9. Benjamin B. Warfield, "Redeemer" and "Redemption," http://www.theologue.org/Redeemer&Redemption-BBWarfield.html.
10. Daniel Peterson, "Focus on Similarities Can Prove Misleading," *Mormon Times*, November 6, 2011, 8.
11. *Teachings of Presidents of the Church: Brigham Young*, 34.
12. *Journal of Discourses*, 23:343–44.
13. Roberts, *Defense of the Faith and the Saints*, 2:570.
14. Jeffrey R. Holland, "The Only True God and Jesus Christ Whom He Hath Sent," *Ensign*, November 2007, 40.
15. *Journal of Discourses*, 2:210.
16. Bernard P. Brockbank, "The Living Christ," *Ensign*, May 1977, 26.
17. Gordon B. Hinckley, "We Look to Christ," *Ensign*, May 2002, 90.
18. Talmage, *The Articles of Faith*, 98.

19. Richards, *A Marvelous Work and a Wonder*, 24.

20. McConkie, *Mormon Doctrine*, 287.

21. Kimball, *The Miracle of Forgiveness*, 206. Also see *Book of Mormon Student Manual: Religion 121 and 122*, 36.

22. Joseph Smith, *Teachings of the Prophet Joseph Smith*, 310. See also *History of the Church of Jesus Christ of Latter-day Saints*, 5:425.

23. "Letter Reaffirms Use of King James Version of Bible," *Church News*, June 20, 1992, 3.

24. Jeffrey Holland, "My Words . . . Never Cease," *Ensign*, May 2008, 91.

25. McConkie, *Mormon Doctrine*, 525.

26. "Frequently Asked Questions," accessed August 10, 2011, http://newsroom.lds.org /article/frequently-asked-questions. The LDS Newsroom is connected with the LDS Church's official Web site.

27. Dallin H. Oaks, "Apostasy and Restoration," *Ensign*, May 1995, 84.

28. Gomes, *Unmasking the Cults*, 7.

29. Ibid., 10.

30. Ibid., 15–16.

31. Ibid., 16.

32. Mark E. Petersen, "Evidence of Things Not Seen," *Ensign*, May 1978, 62.

33. McConkie, *Doctrinal New Testament Commentary* 2:179.

34. McConkie, *The Millennial Messiah*, 48.

35. M. Russell Ballard, "The Importance of a Name," *Ensign*, November 2011, 81.

Chapter 2

1. Thomas S. Monson, "God Reveals Truth to His Prophets and to Us," *Ensign*, March 2011, 8.

2. Joseph Smith—History 1:12, 19 (PoGP).

3. *Gospel Principles*, 45.

4. Alma P. Burton, "Doctrine: Distinctive Teachings," in Ludlow, *Encyclopedia of Mormonism*, 1:398.

5. *Preach My Gospel*, 37.

6. Dieter F. Uchtdorf, "Why Do We Need Prophets?" *Ensign*, March 2012, 5.

7. D. Todd Christofferson, "The Doctrine of Christ," *Ensign*, May 2012, 86–87.

8. Grudem, *The Gift of Prophecy in the New Testament and Today*, 160.

9. Ibid., 28.

10. Ibid., 57.

11. Ash, *Shaken Faith Syndrome*, 21–22.

12. Ibid, 16.

13. For example, he pointed to the issue of the location of the Book of Mormon lands, saying "prophets may offer speculations like any other student or scholar" (ibid., 25).

14. *Teachings of Presidents of the Church: Wilford Woodruff*, 199.

15. *Teachings of Presidents of the Church: George Albert Smith*, 60.

16. *Conference Reports*, Oct. 1970, 152; *Improvement Era*, Dec. 1970, 126. Obviously, Lee's talk was considered important or it wouldn't have been quoted word for word in church manuals such as *Old Testament Seminary Student Study Guide; The Latter-day Saint Woman: Basic Manual for Women Part A; New Testament Teacher's*

Gospel Doctrine Manual; Teachings of Presidents of the Church: Harold B. Lee; Book of Mormon: Gospel Doctrine Teacher's Manual; and *Doctrine and Covenants and Church History Gospel Doctrine Teacher's Manual.* It was also quoted in the October 1993 general conference by Seventy Joe J. Christensen.

17. *Teachings of Presidents of the Church: Spencer W. Kimball,* 256.

18. *Teachings of the Living Prophets Student Manual: Religion 333* (2010), 85.

19. Ibid, 25.

20. *Teachings of the Living Prophets Teacher Manual: Religion 333,* 13. On the same page, teachers are instructed to "help your students understand how important the role of revelation from the Lord to His prophet is in the process of calling Apostles."

21. M. Russell Ballard, "His Word Ye Shall Receive," *Ensign,* May 2001, 65. Quoted in *Teachings of the Living Prophets Teacher Manual: Religion 333,* 6.

22. *Larry King Live,* September 8, 1998.

23. Lee, *Stand Ye in Holy Places,* 129.

24. Claudio R. M. Costa, "Obedience to the Prophets," *Ensign,* November 2010, 11–13.

25. Kevin R. Duncan, "Our Very Survival," *Ensign,* November 2010, 34–36.

26. It should be noted that Benson's speech was also included in the 2010 edition of the *Teachings of the Living Prophets Student Manual: Religion 333* (2010), 22–27.

27. When a Mormon uses this point, determine what the living prophet has said that is supposed to be contradicting a previous prophet. Certainly the Mormon Church leaders have changed official views on issues such as polygamy and race. Yet, while the emphasis may have changed, doctrines involving the Godhead, Scripture, and salvation generally have remained the same over the decades. In addition, common sense would dictate that if the LDS leaders were getting their truth from the same source—presumably God—the teaching should remain constant.

28. Claudio R. M. Costa, "Obedience to the Prophets," *Ensign,* November 2010, 13.

29. *History of the Church of Jesus Christ of Latter-day Saints,* 5:265. Also see Widtsoe, *Evidences and Reconciliations,* 236–39. All things being equal, however, this non-canonical comment from Smith's journal really becomes no more authoritative than the quotes the Mormon might be trying to sidestep.

30. D. Todd Christofferson, "The Doctrine of Christ," *Ensign,* May 2012, 88.

31. Ibid, 89.

32. *Conference Reports,* April 1937, 34.

33. Joseph Fielding Smith, *Doctrines of Salvation,* 3:296. According to page 295, the "class" Smith refers to are the "ungodly," "the bigoted," and "those who love iniquity."

34. "Mormon President Warns Students of Pornography, Criticizing Church Leaders," *Salt Lake Tribune,* January 27, 1996, C1.

35. "Use Proper Sources," *Church News,* January 9, 2010, 16.

36. *Doctrine and Covenants and Church History Gospel Doctrine Teacher's Manual,* 244–45.

37. "Teachings of Our Time," *Ensign,* November 2008, 121.

38. "The Church and New Media: Clarity, Context and an Official Voice," accessed November 17, 2011, http://newsroom.lds.org/article/the-church-and-new-media :-clarity,-context-and-an-official-voice-newsroom-lds.org-full-story.

Chapter 3

1. *Conference Reports*, April 1926, 139.
2. Robinson, *Are Mormons Christians?*, vii.
3. McConkie, *Mormon Doctrine*, 139.
4. *History of the Church of Jesus Christ of Latter-day Saints*, 2:63.
5. *A Sure Foundation: Answers to Difficult Gospel Questions*, 195.
6. Ibid, 196.
7. Whitmer, *An Address to All Believers in Christ*, 73.
8. For example, President Joseph Fielding Smith referred to the Reorganized Church of Jesus Christ of Latter Day Saints (RLDS), based in Independence, Missouri, as a "spurious organization" (*Doctrines of Salvation*, 1:261), and Smith's son-in-law Bruce R. McConkie called the RLDS a "cult" and an "apostate faction" (*Mormon Doctrine*, 629). The Reorganized Church of Jesus Christ of Latter Day Saints is now known as the Community of Christ.
9. See Rom. 12:5 and 1 Cor. 12:12, 27.

Chapter 4

1. Carlos E. Asay, "Opposition to the Work of God," *Ensign*, November 1981, 67.
2. *Webster's New World College Dictionary*, http://www.yourdictionary.com/persecute.
3. Quinn, *The Mormon Hierarchy*, 91.
4. Allen and Leonard, *The Story of the Latter-day Saints*, 93.
5. LeSueur, *The 1838 Mormon War in Missouri*, 3.
6. Allen and Leonard, *The Story of the Latter-day Saints*, 94.
7. LeSueur, *The 1838 Mormon War in Missouri*, 4.
8. Ibid, 133.
9. McConkie, *A New Witness for the Articles of Faith*, 656–57.
10. Quinn, *The Mormon Hierarchy*, 100. While many Latter-day Saints are quick to mention Governor Boggs's extermination order, they often overlook the fact that Sidney Rigdon's call for a "war of extermination" preceded Boggs's order by four months.
11. Ibid, 99.
12. "Mormon Story of Icelandic Persecution Collides with Fact, July 29, 2010, http://blog.mrm.org/2010/07/mormon-story-of-icelandic-persecution-collides-with-fact/.
13. *Conference Reports*, October 1907, 118–19.
14. Walker, Turley, and Leonard, *Massacre at Mountain Meadows*, 13.
15. For example, see the Voice of the Martyrs Web site at http://www.persecution.com.

Chapter 5

1. Quoted in Lawrence Wright, "Lives of the Saints," *The New Yorker*, January 21, 2002, http://www.newyorker.com/archive/2002/01/21/020121fa_FACT1. The reporter (Lawrence Wright) said that when giving this quote, "Hinckley cautioned [him] against speaking with the Church's many critics."
2. "Growth of the Church," accessed August 10, 2011, http://newsroom.lds.org/topic/church-growth.
3. Daniel Peterson, "The Internet Aids Missionary Effort," *Mormon Times*, April 7, 2011.

4. Peter Henderson and Kristina Cooke, "Mormonism Besieged by the Modern Age," Jan. 30, 2012, http://uk.reuters.com/article/2012/01/30/uk-mormonchurch -idUKTRE80T1CP20120130.

5. David Stewart, "LDS Church Growth, Member Activity, and Convert Retention: Review and Analysis," Chapter V-01: Conclusions, accessed August 24, 2012, http://cumorah.com/index.php?target=church_growth_articles&story_id=21.

6. Generally, a person who stops attending or leaves the LDS Church remains a member in the Mormon church rolls unless the person pursues having his or her name removed. Some who leave Mormonism don't bother with the process, which can be a hassle.

7. Ostling and Ostling, *Mormon America*, 128–29.

8. *Deseret News 2010 Church Almanac*, 30. At first glance, the figures listed on the page appear to be just for 2009. However, in a much smaller font at the bottom of the page, it reads, "TOTAL DONATIONS FROM 1985 TO PRESENT."

9. "The Salvation Army in the Body of Christ: An Ecclesiological Statement," 2008, http://www1.salvationarmy.org/ihq/documents/Ecclesiological-Statement.pdf.

10. E.g., see "Can Atheists Be Charitable?" http://www.squidoo.com/Atheist-Chari ties.

11. "New Survey Highlights Causes, Costs of Mormon Faith Crises," rev. February 6, 2012, http://whymormonsleave.com/wp-content/uploads/2012/01/Mormon _Stories_FC.pdf.

12. "Nearly 1 in 5 Utah women use antidepressants," *Salt Lake Tribune*, September 16, 2010, A1.

13. Kent Ponder, "Mormon Women, Prozac, and Therapy," http://www.concerned christians.com/index.php?option=com_fireboard&Itemid=42&func=view&id =74625&catid=526.

14. "Ranking America's Mental Health: An Analysis of Depression Across the States," accessed August 24, 2012, http://www.nmha.org/go/state-ranking.

15. Dennis Romboy, "Utahans Think About Suicide More Than Other Americans, study shows," October 21, 2011, http://www.deseretnews.com/article/705392958 /Utahns-think-about-suicide-more-than-other-Americans-study-shows.html?s _cid=Email-1. The study was based on the 2008–09 National Survey of Drug Use and Health.

Chapter 6

1. Van Wagoner, *Mormon Polygamy*, 212.

2. Technically, polygamy speaks of either a man or woman being married to multiple spouses. Polygyny involves the marriage of a man to more than one spouse. Polyandry involves the marriage between a woman and multiple husbands.

3. Newell and Avery, *Mormon Enigma*, 96. Van Wagoner notes that "'Polygamy,' 'spiritual wifery,' 'spiritual marriage,' and 'plural marriage' were all apparently interchangeable in Mormon and non-Mormon contexts during the early 1840s" (Van Wagoner, *Mormon Polygamy*, 26).

4. Copan, *Is God a Moral Monster?*, 112.

5. Ibid., 117.

6. Millet et al, *LDS Beliefs*, 493.

7. Widtsoe, *Evidences and Reconciliations*, 391.

8. Stanley Ivans, "Notes on Mormon Polygamy," in Quinn, *The New Mormon History*, 177.

9. Compton, *In Sacred Loneliness,* 2.

10. Ibid., 15. LDS historian Richard L. Bushman places Smith's polyandrous marriages at ten (Bushman, *Joseph Smith,* 439).

11. "Polygamy book/Children of Polygamous Marriages," http://fairmormon.org/Polygamy_book/Children_of_polygamous_marriages.

12. *Conference Reports,* October 1947, 165.

13. *Doctrine and Covenants Student Manual: Religion 324–325,* 362.

14. Ibid. See also Woodruff, *Discourses of Wilford Woodruff,* 215.

15. Kenneth L. Cannon II, "After the Manifesto: Mormon Polygamy 1890–1906," in Quinn, *The New Mormon History: Revisionist Essays on the Past,* 202–3.

16. Ibid., 204.

17. Buerger, *The Mysteries of Godliness,* 58–59.

18. Alexander, *Mormonism in Transition,* 60.

19. *History of the Church of Jesus Christ of Latter-day Saints,* 5:xxxii.

20. *Journal of Discourses,* 16:166.

21. Hardy, *Solemn Covenant,* 298.

22. Clark, *Messages of the First Presidency,* 5:329.

23. *A Comprehensive History of The Church of Jesus Christ of Latter-day Saints,* 2:407.

24. *Journal of Discourses,* 20:276.

25. Ibid., 22:147–48.

26. Van Wagoner, *Mormon Polygamy,* 141. Woodruff signed the Manifesto two years later.

27. McConkie, *Mormon Doctrine,* 578.

28. James E. Faust, "The Light in Their Eyes," *Ensign,* November 2005, 21.

29. *Handbook 1: Stake Presidents and Bishops,* 20.

30. Ibid.

31. Dallin H. Oaks, "Timing," January 29, 2002, BYU Devotional, http://speeches.byu.edu/?act=viewitem&id=229.

32. George D. Smith, *Nauvoo Polygamy,* 51.

Chapter 7

1. *Teachings of Presidents of the Church: George Albert Smith,* 125.

2. Tad R. Callister, "The Book of Mormon—A Book from God," *Ensign,* November 2011, 75. Callister's conclusion seems to ignore the fact that there are numerous splinter groups of Latter-day Saints who all use the Book of Mormon.

3. Craig L. Blomberg, "Is Mormonism Christian?" in Beckwith et al., *The New Mormon Challenge,* 322–23.

4. For a detailed study, see Shields, *Divergent Paths of the Restoration.* The third edition, published in 1982, includes references to certain movements that were only rumored to be in existence. In addition, he certainly couldn't cover the many splinter groups formed after 1982.

5. *History of the Church of Jesus Christ of Latter-day Saints,* 6:408–9.

6. For an example of this freedom, see how Paul explains the issue of meat offered to idols in 1 Cor. 8:1–13; 10:23–33.

Chapter 8

1. M. Russell Ballard, "The Importance of a Name," *Ensign*, November 2011, 80.
2. *True to the Faith*, 13.
3. *Gospel Principles*, 95.
4. Gordon B. Hinckley, "We Bear Witness of Him," *Ensign*, May 1998, 4.
5. *Joseph Smith—History* 1:19 (PoGP). This passage is found in the Pearl of Great Price, one of Mormonism's standard works.
6. For example, presidents Brigham Young (*Discourses of Brigham Young*, 83); Wilford Woodruff (Stuy, *Collected Discourses*, 2:124); Heber J. Grant (*Conference Reports*, April 1926, 13); David O. McKay (*Conference Reports*, October 1966, 86); Joseph Fielding Smith (*Answers to Gospel Questions*, 1:97; 5:xi); Spencer W. Kimball (*The Teachings of Spencer W. Kimball*, 423); Ezra Taft Benson (*Ensign*, January 1973, 58, and November 1988, 86); and Gordon B. Hinckley (*Ensign*, June 2004, 3) all taught that the authority of the Christian church was absent until it was restored by Joseph Smith.
7. Talmage, *The Great Apostasy*, iii.
8. *Preach My Gospel*, 35–36. Notice in this quote that the missionaries are instructed to provide just enough information to show a "need for the Restoration." Since the very heart of this argument involves a topic (universal apostasy) that can (and should) be quite offensive to Christians, many Mormon missionaries on the field who heed this advice end up becoming more politically correct than some of their former leaders, who taught that Christians "are shrouded in ignorance" (Brigham Young in *Journal of Discourses*, 7:333) and have "inherited many myths, legends, and traditions from their ancestors—all of which views they falsely assume are part of true religion" (McConkie, *Mormon Doctrine*, 525).
9. Even D&C 18:5 quotes this verse, substituting the word "you" for "it."
10. *Journal of Discourses*, 13:125.

Chapter 9

1. Woodruff, *The Discourses of Wilford Woodruff*, 17.
2. The JST "translation" of this verse is actually a conflation of Matt. 7:1 and John 7:24 in other Bible versions.
3. Matt. 7:8 in the JST; Matt. 7:5 in all other versions.
4. For example, see Luke 18:10ff and John 8:44.
5. Quoted in Strobel, *The Case for Faith*, 210.
6. *History of the Church of Jesus Christ of Latter-day Saints*, 5:499.
7. Young, *Discourses of Brigham Young*, 126.
8. Ibid., 251.
9. *Teachings of Presidents of the Church: Joseph F. Smith*, 53.
10. McConkie, *The Promised Messiah*, 295.
11. Hodge, *Systematic Theology*, 3:437.
12. *Journal of Discourses*, 14:216.
13. Pratt, *The Seer*, 15–16.

Chapter 10

1. *Conference Reports*, October 1968, 113.
2. *Journal of Discourses*, 16:44–45.

3. Joseph Fielding Smith, *Answers to Gospel Questions*, 3:79.
4. Stephen D. Nadauld, "Financial Contributions," in Ludlow, *Encyclopedia of Mormonism*, 510.
5. Smith and Sjodahl, *Doctrine and Covenants Commentary*, 234.
6. Spencer J. Condie, "Missionary/Missionary Life," in Ludlow, *Encyclopedia of Mormonism*, 910.

Chapter 11

1. Kimball, *The Teachings of Spencer W. Kimball*, 494.
2. Joshua J. Perkey, "Power in the Priesthood Restored," *Ensign*, June 2012, 28–29.
3. Joseph Fielding Smith, *Doctrines of Salvation*, 3:103.
4. According to the *History of the Church of Jesus Christ of Latter-day Saints*, 1:41, this priesthood was bestowed sometime between May 15, 1829 and April 1830.
5. Russell M. Nelson, "Honoring the Priesthood," *Ensign,* May 1993, 40.
6. Kimball, *The Teachings of Spencer W. Kimball*, 51.
7. Boyd K. Packer, "The Honor and Order of the Priesthood," *Ensign*, June 2012, 24, quoting from "The Aaronic Priesthood," *Ensign*, November 1981, 32–33.
8. *Teachings of Presidents of the Church: George Albert Smith*, 124–25.
9. McConkie, *Mormon Doctrine*, 479.
10. Boyd K. Packer, "The Honor and Order of the Priesthood," *Ensign*, June 2012, 24.
11. *Conference Reports,* April 1921, 108.
12. Penrose, *Mormon Doctrine Plain and Simple*, 51. This pamphlet was published by the Juvenile Instructor's Office, a nineteenth-century LDS publisher in Salt Lake City. The words "power to bring up his wife" were later changed to "his resurrected wife," making the one responsible for her resurrection vague.
13. *Journal of Discourses*, 5:291.
14. While some might say that "order of Melchizedec" refers to a group of people, this is not what is meant in this context. Melichizedek as an individual is compared to Jesus as an individual, the only ones who were both priests and kings.
15. Modern versions correctly translate the term "children of God" rather than the KJV's "sons of God" in both passages written by the apostle John.
16. D&C 11:30 and 35:2 both quote John 1:12.

Chapter 12

1. *Achieving a Celestial Marriage*, 65.
2. For example, see Joseph Smith, *History of the Church of Jesus Christ of Latter-day Saints*, 5:391; Joseph Fielding Smith, *Doctrines of Salvation*, 2:43–44; Brown, *You and Your Marriage*, 22; Dallin H. Oaks, "Fundamental to Our Faith," *Ensign*, January 2011, 25–26.
3. Petersen, *For Time or Eternity?*, 25–26. In a lecture titled "A Commitment to Temple Marriage," Mark Petersen was very strong in making his point about not dating or marrying outside the LDS faith, imploring that Latter-day Saints should date only other "good" Latter-day Saints (Provo, UT: Brigham Young University, 1962).
4. Kimball, *The Miracle of Forgiveness*, 241–42.
5. Spencer W. Kimball, "The Marriage Decision," *Ensign*, February 1975, 2–6.

6. "Dating FAQs," *New Era*, April 2010, 20–32.

7. "Relationship with Others," accessed August 24, 2012, http://www.lds.org /library/display/0,4945,30-1-7-4,00.html.

8. Thomas S. Monson, "Preparation Brings Blessings," *Ensign*, May 2010, 64.

9. Sandra Tanner, e-mail message to the authors, July 21, 2010. Printed with permission.

Chapter 13

1. Hickenbotham, *Answering Challenging Mormon Questions*, 114.

2. D&C 93:29.

3. "The Fulness of the Gospel: Life Before Birth," *Ensign*, February 2006, 30–31. This comes from an article that was part of "a continuing series explaining basic beliefs of the restored gospel, doctrines unique to The Church of Jesus Christ of Latter-day Saints."

4. *Presidents of the Church Teacher's Manual*, 1.

5. *True to the Faith*, 115–16.

6. *Gospel Principles*, 13, 15.

7. Ibid., 15–16.

8. *Teachings of Presidents of the Church: George Albert Smith*, 70–71.

9. *Teachings of Presidents of the Church: Spencer W. Kimball*, 3.

10. *Conference Reports*, April 1941, 49.

11. Joseph Fielding Smith, *The Way to Perfection*, 48.

12. Mark E. Petersen, "Race Problems as They Affect the Church," August 27, 1954, p. 11, http://www.mormonismi.net/mep1954/.

13. Terry B. Ball, "To Confirm and Inform: A Blessing of Higher Education," March 11, 2008, BYU Devotional, http://speeches.byu.edu/?act=viewitem&id=1764.

14. *Conference Reports*, October 1947, 57.

15. Quoted in Bryant Hinckley, *Sermons and Missionary Service of Melvin Joseph Ballard*, 248.

16. "LDS Marking 30-Year Milestone," *Deseret News*, June 7, 2008.

17. "Mormon and Black: Grappling with a Racist Past," *Salt Lake Tribune*, June 7, 2008.

18. "Church Statement Regarding 'Washington Post' Article on Race and the Church," February 29, 2012, http://www.mormonnewsroom.org/article/racial -remarks-in-washington-post-article.

19. Official statement of the First Presidency to BYU President Ernest L. Wilkinson, dated August 17, 1951, quoted in Lund, *The Church and the Negro: A Discussion of Mormons, Negroes and the Priesthood*, 89–90.

20. *Journal of Discourses*, 7:290–91.

21. For example, see Rom. 9.

22. "God Is Truly Our Father," *Ensign*, January 2010, 15.

23. Everett Ferguson, "Origen," in Dowley and Alexander, *The History of Christianity*, 107.

24. Olson, *The Story of Christian Theology*, 104.

25. Gonzales, *The Story of Christianity*, 1:79–80.

26. See John 6:46; 7:28–29; 8:23–24, 54–59; 17:24–25.

Chapter 14

1. "Increase in Visibility Brings Questions, Answers Mormon Moment," Newsroom, July 26, 2007, http://newsroom.lds.org/article/increase-in-visibility-brings-questions,-answers-mormon-moment.

2. Talmage, *The Articles of Faith*, 430.

3. Mormons have been told that "these words came by revelation to Lorenzo when he was a young man in Nauvoo" (Williams, *The Teachings of Lorenzo Snow*, viii).

4. Joseph Smith, *Teachings of the Prophet Joseph Smith*, 345. See also *Journal of Discourses*, 6:3.

5. Joseph Fielding Smith, *Doctrines of Salvation*, 2:47.

6. http://www.theoi.com/Text/AratusPhaenomena.html.

7. *Journal of Discourses*, 6:4; Joseph Smith, *Teachings of the Prophet Joseph Smith*, 346.

8. *Journal of Discourses*, 3:93.

9. McConkie, *Mormon Doctrine*, 237.

10. Dieter F. Uchtdorf, "You Matter to Him," *Ensign*, November 2011, 20.

11. *Journal of Discourses*, 17:143.

12. Ibid., 18:259.

13. *Eternal Marriage Student Manual: Religion 234 and 235*, 167, quoting McConkie's *Mormon Doctrine*, 517.

14. Pratt, *The Seer*, 37.

15. *Doctrines of the Gospel Student Manual: Religion 430–431*, 29.

16. *Presidents of the Church Student Manual: Religion 345*, 90.

17. L. Tom Perry, "The Tradition of a Balanced, Righteous Life," *Ensign*, August 2011, 51. Perry cited this same quotation in a conference message titled "Receive Truth" (*Ensign*, November 1997, 60). References to exalted beings forming and ruling over their own worlds, as well as engaging in eternal increase, are numerous. See also Joseph Smith, *Teachings of the Prophet Joseph Smith*, 300–301; Joseph Fielding Smith, *Doctrines of Salvation*, 2:48; and *Achieving a Celestial Marriage*, 129, 132, 135.

18. "Mormonism 101: FAQ," accessed May 4, 2012, http://www.mormonnewsroom.org/article/mormonism-101.

19. Taken from the Latin *pater* (father), patristic writers, known as church fathers, lived during the postapostolic age.

20. Quoted in Ostling and Ostling, *Mormon America*, 311.

21. It should be noted that these passages from Isaiah read virtually the same in the Joseph Smith Inspired Version of the Bible.

22. Kimball, *The Miracle of Forgiveness*, 286.

23. Talmage, *Jesus the Christ*, 501.

24. For example, J. J. Stewart Perowne, *The Book of Psalms: A New Translation* (Andover: Warren F. Praper, 1889); H. C. Leupold, *Exposition of the Psalms* (Grand Rapids: Baker, 1970); and A. F. Kirkpatrick, *The Book of Psalms with Introduction and Notes* (Cambridge: University Press, 1895).

25. Kidner, *Psalms 73–150: A Commentary*, 296–97.

26. Kimball, *The Miracle of Forgiveness*, 2.

27. Kistemaker, *New Testament Commentary: James, Epistles of John, Peter, and Jude*, 295.

Chapter 15

1. Dallin H. Oaks, "Apostasy and Restoration," *Ensign*, May 1995, 84.
2. Joseph Smith, *Teachings of the Prophet Joseph Smith*, 372.
3. Widtsoe, *Evidences and Reconciliations*, 58.
4. Bruce R. McConkie, "What Think Ye of Salvation by Grace?" BYU devotional address given January 10, 1984, http://speeches.byu.edu/?act=viewitem&id=597.
5. Jeffrey R. Holland, "The One True God and Jesus Christ Whom He Hath Sent," *Ensign*, November 2007, 40.
6. Marshall, *Tracting and Member Missionary Work*, 73–74.
7. Schaff, *The Creeds of Christendom with a History and Critical Notes*, 1:5.
8. Ibid.
9. Strauss, *Four Portraits, One Jesus*, 489.
10. E.g., Deut. 6:4; Isa. 43:10; 44:6, 8; 45:5–6, 14, 21–22; 46:9–10; Mark 12:29; James 2:19.
11. White, *The Forgotten Trinity*, 20, 26.
12. Two helpful resources that explain apparent contradictions are Gleason Archer's *New International Encyclopedia of Bible Difficulties* (Grand Rapids: Zondervan, 2001) and Norman Geisler and Thomas Howe's *The Big Book of Bible Difficulties: Clear and Concise Answers from Genesis to Revelation* (Grand Rapids: Baker: 2008).
13. Tozer, *The Knowledge of the Holy*, 21.
14. Scharffs, *The Missionary's Little Book of Answers*, 22.
15. Olson, *The Story of Christian Theology*, 154.
16. Joseph Smith, *Teachings of the Prophet Joseph Smith*, 370.
17. This concept is also taught in the D&C. For example, D&C 20:28 reads, "Which Father, Son, and Holy Ghost are one God, infinite and eternal, without end."
18. Zeezrom had asked Amulek—a prophet who could "say nothing which is contrary to the Spirit of the Lord" (v. 22)—if there was more than one "true and living God." If Amulek really believed in a plurality of gods, it would seem that he would have related this to Zeezrom. If there is only one true and living God, as Amulek said, which god within the tritheistic Mormon Godhead is not true and living?

Chapter 16

1. Michaelene P. Grassli, "Helping Children Know Truth from Error," *Ensign*, November 1994, 13.
2. This is hardly a good proof text for Mormons to support the notion that people can see God since many Mormons agree that this "God" was really an angel. For example, Apostle Rudger Clawson (1857–1943) said, "On one occasion Jacob wrestled with an angel all night, and would not let him go until he had received a blessing" (*Conference Reports*, April 1922, 46).
3. Joseph Smith—History 1:17 (PoGP). For more information on the First Vision, see chapter 31.
4. Geisler and Rhodes, *When Cultists Ask*, 30.
5. "How can I respond when my friends say that no man can see God," *Liahona*, August 2011, http://lds.org/liahona/2011/08/how-can-i-respond-when-my-friends -say-that-no-man-can-see-god?lang=eng&query=contradict. Article 8 of the LDS

Articles of Faith is quoted here to show that the Bible is correct only when it is "translated" correctly.

6. For more information on the Joseph Smith Translation, see chapter 25.

7. G. W. Bromiley, "Anthropomorphism," in *The International Standard Bible Encyclopedia*, ed. Bromiley, 1:136–37.

Chapter 17

1. *True to the Faith*, 45–46.
2. Nyman and Tate, *Third Nephi 9–30: This Is My Gospel*, 14.
3. Matthews, *A Bible! A Bible!*, 282.
4. Skinner, *Gethsemane*, 5.
5. M. Russell Ballard, "The Atonement and the Value of One Soul," *Ensign*, May 2004, 85.
6. Gordon B. Hinckley, *Teachings of Gordon B. Hinckley*, 281.
7. Joseph C. Winther, "Because of His Love," *Ensign*, April 2002, 19.
8. Ps. 22:1, 6–8, 15, 16.
9. Gordon B. Hinckley, "The Symbol of Our Faith," *Ensign*, April 2005, 3.
10. For example, see *Encyclopedia of Mormonism*, 3:1243.
11. Piper, *Fifty Reasons Why Christ Came to Die*, 33.
12. J. C. Ryle, "Calvary!," accessed August 24, 2012, http://www.biblebb.com/files/ryle/calvary.htm.
13. Copan, *Is God a Moral Monster?*, 33.

Chapter 18

1. *Conference Reports*, April 1965, 43.
2. Widtsoe, *Joseph Smith*, 178.
3. McConkie, *Mormon Doctrine*, 468.
4. M. Catherine Thomas, "Hell," in Ludlow, *Encyclopedia of Mormonism*, 2:585.
5. Joseph Fielding Smith, *Answers to Gospel Questions*, 2:210.
6. Richard Neitzel Holzapfel, "Damnation," in Ludlow, *Encyclopedia of Mormonism*, 1:353.
7. Woodruff, *Waiting for World's End*, 167.
8. *Conference Reports*, October 1945, 172, as cited in *Search These Commandments*, 1984, 81; Kimball, *The Teachings of Spencer W. Kimball*, 50; Bruce R. McConkie, "The Seven Deadly Heresies," BYU Fireside, June 1, 1980, http://speeches.byu.edu/?act=viewitem&id=658.
9. Joseph Fielding Smith, *Doctrines of Salvation*, 2:31.
10. *Conference Reports*, April 1954, 134.
11. While this passage says it is Satan who tells people there is no hell, let's not forget that John A. Widtsoe and Bruce R. McConkie also have said hell does not exist, as noted above.
12. *True to the Faith*, 81.
13. Joseph Fielding Smith, *Doctrines of Salvation*, 2:220.
14. Joseph Smith, *Teachings of the Prophet Joseph Smith*, 358.
15. Joseph Fielding Smith, *Doctrines of Salvation*, 1:49.

Chapter 19

1. Ridges, *Mormon Beliefs and Doctrines Made Easier*, 94.
2. *Teachings of Presidents of the Church: Wilford Woodruff*, 71.
3. *Journal of Discourses*, 20:30.
4. *Teachings of Presidents of the Church: Heber J. Grant*, 38.
5. Henry D. Moyle, "The Church Security Program: Its Present and Future," *Improvement Era*, December 1937, 787.
6. Joseph Fielding Smith, *Doctrines of Salvation*, 2:5.
7. McConkie, *The Promised Messiah: The First Coming of Christ*, 242.
8. L. Tom Perry, "That Spirit Which Leadeth to Do Good," *Ensign*, May 1997, 70.
9. Neal A. Maxwell, "Apply the Atoning Blood of Christ," *Ensign*, November 1997, 23.
10. James E. Faust, "Dear Are the Sheep That Have Wandered," *Ensign*, May 2003, 62.
11. *Preach My Gospel*, 53, 61, 62, 66.
12. Joseph Fielding Smith, *Doctrines of Salvation*, 1:134.
13. McConkie, *Mormon Doctrine*, 234.
14. Ibid., 641.
15. Clyde J. Williams, "Plain and Precious Truths Restored," *Ensign*, October 2006, 53.
16. Thomas S. Monson, "An Invitation to Exaltation," *Ensign*, May 1988, 53.
17. McConkie and Millet, *Doctrinal Commentary on the Book of Mormon*, 2:258.
18. Millet and McDermott, *Claiming Christ*, 188.
19. Bruce C. Hafen, "Grace," in Ludlow, *The Encyclopedia of Mormonism*, 2:562.
20. Lee, *Stand Ye in Holy Places*, 246. See also *Teachings of Presidents of the Church: Harold B. Lee*, 24.
21. Dallin H. Oaks, "Two Line of Communication," *Ensign*, November 2010, 84.
22. Found under the word *grace* on page 697 of the 1986 version of the "Bible Dictionary" appendix located in the back of the LDS Church-produced King James Version Bible.
23. *True to the Faith*, 77.
24. *Book of Mormon Seminary Student Study Guide*, 53.
25. White, *The God Who Justifies*, 344–45.
26. J. I. Packer, "Justification," in Elwell, *Evangelical Dictionary of Theology*, 593.
27. Strauss, *How to Read the Bible in Changing Times*, 35–36.

Chapter 20

1. Henry Eyring, "That We May Be One," *Ensign*, May 1998, 68.
2. White, *The God Who Justifies*, 98.
3. Describing this passage, one church manual advises the teacher, "Explain that 'deny yourselves of all ungodliness' means 'give up your sins'" (*Preparing for Exaltation Teacher's Manual*, 123).
4. A related verse is D&C 95:12, which says, "If you keep not my commandments, the love of the Father shall not continue with you, therefore you shall walk in darkness."

5. According to the 1997 manual *Teachings of Presidents of the Church: Brigham Young*, 37–38, Brigham Young said, "Joseph [Smith] also told us that the Savior requires strict obedience to all the commandments, ordinances and laws pertaining to his kingdom, and that if we would do this we should be made partakers of all the blessings promised in his Gospel."

6. According to LDS General Authorities, repentance involves not repeating the sin again. President Harold B. Lee wrote, "In one sentence, repentance means turning from that which we have done wrong in the sight of the Lord and never repeating that mistake again. Then we can have the miracle of forgiveness" (Lee, *Ye Are the Light of the World*, 321). President Wilford Woodruff said, "And what is repentance? The forsaking of sin. The man who repents, if he be a swearer, swears no more; or a thief, steals no more; he turns away from all former sins and commits them no more. It is not repentance to say, I repent today, and then steal tomorrow; that is the repentance of the world, which is displeasing in the sight of God" (*Teachings of Presidents of the Church: Wilford Woodruff*, 71–72). In the 1984 LDS gospel tract "Repentance Brings Forgiveness," Spencer W. Kimball quoted D&C 58:43 and said, "The forsaking of sin must be a permanent one. True repentance does not permit making the same mistake again." Kimball also said, "And incomplete repentance never brought complete forgiveness" (Kimball, *The Miracle of Forgiveness*, 212). Apostle D. Todd Christofferson explained, "For our turning to the Lord to be complete, it must including nothing less than a covenant of obedience to Him" ("The Divine Gift of Repentance," *Ensign*, November 2011, 39).

7. Sweat, *I'm Not Perfect*, viii. The poll asked, "If you died and were judged today, what eternal kingdom do you think you would go to?" Two percent answered "outer darkness," or "sons of perdition," even though this was not a choice in the multiple-choice question.

8. Ibid., viii–ix.

9. "BYU president warns about perils of perfectionism," *Salt Lake Tribune*, September 7, 2011, http://www.sltrib.com/sltrib/news/52529038-78/samuelson-students -perfectionism-brigham.html.csp.

10. Ibid.

11. Kimball, *The Miracle of Forgiveness*, 286.

12. Thomas S. Monson, "An Invitation to Exaltation," *Ensign*, May 1988, 54.

13. *Teachings of Presidents of the Church: Heber J. Grant*, 49. The manual is from 2002.

14. *Preparing for Exaltation Teacher's Manual*, 123–24.

15. Kimball, *The Miracle of Forgiveness*, 9–10.

16. Ibid., 15.

17. *Teachings of Presidents of the Church: Spencer W. Kimball*, 8.

18. Spencer W. Kimball, "The Gospel of Repentance," *Ensign*, October 1982, 5.

19. Richard G. Scott, "Finding Forgiveness," *Ensign*, May 1995, 76. Scott was quoting D&C 1:32.

20. *Kimball, The Miracle of Forgiveness, 212.*

21. Jay E. Jensen, "The Message: Do You Know How to Repent?" *New Era*, November 1999, 7.

22. Geisler and Rhodes, *When Cultists Ask*, 100–101.

23. For more information on the difference between justification and sanctification, see chapter 11 in McKeever and Johnson, *Mormonism 101*.

24. J. C. Ryle, "Justification and Sanctification: How Do They Differ?" accessed August 24, 2012, http://www.monergism.com/thethreshold/articles/onsite/sanct _just_ryle.html.

25. Benjamin B. Warfield, "Justification by Faith, Out of Date?" *The Christian Irishman,* Dublin, May 1911, 71.

Chapter 21

1. Spencer J. Condie, "The Savior's Visit to the Spirit World," *Ensign,* July 2003, 32.

2. *Gospel Principles,* 116.

3. *Preach My Gospel,* 64.

4. For instance, see Alma 7:14; 3 Nephi 11:34; 30:2; Moroni 8:25; D&C 20:37. However, 3 Nephi 7:25 makes it appear that those needing to be baptized already had a "remission of their sins." It says, "Therefore, there were ordained of Nephi, men unto this ministry, that all such as should come unto them should be baptized with water, and this as a witness and a testimony before God, and unto the people, that they had repented and received a remission of their sins."

5. See chapter 7 for more on Campbell.

6. Brooks and Winbery, *Syntax of New Testament Greek,* 60.

7. Richard N. Longenecker, "Acts," in Gaebelein, *The Expositor's Bible Commentary,* 9:283–84.

8. Ibid., 284.

9. Beasley-Murray, *Baptism in the New Testament,* 105.

10. Ibid., 101.

11. For more information on salvation and how grace and works fit together, see chapters 19 and 20. In addition, see chapter 13 in McKeever and Johnson, *Mormonism 101,* which gives short explanations of other verses used by Mormons to support baptismal regeneration.

12. James Faust, "The Atonement: Our Greatest Hope," *Ensign,* November 2001, 18.

13. Williams, *The Teachings of Lorenzo Snow,* 20.

14. Adam Clarke, *Clarke's Commentary on the Bible,* notes on chapter 8, http://www .ccel.org/c/clarke/commentary/vol1.txt.

15. Kaiser et al. *Hard Sayings of the Bible,* 717.

16. Ibid., 717–18.

Chapter 22

1. Howard W. Hunter, "A Temple-Motivated People," *Ensign,* March 2004, 41.

2. Millet, *A Different Jesus?,* 129.

3. *Teachings of Presidents of the Church: Joseph Smith,* 473.

4. *Teachings of Presidents of the Church: John Taylor,* 187.

5. *Teachings of Presidents of the Church: Wilford Woodruff,* 189.

6. *True to the Faith,* 63.

7. Gordon B. Hinckley, "Why These Temples," *Ensign* special edition, October 2010, 26.

8. Henry Eyring, "Hearts Bound Together," *Ensign,* May 2005, 78.

9. Talmage, *The House of the Lord,* 68.

10. Spencer J. Condie, "The Savior's Visit to the Spirit World," *Ensign,* July 2003, 36.

11. Because of public controversy with some Mormons performing temple ordinances

for Jewish victims of the Holocaust, the LDS leadership issued a statement on February 21, 2012 instructing "members who are submitting names for baptisms for the deceased to work on their own family lines, not to submit names of celebrities, and not to submit names of unauthorized groups, such as Jewish Holocaust victims" ("Church Asks Members to Undertand Policies," *Ensign*, June 2012, 77).

12. Joseph Fielding Smith, *Doctrines of Salvation* 2:183.

13. Bruce R. McConkie, "The Seven Deadly Heresies," BYU Fireside, June 1, 1980, http://speeches.byu.edu/?act=viewitem&id=658. How many sincere Mormons who have done temple work for those who had already heard the gospel know that one of their own apostles called such work a "total and complete waste of time"?

14. In addition, consider Mosiah 3:25; 16:11; 26:25–27 in the Book of Mormon.

15. *Teachings of Presidents of the Church: David O. McKay*, 129.

16. Millet, *A Different Jesus?*, 130–31.

17. D. A. Carson, "Directions: Did Paul Baptize for the Dead? *Christianity Today*, August 10, 1998, http://www.christianitytoday.com/ct/1998/august10/8t9063.html.

18. D. A. Carson, "Must I Learn How to Interpret the Bible?" *Modern Reformation* 5:3 (May/June 1996): 18–22.

19. G. W. Bromiley, "Baptism for the Dead," in *The International Standard Bible Encyclopedia,* ed. Bromiley, 1:426.

20. E-mail message to the authors, October 11, 2011. Printed with permission.

21. Geisler and Rhodes, *When Cultists Ask*, 296.

22. Archer, *Encyclopedia of Bible Difficulties*, 424.

23. For more information on this topic, please see pages 214–16 in McKeever and Johnson, *Mormonism 101.*

Chapter 23

1. This quote is from an introductory DVD shown at various LDS temple open house events.

2. *Teachings of Presidents of the Church: George Albert Smith*, 83–84.

3. *Gospel Principles*, 277.

4. *Achieving a Celestial Marriage*, 129.

5. *History of the Church of Jesus Christ of Latter-day Saints* 5:391.

6. *Doctrines of the Gospel Student Manual: Religion 430–431*, 78.

7. *Gospel Principles*, 209.

8. President Thomas S. Monson, "He Is Not Here, but Is Risen," *Ensign*, April 2011, 5. This same quote, almost word for word, can be found in the same author's "An Invitation to Exaltation," *Ensign,* May 1988, 56, as well as in the First Presidency Message, "Invitation to Exaltation," in the June 1993 *Ensign*, 6. In both of these other addresses, he added the words, "Such blessings must be earned," along with "(See 2 Nephi 25:23.)" in the latter reference.

9. Apostle Dallin H. Oaks, "The Family Is Central to the Creator's Plan," *Ensign*, December 2004, 51.

10. *True to the Faith*, 93.

11. Dallin H. Oaks, "Fundamental Premises of Our Faith," *Newsroom*, March 5, 2010, http://www.mormonnewsroom.org/article/fundamental-premises-of-our-faith -talk-given-by-elder-dallin-h-oaks-at-harvard-law-school.

12. *Teachings of Presidents of the Church: Joseph F. Smith*, 386.
13. Gordon B. Hinckley, "Why These Temples," *Ensign* special edition, October 2010, 24.
14. Scharffs, *The Missionary's Little Book of Answers*, 62.
15. Joseph Fielding Smith, *The Way to Perfection*, 206.

Chapter 24

1. Taylor, *The Gospel Kingdom*, 50.
2. For more on this issue, see chapters 19 and 20.
3. Joseph Fielding Smith, *Doctrines of Salvation* 2:15.
4. For more information on the topic of hell, see chapter 18.
5. Keller, *The Reason for God*, 72–73.

Chapter 25

1. Petersen, *As Translated Correctly*, 4.
2. *Teachings of Presidents of the Church: Brigham Young*, 121.
3. David Rolph Seely, "The Joseph Smith Translation: 'Plain and Precious Things Restored,'" *Ensign*, August 1997, 9. The quote from Smith comes from the *Teachings of the Prophet Joseph Smith*, 327.
4. *Church News*, June 20, 1992, 3.
5. Neil A. Maxwell, "The Wondrous Restoration," *Ensign*, April 2003, 35.
6. Scharffs, *The Missionary's Little Book of Answers*, 64.
7. Archer, *A Survey of Old Testament Introduction*, 25.
8. Quoted in Strobel, *The Case for Christ*, 81–82.
9. Clay Jones, "The Bibliographical Test Updated," *Christian Research Journal* 35, no. 3 (May 2012): 34, 36.
10. Bruce, *The New Testament Documents*, 14–15.
11. *Fourteenth Annual Symposium of the Archaeology of the Scriptures*, 58–59.
12. This was the original name of Smith's church. In 1834, the name was changed to "The Church of the Latter-day Saints" before eventually being changed to the "Church of Jesus Christ of Latter-day Saints" in 1838.
13. Widtsoe, *Evidences and Reconciliations*, 353. See also D&C 45:60–62. On March 7, 1831, Smith was "instructed to begin the translation of the New Testament, through which important information would be made known."
14. David Rolph Seely, "The Joseph Smith Translation: 'Plain and Precious Things Restored,'" *Ensign*, August 1997, 10.
15. Ibid., 11.
16. Robert L. Millet, "Joseph Smith's Translation of the Bible: A Historical Overview," in *The Joseph Smith Translation: The Restoration of Plain and Precious Things*, ed. Millet and Nyman, 26–27.
17. David Rolph Seely, "The Joseph Smith Translation: 'Plain and Precious Things Restored,'" *Ensign*, August 1997, 10.
18. Ibid., 13–14.
19. Ibid., 15. There is no evidence that Smith's genealogy can be traced back to the patriarch Joseph.
20. *Book of Mormon Student Manual: Religion 121 and 122*, 24.
21. Verse 6 in Smith's version reads, "I am the first, and I am the last; and besides me

there is no God," while verse 8 says, "Is there a God besides me? yea, there is no God; I know not any."

22. Emphasis ours.

23. *History of the Church of Jesus Christ of Latter-day Saints*, 1:368. Quoted by David Rolph Seely, "The Joseph Smith Translation: 'Plain and Precious Things Restored,'" *Ensign*, August 1997, 11. Emphasis ours.

24. Jensen, *Church Chronology*, 9.

25. *Deseret News 1993–1994 Church Almanac*, 339.

26. *Deseret News 2001–2002 Church Almanac*, 510.

27. *History of the Church of Jesus Christ of Latter-day Saints*, 1:324.

28. David Rolph Seely, "The Joseph Smith Translation: 'Plain and Precious Things Restored,'" *Ensign*, August 1997, 11.

29. *History of the Church of Jesus Christ of Latter-day Saints*, 6:57.

Chapter 26

1. Matthews, *Selected Writings of Robert J. Matthews*, 146.

2. Two helpful resources that deal with apparent contradictions are Gleason Archer's *New International Encyclopedia of Bible Difficulties* (Grand Rapids: Zondervan, 2001) and Norman Geisler and Thomas Howe's *The Big Book of Bible Difficulties: Clear and Concise Answers from Genesis to Revelation* (Grand Rapids: Baker, 2008).

3. For more on works, see chapter 19.

4. Jewish translations still use the word *lion* in Psalm 22:16. For more information on this manuscript discovery, see Tim Hegg, "Psalm 22:16—'like a lion' or 'they pierced'?" http://www.torahresource.com/EnglishArticles/Ps22.16.pdf.

5. For more information on this topic, see Paul Copan's *Is God a Moral Monster? Making Sense of the Old Testament God* (Grand Rapids: Baker, 2011).

Chapter 27

1. Hugh Pinnock, "Being a Missionary Church," *Ensign*, August 1996, 42–43.

2. For more, see chapter 31 on the First Vision.

3. Tad R. Callister, "The Book of Mormon—A Book from God," *Ensign*, November 2011, 76.

4. "I Have a Question," *Ensign*, March 1986, http://www.lds.org/ensign/1986/03/i-have-a-question/i-have-a-question?lang=eng&query=%22God+cannot+and+does+not+lie%22.

5. See James 1:3–4, 12–15 to understand the context.

Chapter 28

1. Talmage, *Jesus the Christ*, 419.

2. *Conference Reports*, April 1963, 117–18.

3. Dallin H. Oaks, "All Men Everywhere," *Ensign*, May 2006, 79.

4. E.g., Deut. 27:10; 1 Sam. 12:15; 2 Kings 18:12.

5. John Calvin, "Commentary on John, Volume 1," http://www.ccel.org/ccel/calvin/calcom34.xvi.iv.html.

6. Edwin A. Blum, "John," in Walvoord and Zuck, *The Bible Knowledge Commentary: New Testament*, 310.

7. Merrill C. Tenney, "John," in Gaebelein, *The Expositor's Bible Commentary*, 9:109.

8. Bruce, *The Gospel & Epistles of John*, 228.
9. Cf. Exod. 12:48; 22:21; Lev. 17:15; Acts 7:29.

Chapter 29

1. Russell M. Nelson, "Prepare for the Blessings of the Temple," *Ensign* special edition, October 2010, 42.
2. For more information on baptism for the dead, see chapter 22.
3. Russell M. Nelson, "Face the Future with Faith," *Ensign,* May 2011, 36.
4. Russell M. Nelson, "Prepare for the Blessings of the Temple," *Ensign* special edition, October 2010, 50.
5. "Commonly Asked Questions," *Ensign* special edition, October 2010, 79.
6. *Teachings of Presidents of the Church: Harold B. Lee*, 111.
7. "Commonly Asked Questions," *Ensign* special edition, October 2010, 79.
8. Ibid., 80.
9. *Gospel Principles*, 222–23.
10. Boyd K. Packer, "The Holy Temple," *Ensign* special edition, October 2010, 30–31. Regarding the importance of tithing, Apostle Russell M. Nelson said, "Tithing will keep your name enrolled among the people of God and protect you in 'the day of vengeance and burning'" ("Face the Future with Faith," *Ensign*, May 2011, 35).
11. Russell M. Nelson, "Prepare for the Blessings of the Temple," *Ensign* special edition, October 2010, 43.
12. Thomas S. Monson, "The Holy Temple—a Beacon to the World," *Ensign*, May 2011, 93.
13. Petersen, *Why Mormons Build Temples*, 2.
14. *Gospel Principles*, 98.
15. Ibid., 151.
16. Cavendish, *The Black Arts*, 265.
17. Hartman, *Magic—White and Black*, 290–91.
18. Guiley, *The Encyclopedia of Witches and Witchcraft*, 266.
19. Charles W. Allen, *Window Maker*, 182.
20. For more information about the temple, with a focus on the ceremonies and what takes place there, see chapter 15 of McKeever and Johnson, *Mormonism 101*.

Chapter 30

1. Ludlow, *A Companion to Your Study of the New Testament: The Four Gospels*, 311.
2. *Preach My Gospel*, 53. According to D&C 131:1, "In the celestial glory there are three heavens or degrees." The highest of the three degrees is called The Church of the Firstborn. A detailed description of the two lower degrees within the celestial kingdom is rarely discussed by church leaders or in church manuals.
3. Hughes, *The New International Commentary on the New Testament*, 433.
4. B. Renato Maldonado, "The Three Degrees of Glory," *Ensign*, April 2005, 62. The interpretation made by Maldonado (as well as Joseph Smith) is undermined on the official LDS Church Web site (Mormon Newsroom), which declared, "The Church does not and has never purported to fully understand the specifics of Christ's statement that 'in my Father's house are many mansions' (John 14:2)" (accessed May 16, 2012, http://www.mormonnewsroom.org/article/mormonism-101.)

5. Merrill C. Tenney, "John," in Gaebelein, *The Expositor's Bible Commentary*, 9:143.

6. For more information on this topic, see chapter 14.

Chapter 31

1. *Teachings of Presidents of the Church: Joseph Smith*, 545; *Teachings of Presidents of the Church: Joseph F. Smith*, 14.

2. Benson, *The Teachings of Ezra Taft Benson*, 101. Also see *Church History in the Fulness of Times Teacher Manual*, http://institute.lds.org/manuals/church-history -institute-teacher-manual/chft-tch-3.asp.

3. Gordon B. Hinckley, "Testimony of the First Vision," *Church News*, July 1, 2006, 2.

4. *True to the Faith*, 90.

5. Quoted in "One's Salvation Rests on Belief in First Vision," *Church News*, May 7, 2005, 7.

6. See Wesley Walters's *The Palmyra Revival and Mormon Origins*, available through Mormonism Research Ministry. Walters provides evidence to show that there was no religious excitement in the Palmyra area in 1820. Statistics refute the notion that great multitudes were added to any of the three churches in 1820. That year the Methodist church actually lost six members.

7. James B. Allen, "The Significance of Joseph Smith's 'First Vision' in Mormon Thought," *Dialogue: A Journal of Mormon Thought*, autumn 1966, 30.

8. Ibid., 30–31.

9. Ibid., 31.

10. Ibid.

11. Ibid., 32. The 1842 report of the First Vision can be found in *Times and Seasons*, April 1, 1842, 3:743.

12. Ibid., 34.

13. *Journal of Discourses*, 2:171.

14. Ibid., 10:127; 20:167.

15. Ibid., 12:334.

16. *Joseph Smith's 1832–34 Diary*, 5.

17. For more on the possibility of man seeing God, see chapter 16.

18. *A Sure Foundation*, 79.

19. Harrell, *"This Is My Doctrine,"* 146 n. 65.

20. *Conference Reports*, October 1961, 116.

21. *Preach My Gospel*, 38.

Chapter 32

1. Holland, *Christ and the New Covenant*, 345. Apostle Joseph B. Wirthlin quoted this in the "The Book of Mormon: The Heart of Missionary Proselyting," *Ensign*, September 2002, 14.

2. According to Mormonism, Moroni was the last living Nephite and the one who buried the gold plates in New York. He is said to have appeared later as an angel to Joseph Smith beginning in 1823.

3. *Joseph Smith—History* 1:34 (PoGP).

4. Lucy Mack Smith, *History of Joseph Smith: By His Mother, Lucy Mack Smith*, 108. See also *Church History in the Fulness of Times Student Manual*, 45.

5. *History of the Church of Jesus Christ of Latter-day Saints* 4:537.

6. Daniel Peterson, "John Whitmer Left Church, but Kept Testimony of Book of Mormon," *Deseret News*, Jan. 25, 2012, http://www.deseretnews.com/article/700218869/John-Whitmer-left-church-but-kept-testimony-of-Book-of-Mormon.html?pg=2. Peterson concluded that Whitmer was "a witness whose testimony cannot lightly be dismissed."

7. 1204 divided by 6 = 200.66 pounds.

8. In addition, no LDS leader speaking in official capacity has intimated that the carrying of the plates was a miraculous event.

9. *Joseph Smith—History* 1:34 (PoGP).

10. Widtsoe, *Joseph Smith*, 38.

11. Widtsoe and Harris, *Seven Claims of the Book of Mormon*, 37.

12. At the Utah Lighthouse Bookstore located in Salt Lake City, Sandra Tanner has a display of "plates" made of lead. Made to the dimensions given by Joseph Smith (6 x 8 x 6), these plates weigh only one pound more (118 lbs.) than Widtsoe's estimate. Most of the visitors attempting to pick up this replica barely can budge them, much less walk with them.

13. Reed C. Putnam, "Were the Golden Plates Made of Tumbaga?" *Improvement Era*, September 1966, 830–31.

14. Putnam's estimate of fifty-three pounds would be comparable to carrying a bag of ready-mix concrete under one's arm.

15. "Last Testimony of Sister Emma," *Saints Herald*, October 1, 1879, 289. Apostle Russell M. Nelson confirmed the use of a seer stone and hat on page 61 of a July 1993 *Ensign* article titled "A Treasured Testament."

16. "'The Mormons.' Act One: Revelation." Public Broadcasting System, http://www.pbs.org/mormons.

17. Hiram Page became the Whitmers' brother-in-law when he married their sister Catherine in 1825. Oliver Cowdery joined the Whitmer family when he married their sister Elizabeth Ann Whitmer in 1832.

18. *History of the Church of Jesus Christ of Latter-day Saints*, 1:52.

19. Ibid., 1:52–55.

20. Ronald W. Walker, "Martin Harris: Mormonism's Early Convert," *Dialogue: A Journal of Mormon Thought*, winter 1986, 38.

21. Quinn, *Early Mormonism and the Magic World View*, 240.

22. Marvin S. Hill, "Brodie Revisited: A Reappraisal," *Dialogue: A Journal of Mormon Thought*, winter 1972, 84.

23. Ibid.

24. Ibid., 84–85.

Chapter 33

1. *Gospel Principles*, 254.

2. Russell M. Nelson, "Scriptural Witnesses," *Ensign*, November 2007, 44.

3. Harrell, *"This Is My Doctrine*," 92.

4. Ibid. On page 52, Harrell traces this misinterpretation to Joseph Smith, who saw the bringing forth of the Book of Mormon as a direct fulfillment of Isaiah 29.

5. Richards, *A Marvelous Work and a Wonder*, 66–67.

6. Keith H. Meservy, "Ezekiel's Sticks," *Ensign*, September 1977, 25. See also his article, "Ezekiel's Sticks and the Gathering of Israel," *Ensign*, February 1987.

7. Brian E. Keck, "Ezekiel 37, Sticks, and Babylonian Writing Boards: A Critical Reappraisal," *Dialogue: A Journal of Mormon Thought,* spring 1990, 128. At the time of this article, Keck had a BA from the University of Arizona in Hebrew and Old Testament and an MA in Assyriology with emphasis on Babylonian language and literature from the University of Michigan, where he was then working on a PhD in that same field.
8. Ibid.
9. Ibid., 136–37.

Chapter 34

1. Maxwell, *Plain and Precious Things,* 4.
2. One city was often built upon the ruins of another because the site was near water sources, as well as roads used in trade. This eventually resulted in the tells we see today. When excavating a site, archaeologists deal with strata, or layers, representing the different civilizations. Pottery and coins are helpful in determining the dates of a particular civilization in a stratum.
3. Important historians of the first century included the Roman historians Publius Cornelius Tacitus (A.D. 56–117) and Gaius Suetonius Tranquillus (A.D. 69/75–130), as well as the Jewish historian Titus Flavius Josephus (A.D. 37–100). Much of the outside evidence for biblical people, places, and events comes from these sources, who were not Christian believers.
4. "Archaeology of the Bible," in *Nelson's New Illustrated Bible Dictionary,* ed. Youngblood, 100.
5. Hoerth and McRay, *Bible Archaeology,* 10.
6. P. Kyle McCarter, "Patriarchal Age: Abraham, Isaac, and Jacob," in Shanks, *Ancient Israel,* 7.
7. "Archaeology of the Bible," *Nelson's New Illustrated Bible Dictionary,* ed. Youngblood, 98.
8. McRay, *Archaeology and the New Testament,* 22. It is hard to determine how many biblical sites have been excavated since 1990; however, no archaeologist would pretend that even half of the biblical sites have been studied. Volunteers are requested every year to travel to Israel and become part of teams excavating places all over the Holy Land.
9. "The fight over Book of Mormon geography," *Deseret News,* May 27, 2010, http://www.deseretnews.com/article/700035437/The-fight-over-Book-of-Mormon-geography.html. That same year, 1903, Brigham Young Academy was renamed Brigham Young University.
10. Lund, *Mesoamerica and the Book of Mormon: Is This the Place?,* 9.
11. John E. Clark, "Book of Mormon Geography," in Ludlow, *Encyclopedia of Mormonism,* 1:178.
12. Joseph Fielding Smith, *Doctrines of Salvation* 3:73–74.
13. The Book of Mormon Evidence Web site describes this view in more detail: http://bookofmormonevidence.org/.
14. "Rod L. Meldrum on location at the Great Octagon Earth Works, Newark, Ohio," http://www.youtube.com/watch?v=vmON6b1TrW4&feature=related.
15. Benson, *The Teachings of Ezra Taft Benson,* 587–88.
16. Ash, *Shaken Faith Syndrome,* 31–32.

17. Robert L. Millet, "The Book of Mormon, Historicity, and Faith," *Journal of Book of Mormon Studies*, 2:1.

18. For example, past editions of the Book of Mormon included a photograph of a gold tablet dating to the time of Darius II to give plausibility to Smith's story of the gold plates. Such a similarity does not prove the existence of Smith's gold plates or the alleged content of the plates.

19. See Bill McKeever, "NHM—A Place Name from the Book of Mormon?" www .mrm.org/nhm; and Eric Johnson, "Beit Lei: 'Proof' for the Book of Mormon?" www.mrm.org/beit-lehi.

Chapter 35

1. *Teachings of Presidents of the Church: Harold B. Lee*, 71.

2. Joseph Fielding Smith, *Doctrines of Salvation*, 1:188.

3. *Teachings of Presidents of the Church: Harold B. Lee*, 76.

4. *Teachings of Presidents of the Church: Brigham Young*, 345.

5. Gordon B. Hinckley, "Joseph Smith: Restorer of Truth," *Ensign*, December 2003, 18–19.

6. Kristine Frederickson, "Two December Births to Celebrate: Jesus Christ and Joseph Smith," *Deseret News*, Dec. 18, 2011, http://www.deseretnews.com/article/705 395947/Two-December-births-to-celebrate-Jesus-Christ-and-Joseph-Smith.html.

7. *True to the Faith*, 90.

8. Hymns, no. 27, as quoted in *Teachings of Presidents of the Church: David O. McKay*, 98.

9. For more on this issue, see chapter 14.

10. Gordon B. Hinckley, "Praise to the Man," *Ensign*, August 1983, 6. Hinckley erroneously said thirty-nine years rather than twenty-nine years.

11. Catton, *The Civil War*, 59.

12. *History of the Church of Jesus Christ of Latter-day Saints*, 1:301.

13. *Doctrine and Covenants Student Manual: Religion 324–325*, 194.

14. Ibid.

15. Ibid., 195.

16. Ibid.

17. *Journal of Discourses*, 9:55.

18. *Ibid.*, 9:143.

19. Joseph Fielding Smith, *Answers to Gospel Questions*, 4:112–13.

20. *Journal of Discourses*, 13:362.

21. Ibid., 14:275.

22. Joseph Fielding Smith, *Answers to Gospel Questions*, 4:112.

23. *Journal of Discourses*, 14:260–61.

24. *Conference Reports*, October 1919, 70.

Chapter 36

1. "Praise to the Man," hymn #27, *Hymns of the Church of Jesus Christ of Latter-day Saints*.

2. Philip M. Flammer, "Nauvoo Legion," in Ludlow, *Encyclopedia of Mormonism*, 3:998.

3. *Journal of Discourses*, 7:289. See also *Search These Commandments*, 133.

4. According to Todd Compton's *In Sacred Loneliness: The Plural Wives of Joseph Smith,* of Joseph Smith's thirty-three wives, "eleven (33 percent) were 14 to 20 years old when they married him. Nine wives (27 percent) were twenty-one to thirty years old. Eight wives (24 percent) were in Smith's own peer group, ages thirty-one to forty. In the group aged forty-one to fifty, there is a substantial drop off: two wives, or 6 percent, and three (9 percent) in the group fifty-one to sixty" (p. 11). In addition, Compton reports that "fully one-third of [Smith's] plural wives, eleven of them, were married civilly to other men when he married them. If one superimposes a chronological perspective, one sees that of Smith's first twelve wives, nine were polyandrous [married to other men]" (p. 15). For more on the topic of polygamy, see chapter 6.

5. Petersen, *Hearts Made Glad*, iii.

6. Ibid., 166.

7. Quinn, *The Mormon Hierarchy*, 139.

8. *History of the Church of Jesus Christ of Latter-day Saints*, 6:432.

9. Reed C. Durham, "Nauvoo Expositor," in Ludlow, *Encyclopedia of Mormonism*, 3:997. The legality of this action has been debated, but even LDS historian B. H. Roberts called the press's destruction "questionable." Yet while Roberts stated that "it must be conceded that neither proof nor argument for legality are convincing," he still insisted that the "action of the mayor [Joseph Smith] and city council of Nauvoo is defensible, even if not on the ground of legality of their procedure" (*History of the Church of Jesus Christ of Latter-day Saints*, 6:xxxviii).

10. *History of the Church of Jesus Christ of Latter-day Saints*, 6:453–54.

11. Ibid., 6:499.

12. Ibid., 6:605.

13. Ibid., 6:607–8. Page 608 records, "Brother Hyrum observed, 'I hate to use such things or to see them used.' 'So do I,' said Joseph, 'but we may have to, to defend ourselves'; upon this Hyrum took the pistol."

14. Ibid., 7:100.

15. Ibid., 6:617. While this reference states that there were "about a hundred armed men," other estimates from church leaders and historians vary. Historian D. Michael Quinn lists the number at "more than 250 men" (*The Mormon Hierarchy*, 141).

16. Bushman, *Joseph Smith*, 550.

17. See Compton, *In Sacred Loneliness*.

18. *History of the Church of Jesus Christ of Latter-day Saints*, 7:103. Though this account has been reprinted in several LDS publications, there is some controversy as to whether or not any of the men who were shot by Smith actually died from their wounds.

19. Ford, *A History of Illinois*, 354. See also *History of the Church of Jesus Christ of Latter-day Saints*, 7:31.

20. Ibid., 354–55.

Glossary

General LDS terms and their Mormon definitions

ITALICIZED WORDS IN THE definitions designate those terms that are defined elsewhere in this section.

Aaronic priesthood: Known as the lesser priesthood. Bestowed upon Joseph Smith via a personal appearance by John the Baptist. Authority is given to worthy males beginning at age twelve, as well as to new adult members.

accountability, age of: Begins at age eight, when Mormon children are allowed to be baptized. Before then, children are considered to be innocent.

agency: Freedom all humans have to choose right from wrong and truth from error.

Apostasy, Great: Idea that the Christian church lost its authority soon after the death of the apostles; the true church was then restored by Joseph Smith in 1830.

apostate: In general, refers to Christianity during the time of the *Great Apostasy*. It can also refer to someone who has been excommunicated from the LDS Church.

atonement: Provided by Jesus' suffering in Gethsemane and on the cross, allowing humankind to have a resurrection, as well as paving the way for potential *exaltation*.

baptism, water: Required for the remission of sins. Performed by immersion and valid only if administered by a Mormon male holding priesthood authority.

baptism for the dead: Ordinance performed in a *temple* by a living LDS

Church member on behalf of someone who is deceased, thus allowing the deceased an opportunity to receive the restored *gospel*.

bishop: Unpaid leader at a local Mormon *ward*. Also known as the "judge in Israel" who determines those who qualify for a *temple recommend*.

bishopric: presiding officers of a *ward*, including a *bishop* and two counselors.

born in the covenant: A child born to Latter-day Saint parents who were married in a Mormon *temple*, automatically sealing the child to his or her parents for eternity.

branch: Congregation of local Latter-day Saints from a particular geographic location not large enough to form a *ward*; usually comprised of fewer than two hundred members.

branch president: Leader of a local *branch*.

Brethren: The *General Authorities*.

brother: Title given to a male church member.

calling: Invitation a member receives for a particular assignment.

celestial kingdom: Highest of three *kingdoms of glory*. Within the celestial kingdom are three additional separate levels. *Exaltation* comes to those who attain the top level of this kingdom.

celestial marriage: Marriage performed in an LDS *temple* and that extends beyond this life and into eternity.

chapel: Latter-day Saint building used for Sunday worship services.

child of God: Idea that all people were literally born to *God the Father* and *Heavenly Mother* in the *premortal life*, making every person on earth a literal offspring of God.

choose the right (CTR): Slogan used to encourage young people to "do good" and obey the *commandments*.

commandments: Laws and rules as taught by the LDS Church.

confirmation: Act of a *Melchizedek priesthood* member laying his hands upon a convert who has first been baptized, thus bestowing membership into the LDS Church and the *gift of the Holy Ghost*.

correlation program: Under the auspices of the First Presidency and *Quorum* of the Twelve, this department maintains doctrinal purity and consistency in LDS teaching materials.

Council in Heaven: Premortal council where God the Father's plan for the earth was announced.

covenants: Promises made to God in *baptism*/confirmation, the weekly *sacrament*, temple *endowment*, and temple marriage (*sealing*), all of which are vital for *exaltation*.

deacon: Office in the *Aaronic priesthood*, usually given to boys ages twelve to thirteen.

elder: Lowest ordained office of the *Melchizedek priesthood*. Only male members are allowed to hold this position. It's the official title used by male *missionaries*.

endowment: Ceremony in a Mormon *temple* in which the *temple patron* learns about creation, the garden of Eden, and the *telestial* and *terrestrial* worlds.

enduring to the end: Remaining faithful until death to obtain *exaltation*.

Ensign: A monthly magazine of the LDS Church that includes regular articles and talks by *General Authorities*. May and November editions contain the *general conference* talks from the previous month.

eternal increase: Ability given to exalted couples to procreate throughout eternity, giving them an unlimited number of spirit children.

eternal life: Gaining *exaltation* in the highest level of the *celestial kingdom* and living forever in the family unit.

eternal progression: Composed of three stages of development, which are the first estate (*premortality*), the second estate (*mortality*), and the third estate (immortality or *eternal life*).

exaltation: Godhood achieved by complete obedience to all the *commandments* and complete *repentance* of sins. Those who are exalted earn the right to *eternal life* in the *celestial kingdom* with their families.

fall: Adam and Eve's transgression of God's commandment, a necessary step in the *eternal progression* of humankind. Second Nephi 2:25 in the Book of Mormon says, "Adam fell that men might be."

family home evening: A once-a-week gathering for families, typically on Monday nights, meant for strengthening relationships, reading church materials, and having fun.

fast and testimony: Practice of members sharing their personal testimonies at church services on the first Sunday of each month. They are encouraged to refrain from two consecutive meals, donating the savings to the church.

first estate: The *premortal life*.

First Vision: Officially understood as the appearing of *God the Father* and *Jesus Christ* to Joseph Smith in the Sacred Grove. Smith said he was told all churches were wrong.

forgiveness: Received only after a member repents of all sins and keeps all the *commandments*.

Friend: Monthly magazine produced for the LDS children.

garments: Special underclothing worn to remind a Mormon about *temple* *covenants* and to give protection from physical and spiritual harm. White outer garments are worn in the *temple*.

genealogy: Research of one's family history. Names are gathered so that those already deceased can have *temple* rituals performed on their behalf.

General Authority: Those who are members of the First Presidency (including the *prophet*), the *Quorum* of the Twelve Apostles, and the First *Quorum* of the Seventy.

general conference: Biannual event held each April and October in Salt Lake City where various leaders give talks on a variety of topics pertinent to LDS life and faith.

gift of the Holy Ghost: Fullness of blessings available to LDS members after water *baptism*. The *Holy Ghost* remains with those who stay worthy, though He will withdraw when *commandments* are not kept.

Godhead: Three gods—*God the Father, Jesus Christ*, and the *Holy Ghost*—who, while distinct in being, are one in purpose.

God the Father: Also known as Heavenly Father, or Elohim. He was once a righteous human in another realm who died and then became God of this world. He has a tangible body of flesh and bones (D&C 130:22).

gospel: All doctrines, principles, laws, *ordinances*, and *covenants* necessary for a Mormon to receive *exaltation*.

Heavenly Mother: Assumed to be the wife of *God the Father*, though she is not mentioned in the *standard works*. Not a being to be worshipped.

hell: Could refer to *spirit prison, outer darkness*, or the regret of those ending up in the *terrestrial* and *telestial* levels of heaven over not qualifying for *celestial kingdom* glory.

Holy Ghost: Usually synonymous with Holy Spirit, though some leaders have distinguished between the two. Third member of the *Godhead*. A son of *God the Father*, as well as a brother of *Jesus Christ*.

home teacher: *Priesthood* holder who is assigned by the church to visit members, build relationships, and provide religious instruction.

house of the Lord: One of the Mormon *temples*.

investigator: Person who takes lessons from Mormon *missionaries* and may be thinking about joining the LDS Church.

Jesus Christ: God the Father's firstborn son and humanity's eldest brother. Prior to his incarnation, he was known as Jehovah.

kingdoms of glory: The three possible eternal destinations of humankind known as the *celestial, terrestrial*, and *telestial* kingdoms.

Lamanites: Descendants of Laman in the Book of Mormon who eventually destroyed the *Nephites.*

laying on of hands: The act of *priesthood* leaders putting their hands on the head of a person to bestow a blessing or ordination.

Liahona: Monthly magazine produced for the Latter-day Saints outside the United States in fifty-one different languages.

Lucifer: Also known as Satan, the brother of *Jesus* in *premortality* who disobeyed and was cast out of heaven with one-third of all spirits.

meetinghouse: Building, church, or chapel where Mormons meet for worship.

Melichizedek priesthood: Known as the higher or greater priesthood. Bestowed upon Joseph Smith via the personal appearance of Peter, James, and John. Available to active male members beginning at the age of eighteen.

missionaries: Young men (ages 18 to 25) serve for two years, young women (minimum age 19) serve for eighteen months, and retired couples serve from six months to three years. Locations assigned by leaders.

mission president: Head of *missionaries* in a particular area who works with local *bishops* and meets regularly with *stake presidents* to coordinate missionary efforts.

Mormon: An ancient Nephite prophet who abridged and compiled the records of the American people into the Book of Mormon. Also a nickname for a Latter-day Saint.

Mormon Tabernacle Choir: The "music *missionaries*" of the Mormon Church. Made up of 360 volunteers, ages twenty-five to sixty.

Moroni: The son of *Mormon* and the last living *Nephite.* Buried the *Book of Mormon* gold plates in upstate New York and later appeared as an angel to Joseph Smith.

Moroni's promise: *Investigators* are encouraged to read the Book of Mormon and pray to verify its truthfulness and gain a *testimony.* Based on Moroni 10:4 in the Book of Mormon.

mortality: From birth to death, physical life on this earth. This is the time for humankind to prepare to meet God in the next life.

mutual: Meeting held during a weeknight for youth ages twelve to seventeen.

Nephites: Descendants of Nephi in the Book of Mormon who were eventually destroyed by the fifth century A.D.

New Era: Monthly magazine produced for LDS youth.

new names: *Temple patrons* receive a name in the temple to be used after death; only a spouse is allowed to know the other's new name.

offerings: Money given above and beyond the *tithe* of one's income. An example is the fast offering given at the *fast and testimony* service.

open canon: The teaching that *scripture* does not end with the Holy Bible but continues even in latter days through God's *prophets*.

ordain: To bestow *priesthood* authority on a worthy male member through the *laying on of hands*.

ordinance: Ceremony in which the Mormon makes a *covenant* with God. It includes *baptism, sacrament,* and work in the *temple*.

outer darkness: Severe punishment for eternity, reserved for Satan and his demons as well as the *sons of perdition*.

paradise: Temporary place in the postmortal *spirit world* for those who have been properly baptized and who remained faithful to the end.

patriarchal blessing: Conditional, personal prophetic utterance given to a Mormon either by a relative or by an ordained patriarch appointed by the LDS Church.

plan of salvation: Instructions given by God to humans that enables them to achieve peace in this life and eternal *exaltation* in the life to come.

plural marriage: Also known as polygamy or polygyny. Officially prohibited by the Manifesto of 1890.

premortal life (preexistence): The *first estate,* the time before earthly *mortality* when all humans existed as *spirit children*.

priesthood: There are two divisions: Aaronic and Melchizedek. Authority to hold the priesthood is for male members only.

priesthood blessing: A blessing given by a member of the *Melchizedek priesthood* to someone needing healing, comfort, or counsel.

primary: Church organization for members' children ages three to eleven.

probation, mortal: Earthly existence of a person, whose faith and behavior will determine the final destiny.

prophet, living: Refers either to the currently living Prophet/President or to any of the three members of the First Presidency and the *Quorum* of the Twelve Apostles.

quorum: Group of men holding the same *priesthood* authority.

relief society: Organization for female members who are eighteen or older.

repentance: The process by which a member receives *forgiveness*. True repentance involves six steps, including confession and a successful abandonment of sins.

restoration: Reestablishment of true *gospel* principles.

revelation, continuing: God's ongoing communication to humankind through the words of *General Authorities* and their ability to receive direct guidance from God in the latter days.

revelation, personal: Ability given to individuals by the *Holy Ghost*, enabling them to see the truthfulness of all things, especially issues pertaining to Mormonism.

Sabbath Day: Sunday, set aside for spiritual reflection and personal study. Members are commanded to refrain from shopping, doing chores around the home, or recreational activities.

sacrament: Similar to the Protestant version of Communion, or the Lord's Supper. Performed weekly in LDS services, with bread and water serving as elements.

salvation: Divided into two categories. (1) General salvation, or resurrection, is salvation by grace given to all people regardless of faith and obedience. (2) Individual salvation, or *exaltation*, is earned by those who truly repent and keep the *commandments*.

scripture: Beside the *standard works,* this could also include inspired words of the *living prophet*, official church writings, and *general conference* addresses.

sealing: *Temple* ceremony binding a husband and wife together for eternity. Children who are not *born in the covenant* also can be sealed to parents.

second estate: Life on earth.

seminary: Daily classes held for Mormon high school students. Topics cover the *standard works* and church history.

sister: Title given to a female church member. Also the official title given to female *missionaries.*

sons of perdition: Mormons who willfully and deliberately deny the *Holy Ghost* and the truth of Mormonism while knowing it is true. This sin will not be forgiven and will result in *outer darkness.*

spirit children: All spirits born to *God the Father* and *Heavenly Mother* in the *premortal life*. One-third of these spirit beings were cast out of heaven for siding with Lucifer in the *war in heaven.*

spirit prison: Temporary place for deceased non-Mormons. Here they await vicarious *temple* work done in their behalf by living Mormons, allowing them the opportunity to accept the LDS *gospel.*

spirit world: Temporary place comprised of *paradise* and *spirit prison.*

stake: Grouping of three or more *wards.*

stake center: Building that houses the *stake president's* office and one (or more) *ward* congregations.

stake president: Overseer of *bishops*, who meets with them monthly to discuss plans and also works with the *mission president*. He is in charge of members and *investigators* in his area.

standard works: Four written *scriptures*, comprised of the Bible (officially, the King James Version), the Book of Mormon, Doctrine and Covenants, and the Pearl of Great Price.

telestial kingdom: Lowest of the three *kingdoms of glory*, reserved for the wicked of this world.

temple: Sometimes called "university of the Lord." Special buildings where members deemed worthy get married and participate in *ordinances*, including work on behalf of the dead.

temple open house: A short period of time—usually two to four weeks—where a new or remodeled LDS *temple* is opened to the public for free tours before it is officially dedicated.

temple patron: Person holding a *temple recommend* and participating in rituals at a Mormon *temple*.

temple recommend: Identification card provided to a member in good standing by the person's *bishop* and allowing access to the *temple*. Renewed every two years.

Temple Square: A city block in downtown Salt Lake City, with the Salt Lake Temple and the Tabernacle as well as visitor centers.

terrestrial kingdom: Second of three *kingdoms of glory*, a place where honorable people who were blinded by Satan's activities will spend eternity.

testimony: Mormons' spiritual conviction that tells them the Book of Mormon and the claims of Mormonism are true.

tithe: A tenth of one's income, which is given to the church. It is required for those desiring a *temple recommend*.

tithing settlement: A private meeting members have with their *bishops*; if less than a tenth of one's income was given to the church, the deficit is encouraged to be made up.

unpaid clergy: Reference to local leaders who volunteer their time in church positions, including the *branch presidents* and *bishops*.

ward: Local Mormon congregation made up of members from a particular geographic location, usually consisting of between two hundred and five hundred members. Three or more wards make up a *stake*.

war in heaven: Conflict in the *premortal life* started by *Lucifer* when his bid to become the savior of the world was rejected.

washing and anointing: initiatory *temple* ceremony that purifies the *patron*.

welfare: The Church Welfare Plan was started in 1936, created to help take care of the physical needs of church members as well as perform humanitarian work.

word of wisdom: Mormon health law given through revelation to Joseph Smith in D&C 89.

Young Women: An organization for girls ages twelve to seventeen, created to help them keep *covenants* and to prepare them for the ordinances of the *temple*.

Bibliography

Achieving a Celestial Marriage. Salt Lake City: Church of Jesus Christ of Latter-day Saints, 1975.

Alexander, Thomas G. *Mormonism in Transition: A History of the Latter-day Saints, 1890–1930*. Urbana, IL: University of Illinois Press, 1996.

Allen, Charles W. *Window Maker*. Nauvoo, IL: Allyn House Publishing, 2002.

Allen, James B., and Glen M. Leonard. *The Story of the Latter-day Saints*. Salt Lake City: Deseret Book, 1992.

Archer, Gleason L. *A Survey of Old Testament Introduction*. Chicago: Moody Press, 2007.

———. *Encyclopedia of Bible Difficulties*. Grand Rapids: Zondervan, 1982.

Ash, Michael. *Shaken Faith Syndrome: Strengthening One's Testimony in the Face of Criticism and Doubt*. Orem, UT: FAIR, 2008.

Beasley-Murray, G. R. *Baptism in the New Testament*. Grand Rapids: Eerdmans, 1962.

Beckwith, Francis J., Carl Mosser, and Paul Owen, eds. *The New Mormon Challenge: Responding to the Latest Defenses of a Fast-Growing Movement*. Grand Rapids: Zondervan, 2002.

Benson, Ezra Taft. *The Teachings of Ezra Taft Benson*. Salt Lake City: Bookcraft, 1988.

Book of Mormon: Gospel Doctrine Teacher's Manual. Salt Lake City: Church of Jesus Christ of Latter-day Saints, 1999.

Book of Mormon Seminary Student Study Guide. Salt Lake City: Church of Jesus Christ of Latter-day Saints, 2000.

Book of Mormon Student Manual: Religion 121 and 122. Salt Lake City: Church of Jesus Christ of Latter-day Saints, 1996.

Bromiley, Geoffrey W., ed. *The International Standard Bible Encyclopedia*. 4 vols. Grand Rapids: Eerdmans, 1979.

Brooks, James A., and Carlton L. Winbery. *Syntax of New Testament Greek*. Lanham, MD: University Press of America, 1979.

Brown, Hugh B. *You and Your Marriage*. Salt Lake City: Bookcraft, 1987.

Bruce. F. F. *The Gospel & Epistles of John*. Grand Rapids: Eerdmans, 1983.

———. *The New Testament Documents: Are They Reliable?* Sixth ed. Grand Rapids: Eerdmans, 1981.

Buerger, David John. *The Mysteries of Godliness: A History of Mormon Temple Worship*. Salt Lake City: Signature Books, 2002.

Bushman, Richard Lyman. *Joseph Smith: Rough Stone Rolling*. New York: Alfred A. Knopf, 2005.

Catton, Bruce. *The Civil War*. Boston: Houghlin Mifflin, 2004.

Cavendish, Richard. *The Black Arts: A Concise History of Witchcraft, Demonology, Astrology, and Other Mystical Practices Throughout the Ages*. New York: Perigee Books, 1967.

Church History in the Fulness of Times Student Manual. Salt Lake City: Church of Jesus Christ of Latter-day Saints, 2003.

Church News. Select issues from the weekly LDS newspaper, published by *Deseret News*, Salt Lake City.

Clark, James R., ed. *Messages of the First Presidency of The Church of Jesus Christ of Latter-day Saints (1833–1951)*. 6 vols. Salt Lake City: Bookcraft, 1965–1975.

A Comprehensive History of the Church of Jesus Christ of Latter-day Saints. 6 vols. Comp. B. H. Roberts. Orem, UT: Sonos Publishing, 1991.

Compton, Todd. *In Sacred Loneliness: The Plural Wives of Joseph Smith*. Salt Lake City: Signature Books, 1997.

Conference Reports. Salt Lake City: Church of Jesus Christ of Latter-day Saints, 1889–1970 (139 total conference reports).

Copan, Paul. *Is God a Moral Monster? Making Sense of the Old Testament God*. Grand Rapids: Baker, 2011.

Deseret News. Select articles from the newspaper, published daily in Salt Lake City, Utah.

Deseret News 1993–1994 Church Almanac. Salt Lake City: Church of Jesus Christ of Latter-day Saints, 1993.

Deseret News 2001–2002 Church Almanac. Salt Lake City: Church of Jesus Christ of Latter-day Saints, 2001.

Deseret News 2010 Church Almanac. Salt Lake City: Church of Jesus Christ of Latter-day Saints, 2010.

Dialogue: A Journal of Mormon Thought. Select issues from the journal, published quarterly by the Dialogue Foundation.

Doctrine and Covenants and Church History Gospel Doctrine Teacher's Manual. Salt Lake City: Church of Jesus Christ of Latter-day Saints, 1999.

Doctrine and Covenants Student Manual: Religion 324–325. Salt Lake City: Church of Jesus Christ of Latter-day Saints, 2001.

Doctrines of the Gospel Student Manual: Religion 430–431. Salt Lake City: Church of Jesus Christ of Latter-day Saints, 1986.

Dowley, Tim, and Pat Alexander. *The History of Christianity: A Lion Handbook*. Scarsdale, NY: Lion Hudson, 1996.

Elwell, Walter A., ed. *Evangelical Dictionary of Theology*. Grand Rapids: Baker, 1989.

Ensign. Select issues from the magazine, published monthly by the Church of Jesus Christ of Latter-day Saints.

Eternal Marriage Student Manual: Religion 234 and 235. Salt Lake City: Church of Jesus Christ of Latter-day Saints, 2001.

Ford, Thomas. *A History of Illinois: From Its Commencement as a State in 1818 to 1847*. Chicago: S. C. Griggs, 1854.

Fourteenth Annual Symposium of the Archaeology of the Scriptures. Provo, UT: Brigham Young University, April 13, 1963.

Gaebelein, Frank E., ed. *The Expositor's Bible Commentary*. 12 vols. Grand Rapids: Zondervan, 1981.

Geisler, Norman L., and Ron Rhodes. *When Cultists Ask: A Popular Handbook on Cultic Misinterpretations*. Grand Rapids: Baker, 1997.

Gomes, Alan W. *Unmasking the Cults*. Grand Rapids: Zondervan, 1995.

Gonzales, Justo. *The Story of Christianity*. 2 vols. New York: Harper One,

2010. *Gospel Principles*. Salt Lake City: Church of Jesus Christ of Latter-day Saints, 2009.

Gospel Principles. Salt Lake City: Church of Jesus Christ of Latter-day Saints, 2009.

Grudem, Wayne. *The Gift of Prophecy in the New Testament and Today*, Rev. ed. Wheaton, IL: Crossway Books, 2000.

Guiley, Rosemary Ellen. *The Encyclopedia of Witches and Witchcraft*. New York: Facts on File, 1999.

Handbook 1: Stake Presidents and Bishops. Salt Lake City: Church of Jesus Christ of Latter-day Saints, 2010.

Hardy, B. Carmon. *Solemn Covenant: The Mormon Polygamous Passage*. Urbana, IL: University of Illinois Press, 1992.

Harrell, Charles R. *"This Is My Doctrine": The Development of Mormon Theology*. Draper, UT: Greg Kofford Books, 2011.

Hartman, Franz. *Magic, White and Black: The Science of Finite and Infinite Life, Containing Practical Hints for Students of Occultism*. London: G. Redway, 1886.

Hendricksen, William. *New Testament Commentary: Exposition of the Gospel According to Matthew*. Grand Rapids: Baker, 2007.

Hickenbotham, Michael W. *Answering Challenging Mormon Questions: Replies to 130 Queries by Friends and Critics of the LDS Church*. Bountiful, UT: Horizon Publishers, 1995.

Hinckley, Bryant. *Sermons and Missionary Services of Melvin Joseph Ballard*. Salt Lake City: Deseret Book, 1949.

Hinckley, Gordon B. *Faith: The Essence of True Religion*. Salt Lake City: Deseret Book, 1989.

———. *Teachings of Gordon B. Hinckley*. Salt Lake City: Deseret Book, 1997.

History of the Church of Jesus Christ of Latter-day Saints. Introduction and notes by B. H. Roberts. 7 vols. Salt Lake City: Deseret Book, 1973.

Hodge, Charles. *Systematic Theology*. 3 vols. Peabody, MA: Hendrickson Publishers, 2003.

Hoerth, Alfred, and John McRay. *Bible Archaeology: An Exploration of the History and Culture of Early Civilizations*. Grand Rapids: Baker, 2005.

Holland, Jeffrey R. *Christ and the New Covenant*. Salt Lake City: Deseret Book, 2003.

Hughes, Philip E. *The New International Commentary on the New Testament: The Second Epistle to the Corinthians*. Grand Rapids: Eerdmans, 1986.

Hymns of the Church of Jesus Christ of Latter-day Saints. Salt Lake City: Church of Jesus Christ of Latter-day Saints, 1985.

Improvement Era. Select issues from the magazine, published from 1897–1970 by The Church of Jesus Christ of Latter-day Saints.

Jensen, Andrew. *Church Chronology*. Second ed. Salt Lake City: Deseret News, 1899.

Journal of Discourses. 26 vols. Liverpool: F. D. Richards, 1854–86.

Kaiser, Walter Jr., Peter H. Davids, F. F. Bruce, and Manfred T. Brauch, *The Hard Sayings of the Bible*. Downer's Grove, IL: InterVarsity Press, 1996.

Keller, Timothy. *The Reason for God: Belief in an Age of Skepticism*. New York: Penguin, 2008.

Kidner, Derek. *Psalms 73–150: A Commentary*. Downers Grove, IL: InterVarsity Press, 1975.

Kimball, Spencer W. *The Miracle of Forgiveness*. Salt Lake City: Bookcraft, 1969.

———. *The Teachings of Spencer W. Kimball.* Compl. Edward L. Kimball. Salt Lake City: Bookcraft, 1982.

Kistemaker, Simon J. *New Testament Commentary: James, Epistles of John, Peter, and Jude.* Grand Rapids: Baker, 1996.

The Latter-day Saint Woman: Basic Manual for Women Part A. Salt Lake City: Church of Jesus Christ of Latter-day Saints, 1998.

Lee, Harold B. *Stand Ye in Holy Places: Selected Sermons and Writings of President Harold B. Lee.* Salt Lake City: Deseret Book, 1975.

———. *Ye Are the Light of the World: Selected Sermons and Writings of Harold B. Lee.* Salt Lake City: Deseret Book, 1974.

LeSueur, Stephen C. *The 1838 Mormon War in Missouri.* Columbia, MO: University of Missouri Press, 1987.

Ludlow, Daniel H., ed. *A Companion to Your Study of the New Testament: The Four Gospels.* Salt Lake City: Deseret Book, 2002.

———, ed. *Encyclopedia of Mormonism.* 5 vols. New York: Macmillan, 1992.

Lund, John Lewis. *The Church and the Negro: A Discussion of Mormons, Negroes and the Priesthood.* N.p.: Paramount Publishers, 1967.

———. *Mesoamerica and the Book of Mormon: Is This the Place?* Orem, UT: Granite Publishing, 2007.

Marshall, Scott. *Tracting and Member Missionary Work.* N.p.: Scott Marshall, 1999.

Matthews, Robert J. *A Bible! A Bible!* Salt Lake City: Bookcraft, 1990.

———. *Selected Writings of Robert J. Matthews: Gospel Scholars Series.* Salt Lake City: Deseret Book, 1999.

Maxwell, Neal A. *Plain and Precious Things.* Salt Lake City: Deseret Book, 1983.

McConkie, Bruce R. *Doctrinal New Testament Commentary.* 3 vols. Salt Lake City: Deseret Book, 2002.

———. *The Millennial Messiah: The Second Coming of the Son of Man.* Salt Lake City: Deseret Book, 1985.

———. *Mormon Doctrine.* Salt Lake City: Bookcraft, 1966.

———. *A New Witness for the Articles of Faith.* Salt Lake City: Deseret Book, 1985.

———. *The Promised Messiah: The First Coming of Christ.* Salt Lake City: Deseret Book, 1978.

McConkie, Joseph Fielding, and Robert L. Millet. *Doctrinal Commentary on the Book of Mormon.* 4 vols. Salt Lake City: Deseret Book, 2007.

McKeever, Bill. *In Their Own Words: A Collection of Mormon Quotations.* Kearney, NE: Morris Publishing, 2010.

McKeever, Bill, and Eric Johnson. *Mormonism 101: Examining the Religion of the Latter-day Saints.* Grand Rapids: Baker, 2000.

McRay, John. *Archaeology and the New Testament.* Grand Rapids: Baker, 1991.

Millet, Robert L. *A Different Jesus? The Christ of the Latter-day Saints.* Grand Rapids: Eerdmans, 2005.

Millet, Robert L., and Gerald R. McDermott. *Claiming Christ: A Mormon-Evangelical Debate.* Grand Rapids: Baker, 2007.

Millet, Robert L., and Monte S. Nyman, eds. *The Joseph Smith Translation: The Restoration of Plain and Precious Things.* Provo, UT: Religious Studies Center, Brigham Young University, 1994.

Millet, Robert L., Camille Fronk Olson, Andrew C. Skinner, and Brent L. Top. *LDS Beliefs: A Doctrinal Reference.* Salt Lake City: Deseret Book, 2011.

Mormon Times. Select issues from the magazine, published weekly by the *Deseret News.*

Newell, Linda King, and Valeen Tippetts Avery. *Mormon Enigma: Emma Hale Smith,* Second ed. Urbana, IL: University of Illinois Press, 1994.

New Era. Select issues from the magazine, published monthly by The Church of Jesus Christ of Latter-day Saints.

New Testament Teacher's Gospel Doctrine Manual. Salt Lake City: Church of Jesus Christ of Latter-day Saints, 1997.

Nyman, Monte S., and Charles D. Tate. *Third Nephi 9–30: This Is My Gospel.* Salt Lake City: Deseret Book, 1993.

Old Testament Seminary Study Guide. Salt Lake City: Church of Jesus Christ of Latter-day Saints, 2002.

Olson, Roger E. *The Story of Christian Theology: Twenty Centuries of Tradition & Reform.* Downer's Grove, IL: InterVarsity Press, 1999.

Ostling, Richard N., and Joan Ostling. *Mormon America: The Power and the Promise.* San Francisco: Harper, 1999.

Penrose, Charles W. *Mormon Doctrine Plain and Simple: or, Leaves from the Tree of Life.* Salt Lake City: Juvenile Instructor's Office, 1888.

Petersen, LaMar. *Hearts Made Glad: The Charges of Intemperance Against Joseph Smith the Mormon Prophet.* Salt Lake City: LaMar Petersen, 1975.

Petersen, Mark E. *As Translated Correctly.* Salt Lake City: Deseret Book, 1966.

———. *For Time or Eternity.* Salt Lake City: Bookcraft, 1969.

———. *Why Mormons Build Temples.* Salt Lake City: Church of Jesus Christ of Latter-day Saints, 1972.

Piper, John. *Fifty Reasons Why Christ Came to Die.* Wheaton, IL: Crossway Books, 2006.

Pratt, Orson. *The Seer.* Salt Lake City: Eborn Books, 1990. Photo reprint of newspapers published between January 1853 through August 1854.

Preach My Gospel: A Guide to Missionary Service. Salt Lake City: Church of Jesus Christ of Latter-day Saints, 2004.

Preparing for Exaltation Teacher's Manual. Salt Lake City: Church of Jesus Christ of Latter-day Saints, 1998.

Presidents of the Church Student Manual: Religion 345. Salt Lake City: Church of Jesus Christ of Latter-day Saints, 2004.

Presidents of the Church Teacher's Manual. Salt Lake City: Church of Jesus Christ of Latter-day Saints, 1996.

Quinn, D. Michael. *Early Mormonism and the Magic World View.* Salt Lake City: Signature Books, 1998.

———. *The Mormon Hierarchy: Origins of Power.* Salt Lake City: Signature Books, 1994.

———, ed. *The New Mormon History: Revisionist Essays on the Past.* Salt Lake City: Signature Books, 1992.

Richards, LeGrand. *A Marvelous Work and a Wonder.* Salt Lake City: Signature Books, 1994.

Ridges, David. *Mormon Beliefs and Doctrines Made Easier.* Springville, UT: Cedar Fort, 2007.

Roberts, B. H. *Defense of the Faith and the Saints*. 2 vols. Salt Lake City: Deseret News, 1907–12.

Robinson, Steven E. *Are Mormons Christians?* Salt Lake City: Bookcraft, 1991.

Salt Lake Tribune. Select articles from the newspaper, published daily in Salt Lake City, Utah.

Schaff, Philip. *The Creeds of Christendom with a History and Critical Notes*. 3 vols. Grand Rapids: Baker, 2007.

Scharffs, Gilbert. *The Missionary's Little Book of Answers*. American Fork, UT: Covenant Communications, 2002.

Search These Commandments. Salt Lake City: Church of Jesus Christ of Latter-day Saints, 1984.

Shanks, Hershel, ed. *Ancient Israel: From Abraham to the Roman Destruction of the Temple*. Washington, DC: Biblical Archeology Society, 1999.

Shields, Steven L. *Divergent Paths of the Restoration (A History of the Latter Day Saint Movement)*. Salt Lake City: Restoration Research, 1982.

Skinner, Andrew C. *Gethsemane*. Salt Lake City: Deseret Book, 2002.

Smith, George D. *Nauvoo Polygamy: "But We Called It Celestial Marriage."* Salt Lake City: Signature Books, 2008.

Smith, Hyrum M., and Janne M. Sjodahl. *Doctrine and Covenants Commentary*. Salt Lake City: Church of Jesus Christ of Latter-day Saints, 1972.

Smith, Joseph. *The Book of Mormon*. Salt Lake City: Church of Jesus Christ of Latter-day Saints, 1981.

———. *The Doctrine and Covenants of the Church of Jesus Christ of Latter-day Saints*. Salt Lake City: Church of Jesus Christ of Latter-day Saints, 1981.

———. *Inspired Version of the Holy Scriptures*. Independence, MO: Price Publishing, 1997.

———. *Joseph Smith's 1832–34 Diary*. Salt Lake City: Modern Microfilm, 1979. Transcription by H. Michael Marquardt.

———. *The Pearl of Great Price*. Salt Lake City: Church of Jesus Christ of Latter-day Saints, 1981.

———. *Teachings of the Prophet Joseph Smith*. Comp. Joseph Fielding Smith. Salt Lake City: Deseret Book, 1938.

Smith, Joseph Fielding. *Answers to Gospel Questions*. 4 vols. Salt Lake City: Deseret Book, 1957–63.

———. *Doctrines of Salvation*. 3 vols. Ed. Bruce R. McConkie. Salt Lake City: Bookcraft, 1954–56.

———. *The Way to Perfection*. Salt Lake City: Deseret Book, 1975.

Smith, Lucy Mack. *History of Joseph Smith: By His Mother, Lucy Mack Smith*. Salt Lake City: Stevens & Wallis, 1945.

Strauss, Mark L. *Four Portraits, One Jesus: An Introduction to Jesus and the Gospels*. Grand Rapids: Zondervan, 2007.

———. *How to Read the Bible in Changing Times: Understanding and Applying God's Word Today*. Grand Rapids: Baker, 2011.

Strobel, Lee. *The Case for Christ: A Journalist's Personal Investigation of the Evidence for Jesus*. Grand Rapids: Zondervan, 1998.

———. *The Case for Faith: A Journalist Investigates the Toughest Objections to Christianity*. Grand Rapids: Zondervan, 2000.

Stuy, Brian H., ed. *Collected Discourses*. 5 vols. Burbank, CA: BHS Publishing 1987–1992.

A Sure Foundation: Answers to Difficult Gospel Questions. Salt Lake City: Deseret Book, 1988.

Sweat, Anthony. *I'm Not Perfect. Can I Still Go to Heaven? Finding Hope for the Celestial Kingdom Through the Atonement of Christ*. Salt Lake City: Deseret Book, 2010.

Talmage, James E. *The Articles of Faith*. Salt Lake City: Deseret Book, 1987.

———. *The Great Apostasy*. Salt Lake City: Deseret Book, 1983.

———. *The House of the Lord*. Salt Lake City: Bookcraft, 1969.

———. *Jesus the Christ*. Salt Lake City: Deseret Book, 2001.

Tanner, Jerald, and Sandra Tanner. *Mormonism: Shadow or Reality?* Salt Lake City: Utah Lighthouse Ministry, 1987.

Taylor, John. *The Gospel Kingdom*. Ed. G. Homer Durham. Salt Lake City: Bookcraft, 1943.

Teachings of Presidents of the Church: Brigham Young. Salt Lake City: Church of Jesus Christ of Latter-day Saints, 1997.

Teachings of Presidents of the Church: David O. McKay. Salt Lake City: Church of Jesus Christ of Latter-day Saints, 2003.

Teachings of Presidents of the Church: George Albert Smith. Salt Lake City: Church of Jesus Christ of Latter-day Saints, 2011.

Teachings of Presidents of the Church: Harold B. Lee. Salt Lake City: Church of Jesus Christ of Latter-day Saints, 2000.

Teachings of Presidents of the Church: Heber J. Grant. Salt Lake City: Church of Jesus Christ of Latter-day Saints, 2002.

Teachings of Presidents of the Church: John Taylor. Salt Lake City: Church of Jesus Christ of Latter-day Saints, 2001.

Teachings of Presidents of the Church: Joseph F. Smith. Salt Lake City: Church of Jesus Christ of Latter-day Saints, 1998.

Teachings of Presidents of the Church: Joseph Smith. Salt Lake City: Church of Jesus Christ of Latter-day Saints, 2007.

Teachings of Presidents of the Church: Spencer W. Kimball. Salt Lake City: Church of Jesus Christ of Latter-day Saints, 2006.

Teachings of Presidents of the Church: Wilford Woodruff. Salt Lake City: Church of Jesus Christ of Latter-day Saints, 2004.

Teachings of the Living Prophets Student Manual: Religion 333. Salt Lake City: Church of Jesus Christ of Latter-day Saints, 1982.

Teachings of the Living Prophets Student Manual: Religion 333. Salt Lake City: Church of Jesus Christ of Latter-day Saints, 2010.

Teachings of the Living Prophets Teacher Manual: Religion 333. Salt Lake City: Church of Jesus Christ of Latter-day Saints, 2010.

Times and Seasons. Select articles from the newspaper, published twice a month in Nauvoo, Illinois, from November 1839 to February 15, 1846.

Tozer, A. W. *The Knowledge of the Holy*. San Francisco: Harper and Row, 1961.

True to the Faith: A Gospel Reference. Salt Lake City: Intellectual Reserve, 2004.

Van Wagoner, Richard S. *Mormon Polygamy: A History*. Salt Lake City: Signature Books, 1989.

Walker, Ronald W., Richard E. Turley Jr., and Glen M. Leonard. *Massacre at Mountain Meadows*. New York: Oxford University Press, 2011.

Walters, Wesley. *The Palmyra Revival and Mormon Origins*. Madison, WI: Mormonism Research Ministry, 2012.

Walvoord, John F., and Roy B. Zuck. *The Bible Knowledge Commentary*. Wheaton, IL: Victor Books, 1986.

White, James R. *The Forgotten Trinity: Recovering the Heart of Christian Belief*. Minneapolis: Bethany House, 1998.

———. *The God Who Justifies: The Doctrine of Justification*. Bloomington, MN: Bethany House, 2001.

Whitmer, David. *An Address to All Believers in Christ: By a Witness to the Divine Authenticity of the Book of Mormon*. N.p.: David Whitmer, 1887.

Widtsoe, John A. *Evidences and Reconciliations*. Comp. G. Homer Durham. 3 vols. 1943–51. Reprint (3 vols. in 1), Salt Lake City: Bookcraft, 1960.

———. *Joseph Smith, Seeker After Truth, Prophet of God*. Salt Lake City: Deseret News Press, 1951.

Widtsoe, John A., and Franklin S. Harris Jr. *Seven Claims of the Book of Mormon: A Collection of Evidences*. Salt Lake City: Deseret News Press, 1937.

Williams, Clyde J., ed. *The Teachings of Lorenzo Snow*. Salt Lake City: Bookcraft, 1984.

Woodruff, Wilford. *The Discourses of Wilford Woodruff*. Comp. G. Homer Durham. Salt Lake City: Bookcraft, 1946.

———. *Waiting for World's End: The Diaries of Wilford Woodruff*. Comp. Susan Staker. Salt Lake City: Signature Books, 1993.

Young, Brigham. *Discourses of Brigham Young*. Comp. John A. Widtsoe. Salt Lake City: Deseret Book, 1978.

Youngblood, Ronald F., ed. *Nelson's New Illustrated Bible Dictionary*. Nashville: Thomas Nelson, 1995.

Scripture Index

DOCTRINE AND COVENANTS

PEARL OF GREAT PRICE

About the Authors

BILL MCKEEVER is president of Mormonism Research Ministry, which he founded in 1979. It is based in the Salt Lake City area of Utah. Bill coauthored *Questions to Ask Your Mormon Friend* (Bethany House, 1994) and *Mormonism 101* (Baker, 2000) with Eric Johnson. He has also compiled *In Their Own Words: A Collection of Mormon Quotations* (Morris, 2010). He and his wife, Tammy, have three children (Kristen, Kendra, and Jamin), as well as eight grandchildren.

ERIC JOHNSON joined Mormonism Research Ministry in 1989. Eric received his BA from San Diego State University and his MDiv from Bethel Seminary San Diego. For seventeen years, Eric was a fixture in the Bible department at Christian High School in El Cajon, California, and for many years taught college and seminary classes. Besides writing two books with Bill, Eric was an associate editor of the *Apologetics Study Bible for Students* (B&H Publishers, 2010). Eric and his wife, Terri, have three daughters (Carissa, Janelle, and Hannah).

IF YOU WOULD LIKE more information about Mormonism Research Ministry and to sign up to receive a free subscription to the bimonthly newsletter *Mormonism Researched*, please visit our Web site at http://www.mrm.org.

In addition, if your church is interested in having us speak, e-mail us: contact@mrm.org.